# My Hill and Gully Ride

The Struggles and Triumphs of a Jamaican Boy's
Journey to America

Fred Rose

Fred A. Rose, Publisher

Publisher: Fred A. Rose

Herndon, Virginia, U.S.A.

ISBN: 979-8-9985595-0-1

Book Cover Concept by Andreen Vanriel

First edition 2025

Printed in United States

# Contents

# Dedication

To my beloved mother, Gloria Forbes, gone but not forgotten! For her unwavering support, love, and sacrifice, especially during my time at Dinthill Technical High School and throughout my journey in life. She believed in my potential even when the road seemed uncertain, and her strength and guidance always carried me through every challenge. I am forever grateful for the foundation she built for my success.

To my beloved son, Wynton — you awakened in me a deeper appreciation and awareness of what truly matters in life. I miss your presence every day, but your spirit lives on, and your love and memories will forever be cherished.

To my stepfather, Sam Forbes, whose presence and support played a significant role in shaping my path. Gone but not forgotten!

To Aunt Philaberta and Leslie Sutherland, whose warmth, hospitality, and guidance when I first arrived in the United States provided me with a strong foundation. Your kindness and support have enriched my life in ways I will always cherish.

And to my Uncle Leslie Toomer, who has been a steadfast source of inspiration and a loving parental figure in my life. His compassion and affection will always hold a special place in my heart.

With all my love and appreciation!

—Fred

# Forward

I am excited to share with you this extraordinary autobiography. In "My Hill and Gully Ride," you will embark on the inspiring journey of a Jamaican immigrant as he navigates his way to the United States. This narrative is more than just a story; it offers a thought-provoking and enlightening experience that encourages reflection. Whether or not you are familiar with Jamaican culture, the insights and perspectives within these pages will surely resonate with you and leave a lasting impression.

This autobiography is born from a genuine passion for knowledge and a commitment to sharing meaningful wisdom. Fred Rose has expertly intertwined his life experiences, expertise, and deep dedication throughout each chapter, ensuring that every word carries authenticity and purpose. This work goes beyond simple storytelling; it acts as a bridge that connects curiosity to understanding and helps transform dreams into impactful contributions to society.

Starting from humble beginnings in rural Jamaica, Fred climbed to prominence as a civil engineer specializing in water resources, facing numerous challenges, along his path. Throughout these pages, he not just recounts moments of celebration, triumph, and joy, but also disasters, crises, and tragedies—providing a historical lens through which these events can be understood and remembered. As you immerse yourself in this book, you will encounter moments of triumph and resilience that will inspire you.

This book is not merely a recollection of milestones and achievements, but a testament to the people and experiences that shaped Fred's journey. I encourage you to let this book be your guiding light, a trusted companion, and a powerful catalyst for your growth and discovery. It will meet and exceed your expectations, providing insights that enrich your personal and professional journey.

So, I invite you to dive into this remarkable work, soak up its invaluable lessons, and let yourself be inspired. Get ready for an enlightening journey ahead!

—Leonie Rose Bovino, PhD, APRN, AGACNP-BC, FAHA

## Testimonials

"This book takes you on a personal journey from the hills of Jamaica to life in America, capturing the resilience, growth, and hope that defines Fred's story. It's a powerful and heartfelt reflection on overcoming challenges and discovering one's true path."

—Y. Gordon

"Fred writes boldly and with vivid skill about success, disappointment, and tragedy—both personal and global. Blended with the spiciness of his Jamaican upbringing, his storytelling stirs every emotion, leaving you both entertained and deeply moved."

—M. Francis

# Acknowledgment

I would like to express my heartfelt thanks and appreciation to my esteemed batchmates of the Class of '72, of Dinthill, who took the time to contribute to my story in this book. Your insights, memories, and support have been invaluable in bringing this narrative to life.

Special mention goes to Alvin, Raymond, Herman, Orett, Carl, Lolita, Rosie, Claudette, Jennifer, and Diane—your contributions and friendship have not merely enriched this story but have also been a constant reminder of the bonds we formed during our unforgettable years at Dinthill.

Special thanks to my dear sister Leonie Rose Bovino who provided me with essential ancestral data, provided inspiration and wrote the Forward.

I also extend my deepest gratitude to Everard O'Neill, Neville Simon, Tony Belcher, Maria Turner, Beresford Lewis, Judith Morroy, Marlene Dunkley, and Yvonne Gordon for your support and shared memories, which have made this journey even more meaningful.

Thank you all for being a vital part of this journey.

With the deepest gratitude!

—Fred

# Chapter 1

# A Jamaican Upbringing

## Introduction

My name is Frederick (Fred) Rose, and I was born in the lush, sun-kissed parish of St. Mary, Jamaica. This breathtaking land, cradled by rolling emerald hills and bordered by the glistening turquoise waters of the Caribbean Sea, was my first world place. The air was thick with the scent of ripe fruits and sea breeze, and life pulsed to the rhythmic heartbeat of reggae music. Here, warmth extended beyond the tropical sun; it radiated from the laughter of the people, the unbreakable bonds of community, and the rich tapestry of our island's culture.

Growing up in Jamaica was an adventure bursting with color, sound, and sensation. The district shops were alive with the hypnotic beats of ska and reggae, the intoxicating aroma of delicious island food sizzling over open flames, and the shouts of children engaged in boisterous games of cricket or marble shooting. Our playgrounds were nature's bounty—towering mango and apple trees, coconut palms swaying like dancers in the wind, and fields that stretched into banana plantations as far as the eye could see. Climbing trees was not just a pastime; it was an art. I became a master navigator of branches, swinging from limb to limb in search of the plumpest, sun-ripened fruit, devouring its juicy flesh with juice dripping down my chin.

Banana plantations sprawled across the countryside like a living quilt, their broad, waxy leaves rustling like whispers in the breeze. I roamed those fields with boyish curiosity. My bare feet sank into the damp, fertile soil. My senses were alive with the symphony of nature—the sights, sounds, and smells of my home district. The chirping of crickets at night, the scent of freshly cut cane, the distant bray of a donkey, and the crowing of roosters in the early morning. The occasional burst of laughter from farmers hard at work remains etched in my memory. These experiences form the foundation of my deep appreciation for the environment. Life was simple yet incredibly rich, woven together by stories, traditions, and an unyielding spirit of perseverance.

Our home was located in the small district of Blue Gate, nestled next to Carron Hall, midway between the towns of Highgate and Guy's Hill. The population of Carron Hall and its immediate surrounding was about 700 to 800 in 1970.

We had the most picturesque views from our property. From the front, we saw the rolling hills and valleys stretching all the way down to the shimmering blue Caribbean Sea in the distance. The vast open pastures and lush green fields painted a serene, almost idyllic landscape. One of the standout landmarks was the Pringle Home for Girls, a symbolic structure perched atop a hill in Carron Hall, with Gordon Land nestled quietly at the bottom, adding depth to the vista.

From the rear of our home, the view was equally breathtaking. A portion of the magnificent Blue Mountain range loomed in the distance; its peaks often shrouded in a misty veil of clouds. The Blue Mountains are renowned in Jamaica, not just for having the island's tallest peak but also for producing its legendary coffee, known worldwide for its rich, smooth flavor. The sight of these majestic mountains provided a constant reminder of the natural beauty that surrounded us.

Highgate, one of the nearby towns, seemed like a long journey from Blue Gate, especially as a child – it was merely about five miles away. The trip involved descending winding roads that twisted and turned through the countryside, passing through Palmetto Grove and Dean Pen along the way. The route was an adventure in itself, with each bend revealing new scenery and hidden corners of our parish.

In the opposite direction lay Guy's Hill, a town that appeared to rise gently as you approached. It marked the entry into the Parish of St. Catherine that was well-known for its expansive sugar cane plantations and orange cultivations. The journey to Guy's Hill passes through several districts, including Windsor Castle near Blue Gate. In between that is Change Hill, another district adjacent to Windsor Castle and connected to Carron Hall. Each of these communities has its own distinct characteristics and history.

Continuing beyond Guy's Hill, the next major town was Linstead. Linstead would later become the center of my world when I attended high school there for four formative years. The town buzzed with activity and opportunities, contrasting with the quieter life in Blue Gate, yet it remained connected to my roots.

I distinctly recall a milestone marker situated just a couple of hundred yards from our home. It indicated that we were 30 miles from Spanish Town, one of Jamaica's oldest and most historically significant towns. Spanish Town itself was about 15 miles from Kingston, the vibrant capital city of Jamaica. This simple marker was a constant reminder of how our small, tranquil district of Blue Gate was connected to the broader, bustling world beyond our hills and valleys.

The community of Blue Gate was small enough that most everyone where somewhat related and you knew all the families. It was a close nit family environment with neighbors helping each other and as a child growing up, you felt others genuinely cared for your well-being and looked out for you. I would say Blue Gate represented a microcosm of communities throughout the rural parts of Jamaica.

## Jamaica Celebrate Independence

Jamaica celebrated its independence on August 6th, 1962, and even though I was just 7 years old, the excitement and energy of that historic day are etched vividly in my memory. At the time, the population of Jamaica was approximately 1.7 million which has grown to almost 3 million today. The entire island buzzed with pride and anticipation, as if the very air was charged with the spirit of freedom.

At school, we gathered in the building, our young voices rising in unison as we sang the newly minted national anthem with all the enthusiasm our little hearts could muster. Each of us clutched small replicas of our new flag—of black, green, and gold fluttering in the breeze, symbolizing the strength and resilience of our people, the wealth of our land's natural resources, and the lush beauty of our island. A large flag was raised on a flagpole next to the school building.

The celebration didn't stop with just songs and flags. Local adults organized a lively *"Jonkonnu"* style performance, bringing the rich traditions of our culture to life right before our eyes. The dancers, adorned in colorful costumes and masks, moved to the infectious rhythms of drums and fifes, their energetic steps and dramatic gestures captivating both young and old. I remember being mesmerized by the spectacle—the mix of music, dance, and folklore filling me with a sense of belonging and pride in my Jamaican heritage. It was more than just a festive day; it was the dawn of a new chapter for our nation, and even at that young age, I felt the weight and wonder of witnessing history unfold.

Amidst the festivities, the symbols of our newfound independence were impossible to ignore. The familiar image of Queen Elizabeth II, once a prominent symbol of colonial rule, gave way to the appointment of Jamaica's first Governor-General, Sir Clifford Campbell, marking a significant step towards full self-governance. Our government transitioned to a parliamentary system, with Sir Alexander Bustamante, who later became one of Jamaica's National Heroes, becoming Jamaica's first Prime Minister.

These changes weren't just political milestones—they were powerful symbols of Jamaica's journey from colonial rule to self-determination. The air was thick with a sense of possibility, and even as a child, I could feel the pride swelling in the hearts of those around me. It was a time of celebration, yes, but also a time of great hope, as Jamaica stood tall and free, ready to embrace its future. Our national motto transformed into *"**Out of Many, One People,**"* symbolizing the country's rich diversity and multi-racial heritage.

## Hurricane Flora in 1963

Jamaica, being located in the western Caribbean Sea, is always susceptible to tropical storms and hurricanes that generate in the eastern Atlantic Ocean every year. Throughout my childhood, I was fortunate not to have experienced a direct or severely damaging hit on the island, except in 1963. Hurricane Flora ravaged through the Caribbean in late September to October that year, reaching as high as a category 4 storm. It caused devastating damage to Haiti and significant flooding to the eastern and northeastern regions of Jamaica.

I distinctly remember how we had to board-up the windows of our house as a precaution. We stayed glued to the radio, listening intently to frequent updates on the storm's status. The anxiety was palpable as we worried about the possibility of a direct hit. Fortunately, Hurricane Flora veered in a more northerly direction, sparing Jamaica from the worst but slamming into Haiti with catastrophic force.

Despite avoiding a direct hit, we still experienced severe thunderstorms and torrential rains. The heavy downpours overwhelmed every low-lying area, leading to widespread flooding and numerous landslides that blocked roadways. The heavy winds ravished banana plantations across the community. Schools were closed for several days as the floodwaters slowly receded and crews worked tirelessly to clear fallen trees and debris from the landslides. Our parents were a source of great comfort during this frightening time, their calm presence helping to soothe our fears.

That memory left a lasting impression on me. It was my first real encounter with the raw, destructive power of nature, and it made me deeply appreciate the potential damaging force of water. This experience served as an early inspiration for my future career as a water resources engineer, where the proper management of stormwater became a core practice. The lessons learned from Hurricane Flora stayed with me, shaping my understanding of the importance of resilient infrastructure and effective water management in mitigating the impacts of natural disasters.

## The Assassination of President John F. Kennedy

It was the day the world stood still. President John F. Kennedy was assassinated on November 22, 1963, in Dallas, Texas, while riding in an open-top limousine through Dealey Plaza. He was accompanied by First Lady Jacqueline Kennedy, Texas Governor John Connally, and Connally's wife. As the motorcade made its way through the city, shots rang out, striking Kennedy and Governor Connally. The President was mortally wounded, and despite being rushed to Parkland Memorial Hospital, he was pronounced dead at 1:00 p.m. CST. He was merely 46 years old.

People grieved all over the world, and I remember the tragedy vividly—it made me weep. The news of Kennedy's assassination spread rapidly, sending shockwaves through the United States and beyond. Schools, businesses, and government offices came to a halt as people gathered around televisions and radios, struggling to process the devastating news. The grief was not just confined to America; leaders and citizens across the globe, including in Jamaica, mourned the loss of a leader who had inspired hope and progress.

Shortly after the assassination, Lee Harvey Oswald was arrested and charged with the murder. However, before he could stand trial, Oswald was shot and killed by nightclub owner Jack Ruby on live television, deepening the mystery surrounding the assassination. The Warren Commission, established to investigate the events, concluded that Oswald acted alone, but skepticism remained. Over the years, numerous conspiracy theories emerged, suggesting involvement by the CIA, the Mafia, or other political groups.

Kennedy's death marked a turning point in history. His vision for a new era of progress was tragically cut short, but his legacy endures. Even today, people reflect on that fateful day and the loss of a leader who had captivated the hearts of millions.

## The Community Experiences

One of my most cherished memories revolves around the rich tradition of storytelling, a timeless practice woven deeply into our cultural tapestry. Picture this: on certain moonlit evenings, nestled under the vast night sky, we'd gather around wise elders whose voices carried the weight of history. Their tales danced between the mischievous exploits of Anansi, the spine-chilling whispers of duppies (ghosts) lurking in shadows, and the heroic deeds of our ancestors.

Among these narratives, the stories of duppies held a special grip on my imagination, casting a veil of fear over moonlit paths and graveyards. But nothing terrified me more than the mere mention of Butchy, the renowned butcher-for-hire. With his blood-streaked apron, a wild, unkempt look in his eyes, and the ever-present scent of white rum on his breath, he was the stuff of nightmares. It was said that Butchy was rarely sober, stumbling through the district with a bottle in one hand and a menacing, makeshift cutlass in the other. His drunken rants, unpredictable temper, and the pleasure he seemed to have slaughtering cows, goats, and pigs just added to his fearsome legend. I often imagined him lurking in the shadows, his sharp blades glinting under the moonlight, ready to strike at anything—or anyone—unfortunate enough to cross his path.

Yet, beneath the eerie tales lay profound lessons of resilience, cunning, and bravery. Each story served as a lantern illuminating the path of our folklore, binding us closer to our heritage with every word spoken. These storytelling sessions weren't just entertainment—they were a rite of passage, stitching the fabric of our community together with threads of shared history and timeless wisdom.

Public transportation was essential to the community, as just a few residents owned vehicles. I especially remember the large country buses that carried between 45 and 75 passengers at their peak, connecting people to towns near and far.

One of the most well-known was the *Benbow Special* (nicknamed *Penny-Penny*), which ran twice daily between Benbow, just north of Guy's Hill, and Highgate, arriving between 8 AM and returning noon, then again between 3 PM and returning at 5 PM. The *NorthStar* bus traveled from Kingston to Oracabessa, St. Mary, arriving around 6 PM and making the return trip at 5 AM. Another key service was the *Time Piece* bus, which ran from Kingston to Port Maria, arriving at about 1 PM and making the return trip between 4 and 5 PM.

These buses faced competition from a local taxi service operated by Mr. George Lewis. He initially drove a sedan but later upgraded to a minibus—what we now call a minivan—offering residents another vital transportation option. His wife, Ghika (Nurse Lewis), served as the primary healthcare provider and midwife for the community. Known as our pillar of support, Nurse Lewis was deeply committed to providing essential medical care to both the young and elderly. She managed a public clinic in Windsor Castle, where she administered immunizations to infants and young children, and also made regular home visits to attend to the needs of the sick and elderly.

I fondly remember dancing to ska and later rock steady rhythms from the juke box in the rear entertainment room at Forbes shop in Blue Gate. Arriving around 1963, the coin-operated juke box made records play, turning our dance into a competition for the best drop-legs (akin to later break dancing). This weekend ritual drew applause and laughter from adults, and it was likely my first introduction to Bob Marley's music, especially his hit "Simmer Down" from 1963.

The shop would come alive every weekend, filled with the vibrant energy of young people eager to showcase their dance moves. The smell of fried snacks and the chatter of excited conversations mingled with the music, creating an unforgettable atmosphere. We would gather around the juke box, eagerly watching as each record dropped, ready to spring into action at the first note. Friends cheered each other on, offering encouragement and playful banter. I did excel in drop-legs, a skill I would enjoy showcasing in later years at Jamaican parties in the U.S. It wasn't just about dancing; it was about community, connection, and the pure joy of shared experience.

That period was magical, bringing people together through music. Bob Marley's "Simmer Down" was an anthem with its lively rhythm and powerful message. Popular records included "My Boy Lollipop" by Millie Small (1964), "Sammy Dead O" by Eric Morris (1964) and "Guns of Navarone" by the Skatalites. Artists like Desmond Decker & the Aces, Alton Ellis, Jimmy Cliff, and Toots & the Maytals created hit records that left lasting memories.

Situated in the heart of a Blue Gate, the Forbes shop was always alive with laughter, chatter, and the rhythmic clack of dominoes slamming down on wooden tables. It served as a meeting ground for locals who sought respite from the heat of the day, a place where stories were shared, friendships were forged, and rivalries played out over competitive games of dominoes.

Every evening, as the sun began its descent, groups of men would gather at the shop. Their faces lit up with anticipation, each holding their lucky set of dominoes—old, worn, but trusted companions. The tables would be swiftly occupied, and games commenced with fervor. The older men, veterans of countless matches, took their usual places, their expressions serious and focused. Newcomers, eager yet nervous, observed closely, hoping to learn the tricks and strategies that defined true mastery.

Inside the Forbes shop, the shelves were stocked with an assortment of goods and snacks—bulla cake with cheese was one of my favorite snack. But what drew people most was the bar to the side. Bottles of rum lined the counter, their amber liquid glistening under the dim lights. Next to them, crates of beer and soda chilled in ice, ready to quench the thirst of patrons.

Domino tournaments at Forbes shop were grand events, awaited eagerly by the entire district. Teams from neighboring areas would travel, sometimes miles, just to participate. These tournaments weren't just about winning; they were celebrations of skill, strategy, and community spirit. The shop would be decorated with colorful streamers and balloons, transforming into a festive arena. As the evening wore on, the sound system would come alive, blasting reggae tunes that got everyone swaying to the beats.

Women, not to be left behind, made their presence felt. Adorned in glittering dresses, their laughter and lively conversations added to the festive atmosphere. They cheered on their favorite teams, offered cold drinks to the players, and occasionally joined in the games themselves, proving their prowess at dominoes. Kids ran around, chasing each other, their giggles mingling with the music and chatter, creating a symphony of joy.

As night fell, the real party began. The dance floor was set up, and Uncle Sam's sound system took center stage. Known for his impeccable taste in music, Uncle Sam had a record collection that spanned decades. He knew exactly which songs would get the crowd moving and which ones would tug at their heartstrings. Under the starlit sky, couples danced to slow, romantic tunes while others broke out into energetic moves, losing themselves in the rhythm.

The aroma of food wafted through the air. Large pots simmered with delicious curry goat, a dish so flavorful that people often queued twice for a serving. Nearby, another pot bubbled with mannish water, a traditional soup made from goat parts, known for its hearty taste and nourishing qualities. Plates piled high with food were passed around, and the sounds of satisfied eating complemented the ongoing celebrations.

In the heart of Blue Gate lived two unforgettable brothers known as "Dampa and Harpa," each a vibrant character in their own right. Dampa, an elderly figure, was a pillar of support for everyone around him. Whether lending a hand to local builders, digging graves, tending fields, or assisting at Forbes' shop with loading and unloading goods. He was also a part time barber, who had groomed my hair a few times, and a respected cook, often preparing food for shop events. Harpa, also an elderly figure, equally industrious, and shared Dampa's dedication. He pitched in around the shop, stepping in behind the grocery counter or bar, and helped with clean-ups.

Forbes' shop was more than just a local store; it was the community's heartbeat where friendships were forged, and memories made. Whether through spirited games of dominoes or shared meals or a drinking session, filled with laughter, every moment there was cherished. It stood as a symbol of unity, tradition, and the simple pleasures of life. Sadly, with the passing of its owner, Mr. Forbes, in 1985, the shop closed its doors. Today, the Dean Family shop nearby continues the tradition, providing essential services and a gathering place for the community to come together.

My mother, Gloria, was the rock of our family, working tirelessly as a teacher to ensure that we never went without. She was a woman of quiet strength, her love as unwavering as the Jamaican sun. She nurtured us with a tenderness that spoke louder than words. She instilled in me the values of hard work, integrity, and the relentless pursuit of a brighter future—principles that would become my guiding stars.

Upon meeting Sam Forbes, who later became my stepfather, we gained another caring individual in our lives, who treated us as his own children. Life with Sam evolved into an enjoyable journey. I recall numerous trips in his Bedford truck to and from the town of Highgate, where I would frequently assist my mother with shopping at the market and for groceries. I would look forward to the delicious treats like ice cream, grapes or American apples.

My educational journey began in this lively environment, where I attended both elementary and high school. The schools were not just institutions of learning but were also community pillars where lifelong friendships were forged, and values were instilled. The teachers were dedicated and passionate, often going above and beyond to ensure that we received a well-rounded education. It was here that I developed a love for learning and a curiosity about the world, traits that would serve me well in the years to come.

Though America eventually became my home, Jamaica never left my heart. I found pieces of it in unexpected places—the reggae music that played from passing cars, the gatherings of fellow Jamaicans who, like me, carried the spirit of the island in their souls. The lessons of my youth remained my compass: the importance of community, the power of perseverance, and the profound beauty in simplicity.

## Attending My First School

My time at Carron Hall Primary/Elementary School was filled with vibrant experiences. Situated slightly over a mile from my home, the commute by foot was generally enjoyable, notwithstanding occasional inconveniences such as rainy weather. The route to school included both asphalt and gravel pavements. I often appreciated the camaraderie of fellow students as we made our way together. This period also offered opportunities to resolve conflicts outside the classroom and to form new friendships. Students came from within a 1 to 3-mile radius. Beyond Carron Hall, other feeder districts included Montreal, Hazard, Change Hill, Windsor Castle, Blue Gate, Breahead, and Palmetto Grove.

The school was nestled in a tranquil setting, surrounded by towering almond trees, dense woodlands, and vast open playing fields where we spent countless hours in play and competition. The main building, a charming timber-framed structure, sat gracefully atop a sturdy stone foundation, elevating it above the ground. This elevation created a shadowy cellar space beneath, accessible through small vent holes—just big enough for a daring child to squeeze through. For us, this dim and dusty undercroft held an air of mystery and adventure, as we wriggled inside on clandestine missions to retrieve lost marbles and coins that had slipped through the gaps of the wooden floorboards.

The building itself was a testament to careful upkeep. During my years there, I remember it being repainted at least once—the crisp white ceilings and window frames contrasted with the deep green doors, while the walls were coated in a warm beige hue. The floor, left in its natural wooden state, bore the marks of time and the relentless dust that drifted in from the dry, compacted schoolyard. At the end of each school day, it was our duty as students to sweep away the dust, ensuring the classrooms remained tidy for the next morning's lessons.

Lunchtime was always special—not just for the break to play, but also for the variety of meal options. I could either bring lunch from home, packed by my mother, or choose from an array of tasty snacks sold by a number of vendors just outside the school yard. Bulla cakes, fried fish, fritters, dried red herring, pudding, coconut drops and grater cakes and refreshing snow cones were all favorites. Aunt Tun was one of my favorites and a well-known vendor. Another option was Roy's shop, located a few yards from the school, where lunchtime patrons could purchase spice buns and cheese or other baked pastries along with soda drinks. However, there was often a large crowd to navigate.

For those craving a hearty meal, there was always the hot lunch prepared daily by Ms. Macy and the canteen staff. This often included white rice or bulgur, cornmeal or flour dumplings, and a flavorful chicken back stew, all served with a cup of milk made from powdered milk.

At the end of each school year, any leftover dry goods—usually provided through an assistance program from the U.S.—were distributed among students to take home, a small but welcome bonus to close out the term.

Presiding over this institution with an unwavering sense of discipline was our headmaster, Mr. Hextall. He was a stern figure, demanding academic excellence and swift to administer punishment with his ever-present leather belt. His authority extended beyond the classroom, ensuring that students upheld discipline in every aspect of school life. His wife, Mrs. Hextall, was also a teacher, and their daughter, Marcia, was one of my classmates. Their presence made the school feel almost like an extension of their household—structured, disciplined, yet undeniably formative for us all.

Ms. Scarlet, our 4th-grade teacher, a legend by all accounts, always required full attention and excellent results, speedily disciplining any distractions with a ruler slap. Despite her stern methods, she was deeply invested in her students' success and often stayed after school to help those who struggled.

Mr. Thomas, our 5th to 6th-grade teacher, was honestly unforgettable. He had a knack for making learning hands-on and exciting, introducing us boys to practical skills like woodworking alongside our basic science lessons. But the real game-changer came when he took us on an eye-opening field trip to the water treatment plant in Palmetto Grove. I was absolutely captivated by the entire process—watching how raw water coming from an underground aquifer was transformed into something safe for public use, and then learning how it traveled through underground pipes all the way to Highgate, a good 4-5 miles away. That day left a lasting impression on me. It didn't just teach me about water treatment, it sparked a lifelong fascination with civil engineering and ultimately shaped my later career in water resources.

Each morning began with an assembly and worship. Afternoons included sports games, various clubs, and groups that encouraged creativity and teamwork, such as 4-H and Boy Scouts. Evening prep classes provided students with special lessons in preparation for the common entrance examination for high school admission. This started when I was around 10 years old. These lessons helped me eventually earned an admission scholarship to attend Dinthill Technical High School in 1968 when I was 13. Admittedly, my first two years in this after-school prep class yielded disappointing results—perhaps due to my own lack of commitment. I can still hear my mother's voice echoing one of her famous sayings: *"Puss and dawg nuh have di same luck,"* a reminder that blindly following others doesn't guarantee the same outcome.

My perspective shifted when several of my peers, including my best friend Vincent (Tim), earned scholarships to attend St. Mary's High School. Their success ignited a newfound determination in me, pushing me to focus and persevere. With renewed motivation, I finally achieved success in 1968.

Cricket was not just a sport, but a way of life; it was the heartbeat of our school days. The excitement brewed from the moment the bell rang for lunch time and evening dismissal, transforming us into eager athletes. We would rush out, forming makeshift teams with an unspoken understanding that everyone had a role to play. The sound of bat hitting ball, the cheers from classmates, and the intense concentration on the faces of my peers are memories that remain vivid. The impromptu matches were filled with raw passion and thrill, each hit and miss cementing lifelong memories. Some of my peers would often try to emulate the famous professional cricketers who played for the West Indies Team at the time – some wanted to be like the legendary all-rounder, Sir Garfield Sobers, and others wanted to be like the legendary *"fast bowler"*, Wes Hall. I was excited when I got the opportunity to imitate Lance Gibbs, the famous *"spin bowler"*. However, my experience was sometimes shattered by giving up the occasional six-run. I remember on one occasion the ball was hit for six so far over the roof of school that it was lost.

Matches against rival schools showcased intense competition and school pride. I was once designated to be an "opening batsman," inspired by the legendary West Indies cricketer Rohan Kanhai - one of the best West Indies Team cricketers during the 1960s-70s. When it came time to face rival schools, the atmosphere turned electric. The intensity of the competition was palpable, with pride and honor on the line. These moments on the field were more than just games; they were lessons in resilience, leadership, and strategic thinking.

I remember the succession of cricket team captains: first Keith Cole, then Beresford Lewis, followed by Winston "Doc" Palmer. Each brought their distinct style of leadership and expertise to the field. They were esteemed leaders, not just by the headmaster but by us students, entrusted with overseeing school clean-up exercises and setting exemplary standards. The lessons of teamwork and collaboration forged through cricket have remained foundational in both my personal and professional journey.

Marble (glassy) games, on the other hand, required precision and patience. We would draw circles in the dirt and take turns flicking our marbles, aiming to knock out our opponents' marbles while keeping ours within the circle. The thrill of winning another's prized marble, along with the friendly rivalries that developed, added excitement to our school days. These games taught us about competition, fair play, and resilience.

Making and flying kites was an activity that connected us to nature. We crafted our kites from coconut palm stems, colorful paper, homemade flour glue, carefully tying knots and ensuring the structure was stable enough to withstand the wind. Flying them was a magical experience using several rolls of thick threads tied together to form hundreds of feet. Watching our creations soar high above, dancing with the breeze, gave us a sense of accomplishment and joy. It was a simple yet profound reminder of the rewards of hard work and creativity.

Playing "Cowboys and Indians" allowed us to delve into the world of imagination. We crafted makeshift bows and arrows, fashioned cowboy hats from old newspapers, and created elaborate scenarios of chases, rescues and gun fights. While the game is now viewed through a more critical lens due to its cultural implications, at the time, it was a source of endless fun and camaraderie. We would spend hours running around, hiding around trees, the school yard and neighboring church building, and plotting our next moves. Inspired by John Wayne and Roy Rogers movies and comic books, we spent hours running, hiding, and planning. This game honed our storytelling and teamwork skills.

Our characters evolved with each session, and so did our plots. We learned to negotiate, create alliances, and even resolve conflicts that arose during play. These sessions were more than just games; they taught us lessons in creativity, empathy, and collaboration. Despite the game's outdated premise, it undeniably sparked endless adventures and cherished childhood memories. This enriched our bonding and shaped our social dynamics in numerous ways, laying a foundation for lifelong friendships and shared stories.

Skipping rope was another beloved activity. We would form groups, turning the rope rhythmically while chanting rhymes. Each jump was a test of timing and agility. As we progressed, we added challenges like double jumps or incorporating dance moves. Skipping was not just a physical exercise; it was a social event. We bonded over shared laughter, encouraging each other to improve and celebrating our successes together.

## Playing a Role in Julius Caesar Play

One of the most significant highlights of my elementary school years was participating in the school's annual concert. In my final year at Carron Hall, I had the honor of being cast in a play as the character Decius Brutus in the adaptation of Shakespeare's "Julius Caesar." The preparation for the play was intense and exhilarating. We spent weeks rehearsing our lines, understanding our characters, and perfecting our performances. Our teachers (Ms. Cuff and my mother) were both strict and inspiring in their role as producers. They encouraged us to delve deep into our roles, often explaining the historical context and motivations behind each character. Ms. Cuff, our 9th grade teacher, was new but very energetic and enthusiastic. She was a perfectionist who made learning fun and enjoyable. My mother's primary responsibility was to design and prepare the costumes for the production.

Portraying Decius Brutus was a transformative experience. Known for his cunning and persuasive traits, Decius convinced Caesar (played by Winston Palmer) to attend the Senate meeting on the Ides of March, ultimately leading to Caesar's assassination. Delving into this character revealed the intricate dynamics of loyalty and betrayal. As I delivered my lines with conviction, I felt deeply connected to the unfolding tension in the story.

Every rehearsal brought new insights into Decius's motivations and how his actions intertwined with the fates of other characters. Working closely with the directors and fellow cast members allowed me to explore different facets of Decius's personality, from his manipulative charm to his underlying ambitions. This immersion into the role helped me understand the weight of each word and gesture, enhancing my portrayal on stage.

Another remarkable performance was by Everard, who played Mark Antony brilliantly. His delivery of the iconic speech beginning with "Friends, Romans, countrymen, lend me your ears" was particularly powerful. Watching Everard's dedication and mastery of his role inspired me to push my own boundaries and strive for excellence in my performance.

The night was electrifying, with a full auditorium erupting in applause, which greatly boosted my confidence and passion for the performing arts. The audience's reaction was a testament to the hard work and commitment of everyone involved in the production. Moments like these remind me why I appreciate acting—the ability to transport audiences, evoke emotions, and bring stories to life. This experience has deepened my appreciation for the art of theatre and the collaborative effort it requires.

I also remember when Jamaica began television broadcasting in 1963 through the Jamaica Broadcasting Corporation (JBC). At that time, broadcasts were in black-and-white. My first experience with television came after school when some of us would sneak over to the nearby vocational school for girls, which was close to the primary school. There, we were warmly welcomed by Ms. Evans, a matron at the school, who allowed us to watch a small black-and-white TV from the steps leading to the teacher's lounge.

Despite the modest setup, we were absolutely thrilled just to be watching television. I recall that we were allowed to watch between 4:00 and 6:00 PM, during a time slot dedicated to young viewers. The programming was primarily cartoons, making the experience even more thrilling for us. Bugs Bunny, the beloved cartoon character, often delighted us with his iconic catchphrase, ***"What's up, Doc?"***. Unfortunately, our home did not have TV until we moved to St. Catherine in 1971.

## The Assassination of Dr. Martin Luther King Jr.

Dr. Martin Luther King Jr.'s assassination on April 4, 1968, sent shockwaves not just across the United States but also through Jamaica, stirring deep sorrow, anger, and solidarity. I still remember the moment I heard the announcement on the radio that day. It was as if time had frozen. The weight of the news pressed down on me, and I wept. Even as a young boy, I understood that something monumental had been taken from the world—a leader whose words had inspired millions, a beacon of hope extinguished far too soon.

Jamaica, with its long history of resistance to oppression and its deep cultural and political ties to the African American struggle, responded with profound grief and outrage. The country had long admired King's tireless work for civil rights, and his message of nonviolent resistance resonated deeply with the island's own fight against colonialism and racial inequality. His death was not just an American tragedy; it was a loss felt by Black people across the world, and for Jamaicans, it was deeply personal.

That evening, the entire country seemed to mourn in unison. Radio stations played tributes, church bells rang, and community leaders spoke out about the significance of King's legacy. Many people gathered in churches and public spaces to pray, sing hymns, and share their sorrow. I recall my own family members discussing the news in hushed, somber tones, grappling with the implications of his assassination.

For many Jamaicans, particularly those involved in the Rastafarian and Pan-African movements, King was more than just an American leader—he was a symbol of justice, liberation, and Black pride. His murder reinforced the belief that the fight against racial injustice was far from over. Rastafarians, who had long championed the struggle for Black self-determination, saw King's assassination as yet another reminder of the systemic oppression faced by people of African descent worldwide. The moment galvanized many within the movement to push even harder for social change.

At the same time, there was also a palpable sense of frustration and anger. How could a man who preached peace and unity be met with such violence? This question lingered in the minds of many Jamaicans who empathized deeply with the struggles of Black Americans. It was a stark reminder that the dream King so eloquently spoke of was still far from being realized. The news sparked discussions about the broader implications of racial injustice, colonialism, and economic disparity—not just in America, but across the world.

Jamaican political leaders also expressed their sorrow, with then-Prime Minister Hugh Shearer denouncing the assassination and calling for the continued pursuit of justice and equality. In schools, teachers spoke about King's impact, ensuring that younger generations understood the importance of his work. His speeches and writings were studied with renewed urgency, reinforcing the idea that the struggle for equality was a shared responsibility.

The moment served to reinforce a sense of global Black unity and further strengthened Jamaica's commitment to social justice and Black empowerment. Several local activists found renewed inspiration in King's words, and his dream lived on through the continued efforts of those who fought for racial and social justice on the island.

For me, King's assassination left a lasting impression. Even as a child, I could sense the collective sorrow that gripped the nation. It was my first real encounter with the harsh realities of racial injustice on a global scale, and it planted a seed in me—a deeper awareness of the struggles that Black people faced, not just in America, but everywhere. It made me more conscious of my own identity and the importance of standing up for what is right.

Though decades have passed since that fateful day, the lessons of Dr. King's life and his tragic death continue to resonate. His unwavering commitment to justice, his belief in the power of unity, and his courage in the face of adversity remain an enduring source of inspiration. Even today, as I reflect on that moment in 1968, I am reminded that the fight for equality is ongoing and that we each have a role to play in carrying his dream forward.

## Building Lifelong Friendships at Carron Hall

Beyond academic and extracurricular activities, the relationships I built at Carron Hall were equally impactful. School was not just a place of learning; it was a community, a space where friendships were forged through shared experiences and mutual respect. My classmates and I formed strong bonds that extended far beyond the classroom walls.

We supported each other through challenges—whether it was tackling difficult subjects, navigating schoolyard conflicts, or dealing with personal struggles. We celebrated each other's successes, no matter how big or small, reinforcing the idea that we were in this journey together.

Some of my fondest memories involve the carefree afternoons we spent after school. When the final bell rang, the playground became our kingdom. I have fond memories of sharing countless experiences with two of my best friends, Tim and Dandan. We would run, climb trees, and engage in spirited games, our laughter echoing through the schoolyard. Sometimes, our adventures took us beyond the school grounds, exploring the nearby woods or visiting each other's homes. Those moments of childhood exploration created bonds that would last a lifetime.

What made these friendships especially special was the deep sense of trust and camaraderie we shared. We confided in each other, offering support in ways that just childhood friends can. Whether it was discussing our dreams for the future or simply sharing a meal at lunchtime, these interactions shaped my understanding of friendship, loyalty, and the importance of human connection.

Even as we grew older and life took us in different directions, the friendships I built at Carron Hall remained significant. Many of my classmates went on to achieve great things, but whenever we reunited, it felt as though no time had passed at all. The foundation of our friendships—mutual respect, shared memories, and an unspoken understanding—remained strong.

Looking back, I realize that the friendships I formed during those years played a crucial role in shaping who I am today. Though decades have passed, the lessons and memories from Carron Hall continue to hold a special place in my heart.

# Chapter 2

---

# Roots and Beginnings

## The Family in the Early Years

I am the second of four children—Maurice, Althea, Kay, and myself—born to my mother, Gloria Forbes (formally Rose), affectionately known as Mama G, and my father, Frederick Rose. We all grew up together in the small district of Blue Gate, I described earlier, where family and community shaped our early years. Maurice, the eldest, arrived in 1953, followed by me in 1955, then Althea in 1959, and finally, our youngest sibling, Kay, in 1963. My birth certificate indicates that I was born in Brea Head, an area located between Blue Gate and Palmetto Grove.

Our parents were married just before the coronation of Queen Elizabeth II in 1953—a moment in history that lingered in our household, symbolized by the commemorative glasses proudly displayed in our china cabinet. My mother, Gloria, hailed from Pear Tree Grove was part of the larger, close-knit Toomer clan. My father, Frederick, came from the sizeable Rose family of Carron Hall. Growing up, I cherished learning from all the uncles and aunts we had on both sides of the family, some of whom played unforgettable roles in shaping my life.

Our parents excelled at creating a safe, nurturing, and comfortable home for us during our early years. Their love and dedication were evident in every aspect of our upbringing, providing a strong foundation that we leaned on even after their separation in 1963.

My father's departure from our family home in 1963 was a heartbreaking turning point in my life. It left a void that was hard to fill, but despite the pain, I cherish many warm memories of him from my early childhood. After leaving, he started a new chapter with his partner, who he eventually married in the early '70s. Together, they had six children before his passing in 2013. Though our paths diverged, the imprint of his presence—both in joy and in absence—remains a significant part of my story.

One particular incident stands out in my mind. My father was raising a young calf in our backyard, which was fenced in, and we had to feed it milk from a bucket with a nipple attached. One morning, eager to help my father prepare the milk, I accidentally bumped into him as he turned around with a pot of hot water. The hot water spilled and burned a large section of my left side really bad. My father rushed me to the clinic in Highgate to receive emergency treatment. The days following were marred with excruciating pain and a large bandage over the burn site. Despite this painful memory, I also remember the joy of helping my father with various tasks related to the cultivation and harvesting of bananas, pineapples, cocoa, coffee, oranges, coconuts, and various ground provisions in the field behind our small three-bedroom house. This wooden house featured a veranda at the front and sat high on wooden posts. The area beneath the floor, or cellar, was a haven for playing. The yard surrounding the house was dotted with several orange trees, along with towering breadfruit and ackee trees—all of which provided the perfect playground for honing my tree-climbing skills.

Tucked away in one of the back corners of the house stood a concrete water catchment tank, about 10 feet square and perched about 7 feet off the ground. Rainwater from the roof would funnel through a series of gutters straight into the tank, supplying us with water for daily use. Looking back, it was a remarkably clever system for harvesting rainwater long before the term *"sustainability"* became popular.

As kids, my brother and I became *"masters"* at retrieving water, especially when the tank's level dipped too low for it to flow through the connected pipe and faucet. Armed with a bucket tied to a rope, we'd balance on a ladder, carefully lowering the bucket into the tank, then hauling it back up with the precision of seasoned engineers. It felt like a routine chore back then, but thinking about it now, it was pretty ingenious.

Nowadays, roof catchment systems like the one we had aren't just relics of rural life—they've become common in both countryside homes and urban areas. People use modern versions to supplement public water supplies or as emergency reserves during water shortages. It's amazing to see how something we grew up with has become a key solution for sustainable living today.

I have fond memories of playing doll house with my sisters and cricket in the front yard with bats made from coconut husks and young hard orange as balls. These play times would sometimes get very competitive between my brother Maurice and myself. Competitive play sometimes involves participation with neighbors.

Interactions with neighbors like Leroy, Lloyd, Faye and Anneth would involve playing various games such as hide and seek, jump rope, board games, and jacks. I was fascinated by their rabbits and guinea pigs raised in coops. It was my first time trying rabbit meat, which they occasionally shared with me for dinner. I still remember the taste of their granny's delicious meals. The boys would engage in activities like picking guavas, ripe bananas, and apples from neighboring properties without permission. Other pastimes included shooting birds with slingshots made from rubber tubing, sliding down hills with makeshift coconut husk skates or with go-carts on the road, fishing for baby shrimps, and swimming in the pristine river most times in Palmetto Grove. The Peggy and Dam water holes were notable spots where swimming skills were developed.

One of our favorite summer pastimes was venturing out in a group of 8 to 12 kids from the district to the *"mango bush"*. This was always an adventure, as the mango bush was typically in Rock Springs, about three to four miles away, near the district of Woodside. The journey itself was part of the thrill—winding through hidden shortcuts, weaving through woods and open fields, until we finally arrived at Rock Springs, where towering mango trees stood heavy with the ripe, delicious fruit. It was nothing short of mango paradise.

After feasting until our bellies could hold no more, we would gather as many mangoes as we could carry, carefully packing them into baskets. Balancing the loaded baskets on our heads, we braced ourselves for the long trek back home, satisfied and already dreaming of our next trip.

I'll never forget the day I had a *"too close for comfort"* encounter with one of the most fearsome creatures of my childhood—the dreaded croaking lizard. As usual, I had climbed the large towering "Otaheite" apple tree next door, my go-to spot for snagging those sweet, juicy apples that hung like little red treasures just out of reach. I was feeling pretty confident, perched high up on a sturdy limb, stretching out to grab the ripest apple in sight. But just as I turned to make my triumphant descent, there it was. A massive and menacing croaking lizard, staring me down with those beady eyes, its body puffed up like it was ready for battle. And trust me, these weren't your ordinary lizards—these things could leap at you from a distance like some kind of scaly, spring-loaded missile. My heart practically stopped. For a split second, I was frozen, clinging to that branch, imagining the lizard launching itself at my face.

But then, survival mode kicked in. I didn't have time to think—I had to move fast. I swung my legs around, barely keeping my balance, and made a daring leap to the limb below. It creaked dangerously under my weight, but I wasn't sticking around to test its strength. Without missing a beat, I launched myself again, this time straight to the ground, landing with a hard thud about 7 or 8 feet below.

I hit the dirt, heart racing, covered in scrapes and leaves, but grateful to be lizard-free. As I dusted myself off, I glanced back up at the tree. That croaking lizard was still there, victorious in its perch, probably thinking it had claimed the tree for good. But I knew one thing for sure—I wouldn't be giving up those apples that easily.

My mother started teaching in the infant section of Carron Hall Primary. After training at Caledonia Teacher's College, she moved to higher grades. Having her as a teacher in my school meant constant support and reinforcement of other teachers' reprimands. She was very passionate about education and dedicated her time to helping each student succeed. The bond we shared extended beyond our home; in school, she provided not just academic guidance but also emotional support. Her presence in my educational journey was a balanced mix of encouragement and discipline, ensuring I stayed focused and driven. One of her well-known sayings was – *"if yuh want gud, yuh nose haffi run"*, indicating that achieving positive outcomes often necessitates sacrifice and effort, even if it feels uncomfortable or difficult.

My paternal grandmother, Isadora (Sis), lived with us until 1963. Her husband, Grandpa David Rose, passed away before I was born. Sis recounted many stories about Grandpa Rose when he was alive. He worked as a builder/tradesman and later moved to the western region of Jamaica for work, where he had children in the parish of Hanover. My extended family has its roots in the western part of the island. I later learnt that the origins of the Rose clan was from the parish of St. Ann and they have ancestral roots from Scotland.

Sis had extensive knowledge of past struggles and African customs passed down by her enslaved ancestors. She often shared stories of overcoming slavery while humming hymns and spirituals like *"Swing Low, Sweet Chariot"* . Sis's tales were filled with resilience and hope, painting vivid pictures of her ancestors' lives. She would sit by her outdoor wood fire, her eyes gleaming with wisdom, recounting different tales of their past struggles. Grandma Isadora also taught us about various African traditions that had endured despite the adversities faced by our forebears. From the intricate braiding of hair, symbolizing tribal identity, to the rich culinary practices that fused African ingredients with new world flavors, she ensured that we appreciated our heritage. Each story and lesson were a reminder of our roots, and the incredible strength embedded in our lineage.

Her presence was a living connection to a time long past, yet crucial to our understanding of who we were. The evenings spent listening to her stories and songs instilled in us a deep respect for our family's journey and an unwavering determination to honor their legacy.

Her culinary expertise in traditional dishes was particularly memorable. A notable dish she prepared included coconut rundown with salted shad or mackerel, accompanied by roasted breadfruit, green bananas, flour dumplings, and susumba berries. She was also a strong advocate for natural healing using various herbs and spices. While I appreciated her cooking, I was less fond of certain teas such as cerasee and fever grass. Nonetheless, she left an enduring impact on my appreciation for the use and benefits of natural herbs and spices, which I continue to incorporate into my adult life. One of her notable quotes was *"Wah sweet nanny goat, a go run him belly,"* meaning some enjoyable things can have negative consequences later. Her wisdom and life experiences were sources of enlightenment, hope, and perseverance. Sadly, Sis passed away in 1971, at the age of 87, taking a significant part of the Rose family's legacy with her.

My maternal grandmother, Rosa Wright—affectionately called Menda—came to live with us in 1968. Before moving in, she had been a long-time resident of Portland Cottage, Vere, Clarendon, a place that would leave a lasting impression on me from a single childhood visit.

I have vivid memories of my initial meeting with Menda in Clarendon, around the 1965-66 timeframe when my baby sister Kay was a toddler. I spent several weeks of summer vacation there, and it was my first- and only time visiting Vere in my childhood. The landscape was unlike anything I had ever seen in St. Mary. Vere was a unique place, characterized by vast flat areas of salt ponds near the coastal region in the southern part of Jamaica. The natural sparse vegetation—punctuated by cactus and sandy surfaces—stood in stark contrast to the lush greenery of St. Mary.

Despite my admiration for the wide, open scenery and the endless sugar cane plantations, I found it hard to enjoy the persistent mosquitos and the prickles that seemed to be everywhere. The sandy ground and thorny plants made every step an adventure of its own. But even with these discomforts, the experience of being in such a different environment was unforgettable.

My sister Kay spent about a year with our grandmother Menda in Vere. When she returned home, we were all amazed—and thoroughly entertained—by how much she had adopted the accent and expressions of the locals in Vere. She would say things in such a distinct way that it cracked us up every time. Her transformation was a constant source of amusement and became one of those family stories we loved to revisit.

That summer in Vere, though brief, gave me a new appreciation for Jamaica's diverse landscapes and the unique cultural flavors that different parishes had to offer. It also deepened my bond with Menda, whose warmth and presence would become an integral part of our household in the years to come.

Grandma Menda came in 1968 to run our household while my mother was going to attend the Moneague Teacher's College in St. Ann for 2 years. She was very instrumental in preparing me for the daily routine commuting when I started attending Dinthill. Throughout the early days, Menda was the essential force behind teaching me self-reliance. I learned to wash and iron my clothes, especially my school uniform, cooking and preparing meals, and other domestic chores. The skills I acquired with my grandma's guidance have served me well throughout my life. Her standout lessons were sometimes imparted through various proverbs, the meanings of which might have escaped me at the time. For instance:

*"Humble calf drink the most milk"* – a lesson in humility.

*"Chicken merry, hawk deh near"* – dangers can lurk in some of the most unexpected places.

*"Yu want all, yu lose all"* – take just what you can comfortably manage, rather than attempt to grab everything for yourself.

*"New broom sweep clean, but old broom know dem corners"* – we should strive for a happy blend between the old and new.

Unfortunately, sometime during my second year at Dinthill, Menda suffered a serious stroke and had to undergo a lengthy period of rehabilitation that left her severely hampered in her movements. At this stage, we had to manage all domestic chores and assist my grandma. Despite the hardship, my mother, who was close to finishing college, was able to arrange for a domestic helper to ease the burden. This was a very challenging and unforgettable time. Grandma Menda continued to live with her disability, demonstrating remarkable strength and resilience until her passing in 1993 at the age of 75.

My maternal grandfather, Cyril (Backus) Toomer, was a distinguished and beloved figure on my mother's side of the family. My mother, the second of several siblings, hailed from Pear Tree Grove, St. Catherine, though Grandpa later relocated to Kingston. By the time I first remember meeting him, he and his sister (Aunt B) were co-owners of a bustling drugstore in the heart of downtown Kingston.

Some of my earliest and fondest memories are of spending time with him at the store while my mother navigated the many shops around Parade. Grandpa had a way of making those moments special—he'd spoil me with toys and sweet treats from the sidewalk vendors, ensuring I never felt bored. My grandaunt, equally warm and caring, always took an interest in my schooling, asking questions and encouraging me in a way that made me felt important.

As I grew older, I began spending parts of my summer vacations at Grandpa's home in the Half Way Tree area of Kingston. Those visits were my first real taste of city life as a grown boy, and I embraced every bit of it. It was during these stays that I got to know my uncles and aunt, but two of them, Uncle Les (Leslie Toomer) and Uncle Lindo (Victor Toomer), became my favorites. Sadly, Grandpa Cyril passed away in 1983, at the age of 81.

Uncle Lindo, who worked with an asphalt paving company, had a treasure-trove of stories about his adventures on road projects across the island. But what honestly made him stand out was his deep love for music. He spent hours spinning vinyl records on his turntable, immersing me in the rich sounds of American R&B, jazz, and local hits. I found myself rocking to the rhythm, fascinated not just by the music but by the entire setup of his sound system.

Lindo also had a love for the great outdoors. On his visits to the countryside, he'd take my brother Maurice and me on thrilling hikes through the woods, armed with handmade slingshots for bird hunting. The best part? He made slingshots for us too, so we could feel like full-fledged adventurers and marksmen. Though

I don't recall ever hitting a single bird, the experience itself—stalking through the brush, maintaining a hush, aiming with precision at the birds, and sharing in Lindo's excitement—was absolutely exhilarating. The trips were often rewarding as Uncle Lindo would roast his haul of birds and share this exotic meat with us after we got home. The memory of Uncle Lindo shines brightly in me even though he has passed on in 2018 at the age of 76.

Uncle Les, who remains my all-time favorite to this day, was a cherished presence in my childhood. He would occasionally visit us in the countryside when I was a young boy, always bringing warmth, laughter, and treats from Kingston. He shared a special bond with my mother, showering her with gifts and affection in a way that showed their deep sibling connection. In the early days, he and my father also became great friends, often accompanying each other on work-related trips, strengthening the family ties even more.

As I grew older and entered my teenage years, my relationship with Uncle Les deepened. I spent many summer vacations and weekends with him in Kingston while I was in high school and college, and this continued until I eventually migrated from Jamaica. He was a highly skilled tailor, crafting stylish pants not just for himself but also for his friends and me. I was always in awe of his craftsmanship, but what stood out even more was his gentle nature, kindness, and the unwavering encouragement he always offered.

Beyond his talent as a tailor, Uncle Les was deeply dedicated to his church and the youth in the community. He was an outstanding member of his church choir, constantly humming his favorite hymns as he went about his day. Some of my fondest memories with him include our trips to the annual pantomime shows at the Little Theatre in Kingston—an experience that brought both cultural enrichment and pure joy.

Even after he migrated to the United States, we remained closely connected. To this day, our bond remains strong, a testament to the love, guidance, and inspiration he has always provided in my life.

My aunt Rhoda was one of my father's sisters who lived in Kingston. During my childhood, I spent a few school holidays—both Christmas and summer—with her, her husband, Mr. Chambers, and my two cousins, Gary and Fern. Although my cousins were a few years older than me, they were always delighted to play around the house and entertain me. We spent countless hours with different toys, playing hide-and-seek and board games, making those visits lively and memorable.

Being exposed to life in Kingston at an early age was eye-opening. The city felt much hotter than Blue Gate, and the streets were wider and bustling with traffic. I was especially fascinated by the sight of the JOS buses, which seemed enormous and full of life compared to anything I had seen back home. Aunt Rhoda's house was large, with a carport in front and a metal gate enclosing the property. The house itself was impeccably maintained, both inside and out. They had beautifully tended flower beds and shrubs, a vegetable garden, and even rabbits and fowls kept in coops at the rear of the property.

Aunt Rhoda, being a teacher, upheld strict discipline, even during school vacations. She encouraged us to study and insisted that I contribute significantly to household chores. Watering the lawn, tending the vegetable garden, and caring for the rabbits were all part of my daily routine while staying there. These tasks, though sometimes tedious, taught me the value of responsibility and hard work.

My most cherished memory of Aunt Rhoda is the delicious black cake and sorrel drink she made at Christmas time—a treat I looked forward to with great anticipation. However, not all her culinary efforts were to my liking. The times when she insisted I eat eggplant and other vegetables were my least enjoyable moments, but they too are part of the vivid tapestry of memories I hold dear from those visits. Those holidays in Kingston not just brought me closer to my cousins but also provided invaluable lessons and experiences that shaped my understanding of life beyond Blue Gate. Sadly, Aunt Rhoda has since passed in 2003.

My father, a trained agriculturalist, advised community farmers and enjoyed grafting citrus trees to create different species from seville (sour) orange trees. He also produced export-quality bananas on his own farm and supported local small farmers in banana cultivation. He was well-liked and respected in the community. My uncle Les, who sometimes visited us from Kingston, would accompany him on the job and saw families offer my father dinner during his daily routine. My father always accepted but told my uncle, *"You still have to eat Gloria's food when we get home, or she'll be very mad."*

## The Banana Export Chain

During the 1960s and 1970s, St. Mary was one of the leading parishes in Jamaica for banana export, playing a crucial role in the island's agricultural economy. The infrastructure supporting this industry relied on a network of independent truckers who would collect bananas bi-weekly from farmers' gates and transport them to the nearest *"boxing plant"*. At these facilities, the bananas were carefully sorted, washed, and packed into boxes for shipping overseas. For many families in the community, banana export was a vital source of income, sustaining their livelihoods for generations.

The export process was well-coordinated, with container ships typically docking in the port town of Port Antonio, located on the northeast end of the island. I recall a time when a large boxing plant in the town of Highgate played a significant role in the process. Once prepared for export, the bananas were loaded onto a train and transported to Port Antonio. This rail system provided an efficient means of moving large quantities of bananas until the railway system began to decline.

As rail transport became less viable, the industry adapted by shifting operations to a closer boxing plant in Palmetto Grove. From there, truckers took on the responsibility of transporting the boxed bananas directly to Port Antonio, ensuring that Jamaica's banana exports continued despite changes in infrastructure. The banana trade was not just an economic activity—it was a way of life for many in St. Mary, shaping the rhythms of daily work and community interactions.

## My Future Stepfather

Sam Forbes, who later became my stepfather, operated a truck transporting bananas to the boxing plant and Port Antonio shipping port bi-weekly. He worked diligently to satisfy customers and ensure they received proper compensation. I knew of my mother's early contributions to his business. Sam had been in the transportation business for years before meeting my mother. His reputation for reliability and efficiency earned him many loyal clients. Their partnership was not just professional but also blossomed into a loving relationship, leading to their marriage in 1971. The synergy between them was apparent, as their combined efforts led to greater business success and a fulfilling personal life.

Sam, who was the son of Mr. Stanford Forbes, owner of the famous shop in Blue Gate. Stanford "Sanki" Forbes was married to Mrs. Amy Forbes, and they became my extended family with several step aunts, uncles and cousins. Neville Forbes, who lived at the family residence, became one of my favorite step-uncles with his cheerful nature and constant encouragement.

Sam was a huge part of my life, from my early childhood right into adulthood, and boy, did he know how to keep things lively! His quick wit and humor were unmatched, and he had a knack for making even the simplest moments unforgettable. One of his first jokes that stuck with me was, *"Yeah, I'm on a seafood diet—I see food and eat it!"* It never failed to get a laugh, no matter how many times we heard it.

Mealtimes with Sam were always a riot. I remember one dinner when someone left a good portion of food on their plate. Sam raised an eyebrow, grinned, and said, *"What happen, the cat touch yu?"* We all burst out laughing, but of course, Sam had a story to go with it. He launched into this tale about a couple invited to dine with a wealthier family. The wife, knowing her husband loved to clean his plate, worried it might make them look bad. So, she told him she'd tap his foot under the table when it was time to stop eating. Well, halfway through dinner, the husband suddenly stops eating, well before his plate is empty. The wife's confused—she hadn't tapped him. Turns out, it wasn't her giving the signal, it was the family's cat brushing against his leg! Classic Sam—he always had a story that left us in stitches.

Sundays were extra special thanks to Sam. Early morning, he'd pile us into his truck and take us down to the river at Palmetto Grove, along with a bunch of other young guys from the neighborhood. Those trips were the highlight of my week—splashing around in the bath holes, laughing at jokes, and learning how to swim with Sam's patient guidance. He wasn't just there for the fun; he was the reason it was fun.

As I got older, Sam became even more involved in our lives. He partnered with my mother to raise chickens for broilers and eggs, turning our backyard into a bustling little farm. That meant my brother and I had front-row seats to the world of poultry farming—feeding the chickens, keeping their coops clean, and making sure everything ran smoothly. I can't say I was a fan of all the chores, especially when it came time to slaughter and package the broilers for sale (let's just say that part wasn't my favorite), but those experiences taught us responsibility and gave us plenty of stories to laugh about later.

Sam wasn't just a family member; he was the heartbeat of so many of my memories. His humor, kindness, and larger-than-life presence made every day a little brighter and every story a little funnier.

One of Sam's closest friends was Barry Ramsey, a highly skilled builder and carpenter whose craftsmanship was well known throughout the community. The two were inseparable drinking buddies, often meeting at Forbes' shop and bar in Blue Gate, where their booming laughter and animated storytelling filled the air. Seeing them together was pure joy—they had a way of turning even the simplest moments into something unforgettable.

Barry wasn't just a drinking companion; he was part of our adventures too. On some Sunday mornings, he'd tag along on our escapes to the river, adding to the fun with his quick wit and easygoing nature. But my most vivid memory of Barry is watching him transform our home. I can still picture him, steady and focused, as he tore down the old wooden veranda and skillfully replaced it with a sturdy concrete one. Every measurement was precise, every movement confident—it was like watching an artist at work.

Little did I know then that those moments of quiet admiration would shape my own path. Looking back, I realize that my deep appreciation for building construction, carpentry and joinery at Dinthill was sparked by watching Barry at work. His skill, patience, and dedication left an impression on me that would last a lifetime. Barry emerged as a prominent figure and served as a mentor to numerous young men in the community, maintaining high regard until his passing in 2023.

## The Carron Hall Presbyterian Church: A 200-year History

Growing up, my family was deeply connected to the Presbyterian Church in Carron Hall, St. Mary. The church was situated near the primary school and the vocational school, a bit over a mile from my home. Sunday services and Sunday School were highlights of my week, filled with laughter and chats with friends. The charm of seeing the girls from the Vocational School across the street, clad in their elegant white dresses and hats, brightened one side of the church congregation. They also took Sunday evening strolls through the community, as a group, they would pass by my home. My mother's participation in the choir added a special touch; her solos at Christmas concerts, especially her favorite, "O Holy Night", were mesmerizing and brought joy to me.

The church stood like a fortress, its solid stone structure adorned with long, colorfully decorated stained glass murals in the windows. Inside, the atmosphere was captivating, with fine stained wooden panels lining the lower walls and surrounding the preacher's pulpit and the platform for the organ and choir. What always impressed me were the well-polished wooden benches arranged in three distinct sections for the congregation, each section meticulously laid out in unison. Adjacent to the pulpit was a designated area for Sunday school sessions.

I have vivid memories of trying to sneak into church late through the rear entrances, just to come face to face with the pastor preparing in the vestry area. As I grew older, I occasionally took on usher duties, responsible for passing the collection plate through the congregation. Despite my nerves, this experience instilled in me a sense of responsibility and importance.

The first pastor I remember was Mr. Bigsby, followed by Mr. Bisnauth, who hailed from Guyana with his family. Pastor Bisnauth, an avid cricket enthusiast and player, had the vacant land next to his residence (Mans) cleared to create a wide-open cricket field—a welcomed addition for the young men and boys in our community. Bisnauth himself often joined in games, demonstrating his skill as a spin bowler. I was so fascinated by his spin bowling techniques, I tried to emulate them whenever I could.

The church boasts a rich history spanning over two centuries. Its origins (around 1823) are deeply intertwined with Jamaica's colonial past, specifically the era of slavery and the subsequent evolution of Jamaican society. From its early days as a missionary outpost to its role in post-emancipation education and social reform, the church has been a cornerstone of the Carron Hall community. The church remains present on the landscape of Carron Hall today. The rich history of both the church and the community it served would make a fascinating subject for a separate book.

## Early Foundations and the Era of Slavery (Late 18th – Early 19th Century)

The presence of the Presbyterian Church in Jamaica began with the arrival of Scottish missionaries in the late 18th and early 19th centuries. These missionaries, many from the Scottish Kirk and the United Presbyterian Church, were part of a broader movement to evangelize enslaved Africans and the free Black population in the British colonies. Carron Hall, situated in the parish of St. Mary, became one of the communities where Presbyterian missionaries established a foothold.

During this period, Jamaica's economy was driven by the brutal plantation system, which relied heavily on the labor of enslaved Africans. The role of Christian churches in this system was complex and often contradictory. While some denominations, including parts of the Presbyterian Church, were complicit in upholding the social structures of slavery, others actively opposed it.

## Missionary Efforts Among the Enslaved

The Presbyterian Church, like other Protestant denominations, sought to convert enslaved Africans to Christianity. Missionaries often faced resistance from plantation owners who feared that Christian teachings could inspire rebellion and undermine the institution of slavery. Nevertheless, the missionaries persisted, offering religious instruction and basic education to the enslaved population, albeit within the constraints of the colonial system.

While some missionaries justified slavery as a means to "civilize" Africans through Christianity, others began to see the inherent contradictions between their faith and the realities of the slave system. Over time, a growing number of Presbyterian missionaries became vocal critics of slavery, aligning themselves with the broader abolitionist movement.

## The Abolition of Slavery and the Church's Role in Emancipation (1834 – 1865)

The abolition of slavery in the British Empire in 1834, followed by the full emancipation in 1838, marked a significant turning point for the Presbyterian Church in Carron Hall and across Jamaica. The church played a critical role in supporting the newly freed population, many of whom continued to face economic hardship and social discrimination.

## Education and Social Upliftment

One of the church's most lasting contributions during this period was its emphasis on education. The Presbyterian Church established schools throughout St. Mary, including Carron Hall, to provide basic literacy and vocational training to the emancipated population. Education was seen as a pathway to empowerment, allowing former slaves to assert their independence and improve their socio-economic status.

The church's schools not merely taught reading and writing but also instilled values of discipline, self-reliance, and community service. Many leaders in the post-emancipation Jamaican society were products of these church-run educational institutions.

The Presbyterian Church in Carron Hall has historically maintained strong ties with several key institutions in the community, including Carron Hall Primary School, the Pringle Home for Girls, and the Vocational School for girls that has evolved into a high school. These institutions reflect the church's longstanding commitment to education, social welfare, and community development.

## Carron Hall Primary School

Carron Hall Primary School was established under the auspices of the Presbyterian Church as part of its broader mission to educate the children of freed slaves and foster literacy in the rural communities of St. Mary. After emancipation in 1838, many Christian denominations saw education as a tool for empowerment and upliftment. The church likely played a pivotal role in providing both financial and organizational support. Church leaders often served on the school boards, ensuring that Christian values were integrated into the curriculum teaching students Presbyterian doctrines alongside academic subjects.

The primary school often acted as an extension of the church, hosting community events, celebrations, and church-related activities. Many teachers were active church members, and the school served as a feeder for the church's youth programs.

## Pringle Home for Girls

The Pringle Home for Girls was another institution closely tied to the Presbyterian Church's mission in Carron Hall. Established as a residential facility for orphaned or disadvantaged girls, the Pringle Home embodied the church's commitment to social welfare and gender equity in education and care.

The Presbyterian Church was likely involved in founding or sponsoring the Pringle Home, either directly or through partnerships with other missionary organizations. This would have been part of the broader mission to support vulnerable populations, especially women and children. In addition to providing shelter and education, the church would have offered spiritual counseling and religious instruction to the girls. Presbyterian values of discipline, integrity, and service were likely central to the home's ethos.

The church may have collaborated with local schools or provided in-house educational programs, ensuring that the girls received both academic and vocational training to prepare them for independence. The Pringle Home girls maintained strong ties with the wider church community, with congregants volunteering time and resources to support the home's residents. The operations of this institution is still in existence today.

## The Practical Training Center (PTC) Vocational School for Girls

The PTC vocational school for girls in Carron Hall, which has now transitioned into a co-ed high school, represented the Presbyterian Church's commitment to practical education and skills development. This institution was established to provide the females with the technical skills needed to secure employment. The church would have influenced the curriculum, ensuring it included moral instruction alongside vocational training in home economics. At the culmination of the academic year, the school organizes an exhibition or open house where students' meticulously prepared and visually appealing dishes and desserts are showcased. The highlight for me was sampling a variety of these culinary creations.

The church may have contributed to the infrastructure of the school, fundraising for buildings, equipment, and teacher salaries. Church members often served as administrators or educators. By promoting vocational education, the church helped equip young people with the skills necessary for leadership roles in the community and the broader Jamaican society.

After Jamaica's independence in 1962, the role of the Presbyterian Church in Carron Hall and its support for local institutions like Carron Hall Primary School, the Pringle Home for Girls, and the former vocational school for girls shifted significantly. This evolution reflected broader national changes, including increased government involvement in education, growing national identity, and the decline of missionary dominance in social services. However, the church remained an important pillar of moral guidance, community cohesion, and supplementary support.

The church's legacy in these institutions continues today, as they remain central to the life of the Carron Hall community. Whether through direct involvement or the enduring influence of its foundational values, the Church's commitment to education, social justice, and community empowerment is deeply embedded in the fabric of Carron Hall's history.

## Land Ownership and Economic Independence

In addition to education, the Presbyterian Church supported initiatives that encouraged land ownership among freed Jamaicans. By promoting self-sufficiency and economic independence, the church helped to lay groundwork for the development of free peasant communities. Carron Hall, like many rural areas in St. Mary, benefited from these efforts, fostering a sense of pride and resilience among its inhabitants.

## The Church and the Morant Bay Rebellion (1865)

The Morant Bay Rebellion of 1865, led by Paul Bogle, now one of Jamaica's National Hero, highlighted the ongoing struggles of the Black population in post-emancipation Jamaica. While the Presbyterian Church in Carron Hall may not have been directly involved in the rebellion, the wider Presbyterian community was deeply affected by the events. Many church leaders sympathized with the plight of the poor and landless, recognizing the systemic injustices that persisted after emancipation. The rebellion and its brutal suppression by the colonial government served as a wake-up call, galvanizing the church to deepen its commitment to social justice and advocacy for the marginalized.

## Growth and Development in the 20th Century

Throughout the 20th century, the Presbyterian Church in Carron Hall continued to evolve, adapting to the changing needs of the community. The church remained a center for worship, education, and social activism, playing a vital role in the cultural and spiritual life of St. Mary.

The church's emphasis on education produced generations of community leaders, teachers, and professionals who contributed to Jamaica's development. Many former students of Presbyterian schools in Carron Hall went on to play significant roles in local government, business, and civil society.

Building on its historical commitment to social justice, the church engaged in various initiatives to address poverty, inequality, and discrimination. It supported efforts to improve healthcare, housing, and access to resources, reflecting its mission to serve both the spiritual and material needs of the community.

## Continuity and the Modern Era

In the 21st century, the Presbyterian Church in Carron Hall remains a pillar of the community. While maintaining its historical legacy, the church has embraced modern challenges and opportunities, from addressing contemporary social issues to leveraging technology for outreach and education.

The Presbyterian Church's journey—from its early missionary efforts during slavery, through the struggles of emancipation, to its role in shaping modern Jamaican society—offers a profound example of how religious institutions can evolve and impact the communities they serve. Its legacy in Carron Hall is one of faith, education, and a steadfast commitment to justice and equality.

The church today has become part of the United Church in Jamaica and the Cayman Islands (UCJCI), which was established in 1992 through the union of the Disciples of Christ in Jamaica and the United Church of Jamaica and Grand Cayman. The latter was itself formed in 1965 from the merger of the Presbyterian Church of Jamaica and the Congregational Union of Jamaica. Therefore, while the Presbyterian Church in Carron Hall has been part of denominational unions, it continues to uphold its Presbyterian heritage within the UCJCI framework.

## The Transition into Teenage Years

As I stepped into my early teenage years, a few memories stood out distinctly—moments of discovery, adventure, and a budding awareness of emotions I had never felt before. It was during this time that I experienced my first crush. Her name was Wanda, a new resident of Pringle Home and a fresh face at Carron Hall Primary School. Wanda was different—she carried an air of elegance that set her apart. Her clothes, which appeared to have been sent from overseas, made her the envy of the other girls, and to me, she was simply captivating.

One rainy afternoon, fate gifted me a moment I would never forget. As the raindrops drummed against the rooftops, Wanda turned to me with a smile and invited me to walk with her under her umbrella. I didn't hesitate for a second. We strolled side by side, sharing laughter and conversation, the world around us fading into the background. It didn't matter that I had to part ways with her long before reaching my home or that I would eventually be drenched by the rain—those precious minutes under Wanda's umbrella were worth every drop. Sadly, our paths never crossed again after I left Carron Hall School in 1968, but that memory remains etched in my heart like a scene from a cherished old movie.

This was the time when I frankly felt I had earned my place among the older boys. At last, I was welcomed into the fold of the big guys—Everton, Maurice, Leroy, Devon, Desmond, Keith, Allan, Teddy, Carl, Ronald, Beresford, Everard, Dalbert, the late Sasso, the late Winston, the late Trevor and others—who looked out for me like a younger brother, offering both guidance and protection. Their presence gave me a sense of belonging, but what made these moments even more special was having my best friends, Tim and Donovan (Dandan), by my side. Together, we immersed ourselves in the excitement of youth, eagerly looking forward to the annual fair and the unforgettable parties at the *"Parnassus"* grounds in Windsor Castle. These gatherings were electric—filled with music, laughter, and boundless youthful energy, creating memories that would stay with me for a lifetime.

I would be remiss if I didn't recognize the equally nurturing role played by the older girls who were like big sisters to me. Their kindness, guidance, and protective presence provided a sense of comfort and belonging during my formative years. Whether it was offering words of encouragement, helping with schoolwork, or simply looking out for me in everyday situations, their support was invaluable. Among this remarkable group were Hermalin, Lorna, Marnel, Winsome, Millicent, Violet, Dorothy, the late Janet, and others, each leaving a lasting impression on my life. Their warmth and generosity of spirit helped shape my sense of community.

One of the most thrilling experiences of that time was attending the indoor movie nights at school, courtesy of Mr. Gordon's roving cinema on wheels. Mr. Gordon, who operated a cinema in Highgate, had a simple philosophy: *"If you can't make it to the cinema, the cinema will make it to you."* And so, on those magical nights, we would gather in the dimly lit schoolroom as the projector flickered to life, bringing Hollywood to our doorstep. I can still recall the larger-than-life figures of John Wayne, Roy Rogers, Clint Eastwood, Jack Palance, Charlton Heston, and, of course, Sean Connery as the suave and unshakable James Bond. The action, intrigue, and spectacle of Bond films made them instant favorites, transporting us into a world of adventure and espionage. Of all the films I watched, none left a deeper impression on me than *"**The Ten Commandments**"*. The grand storytelling, the commanding presence of Charlton Heston as Moses, and the sheer spectacle of the parting of the Red Sea held me spellbound. It was more than just a movie—it was an experience, a story that left me with a sense of awe and wonder.

Looking back, those were golden days filled with adventure, camaraderie, and the thrill of youthful innocence. Each moment—whether a stolen walk in the rain, a night in the school watching a film, or the excitement of a local fair—was a chapter in the story of my coming of age.

In closing, my path from childhood in Blue Gate and Carron Hall is intricately woven into Jamaica's history and development. Though the quaint old house I grew up in no longer stands, I continue to cherish the land and the memories it holds dear in my heart.

The experiences and lessons learned during my formative years have shaped my outlook on life and my approach to problem-solving. Reflecting on my years at Carron Hall Primary/Elementary school, I realize that it was not just the academic lessons that left a lasting impression but also the values and skills we imbibed. The skills and values learned during those years continue to influence my life.

Elementary school was more than just a place of learning; it was a nurturing ground where talents were discovered, friendships were forged, and lifelong memories were created. The sense of community, the dedication of teachers, the spirit of collaboration, and the joy of discovery were integral to our daily lives. These experiences laid a solid foundation, preparing us for future challenges and opportunities. I truly realized living the motto–*"it takes a village to raise a child"*

# Chapter 3

---

# The High School Years

## The Dawn of a New Journey

I still remember the last few weeks at Carron Hall Primary School with vivid clarity. It was 1968, a time when my days were filled with the innocent joys of boyhood in St. Mary. Cricket games with friends, marble competitions during recess, and playing "Cowboys and Indians" in the schoolyard defined my childhood. Studying, to be honest, was often secondary to these pleasures, and the thought of passing the Common Entrance Exam seemed a distant priority. However, fate had different plans for me.

One unforgettable day, my mother received a letter that would change the course of my life. I had secured a half-scholarship to attend Dinthill Technical High School (Dinthill) in Linstead. Despite the financial strain it would place on our family, my mother was adamant that I would take this opportunity. As a teacher herself, she understood the value of education and was determined to ensure I had a chance to better my future. My father was also happy I would be attending Dinthill where he was an alumnus from the inception of the agricultural school for boys.

The transition from the familiar surroundings of Carron Hall to the bustling atmosphere of Dinthill was daunting. Linstead was a world apart, and the daily two-way commute on the *"NorthStar"* bus, which involved traversing the infamous **"Devil's Racecourse,"** was an ordeal. The narrow, steeply sloped, winding road was perilous, and each journey to and from school felt like a gamble with fate. A small consolation was the prospect of street vendors with their colorful displays of snacks and tropical fruits at the base of the course.

My daily commute to Dinthill, a 30-kilometer (19-mile) journey one way, was an adventure filled with memorable experiences even though it felt like a longer distance. I recall on a few occasions being awakened by the sound of the bus horn less than a mile away and having less than 10 minutes to get ready – the bus usually arrived between 5:00am and 5:30 am. Thankfully, the NorthStar bus driver, "*Papa Reni,*" was kind and understanding and would stop the bus and wait for me.

Sharing this commute with my best friend and fellow Carron Hall student, Tim, made the experience even more special. Tim had spent a year at St. Mary's High School but to my delight, he decided Dinthill was a better option for him. Papa Reni would always save seats in the front of the bus for us. His humor and short stories enlivened the journey, and the time he spent living abroad seemed to add a distinctive charm to his personality. Occasionally, he would let Tim and me shift the gears of the Leyland bus, a thrill we both cherished.

The commute was further enriched by the presence of two senior students, Dory and Amy, who acted like our big sisters and provided some guidance and protection on the Dinthill campus. Additionally, Ms. Carmen, the conductor of the NorthStar, looked out for us as if we were her own children. The NorthStar personnel frankly felt like an extended family during that period of my life.

## Baptism by Fire

Arriving at Dinthill for the first time in September 1968 was overwhelming. The campus was vast, a far cry from the intimate confines of Carron Hall Primary School. As I navigated the new environment, I couldn't help but feel a mix of excitement and trepidation. The imposing school buildings, the throngs of students in their crisp uniforms, and the buzz of activity all contributed to the sense that I was embarking on a significant new chapter of my life.

The first day at Dinthill was nothing short of a nightmare for my friend Tim and myself. The senior students wasted no time in asserting their dominance over the newcomers. Ragging was a brutal tradition, and I found myself at the mercy of boys who took pleasure in our discomfort. They called us *"grubs"* and *"grubesses"*, pulled pranks, issued threats, plucked our noses, assigned us strange nick names and ensured that our first taste of high school was a bittersweet experience. I recalled, the two senior students that stood out due to their physicality, persistence and cruelty were Harriott and Gonzales. I later learned that Gonzales was already a graduate student but came back just for the joy of making us miserable.

I remember the throbbing headache I endured that day, more from stress than physical pain. Just when I thought I couldn't take any more, a few sympathetic seniors intervened. They offered a small reprieve from the torment, guiding me to safety. Among our protectors were Maurene Parker and Lawson Rose – the older sister of my classmate and new friend, Orett Parker, and my adopted cousin, respectively.  Despite their attempted help, the teachers seemed indifferent, either unaware or unwilling to disrupt this initiation ritual. A mild consolation was the fact that Tim was also there to offer moral support and be a partner throughout the ordeal. On top of this, we had to complete a placement test that determined the form (1A to 1D) you would be placed in. As fate would have it, I was placed in form 1D and Tim in 1C. Incredibly, the results of the first term exams placed me among the top five students in form 1D which then enabled me to be promoted to form 1A. This was a very motivating accomplishment and served as the impetus for maintaining my status as an A-former the rest of the duration at Dinthill. I would subsequently celebrate the results of term and annual grade reports as being very gratifying and outstanding.

One of the most enjoyable aspects of school life was the mandatory participation in Physical Education (PE). Far from being just another class, PE brought a sense of excitement and camaraderie to our daily routine. The structured activities, led by dedicated teachers, provided a well-rounded mix of exercises, games, and team sports that kept us active and engaged.

It was during these sessions that students from different forms came together, creating a dynamic and spirited environment where friendships were forged beyond our usual classroom circles. Whether it was sprinting on the field, playing a competitive game of football or cricket, or engaging in stretching and calisthenics, PE fostered a sense of teamwork, discipline, and resilience.

For many of us, it was a welcome break from the rigors of academic study—a chance to release energy, challenge ourselves physically, and enjoy the thrill of healthy competition. The laughter, the friendly rivalries, and the sheer joy of movement made these sessions an unforgettable part of school life.

By the time we got to the second year, the daily long-distance commute had become extremely taxing. If we had missed the NorthStar bus in the morning, chances are we would have missed attending school that day. On several occasions we were late due to delays by the bus. Fortunately, Tim and I were able to persuade our parents that residing in Linstead would be more advantageous for us. This arrangement would allow us to dedicate more time to extracurricular activities at the school and have more time for studying and homework. Luckily, one of my father's peers at Dinthill, Mr. Francis, and his family came to our rescue. Tim and I had the good fortune of boarding with the Francis family, whose warm and welcoming home sat just outside Linstead, near Vanity Fair. Beyond providing us with a comfortable place to stay, their home came with the added bonus of lively interactions with their son Evon and daughter Celia, both proud Dinthill alumni. Evon, who had graduated the year before we entered, became an invaluable mentor and role model—his penmanship was a work of art, and his technical drawings were nothing short of masterful.

One of the things that left a lasting impression on me was Evon's love for American R&B music. Almost every evening after returning from work, he would fill the house with the soulful sounds of Isaac Hayes, Smokey Robinson and the Miracles, The Impressions, Junior Walker & the All-Stars, and The Temptations, just to mention a few. Those melodies became the popular soundtracks of our time there. But Evon knew how to balance work and play—despite the good times, he never allowed music or leisure to interfere with our academic focus.

Living in Linstead had its own set of perks—easy access to shopping in town, weekend trips to the cinema, and the occasional visit to classmates' homes. Tim and I were practically inseparable, always finding new adventures to dive into together. Our time with the Francis family came to an end at the end of the 1970 school year, leaving us with deep gratitude and a trove of cherished memories.

For our 3rd and 4th years at Dinthill (1970-1972), Tim and I secured boarding with the Parker family, who lived just a stone's throw from the Francis family. Mr. Parker, a former Dinthill student like my father, was a manager at the condensed milk factory in Bog Walk, St. Catherine. A man of discipline and order, he ran his household with military precision, instilling in us a deep sense of responsibility.

Mornings and evenings came with assigned chores—whether tending to the backyard poultry and pigs, mowing the meticulously kept lawn, or occasionally washing Mr. Parker's car, we were expected to pull our weight. Mealtimes were a true highlight, with an array of delicious dishes and desserts that sometimes felt like a well-earned reward for our efforts.

Just beyond the house stretched a vast orange field, a tempting oasis that Tim and I couldn't resist raiding under the cover of night. The oranges—some of the sweetest I had ever tasted—made every daring escapade feel worth the risk.

One of the biggest perks of living with the Parkers was Mr. Parker's reliable morning rides to school. But there was no room for tardiness—his punctuality was non-negotiable, and we fast learned to be ready on the dot. Some of my fondest memories include the hours we spent studying out on the lawn, shaded by trees, soaking in both knowledge and the serenity of our surroundings.

I will always be grateful to the Parker family for their generosity and the role they played in shaping our Dinthill journey. Their home was more than just a place to stay—it was an invaluable part of our success, and a chapter of our lives filled with discipline, adventure, and unforgettable moments.

## A World of Knowledge

As the weeks passed, the chaos of the first day subsided, and I began to immerse myself in the academic life of Dinthill. The curriculum was far more advanced than what I had been used to, but I found myself intrigued by the new subjects, especially the technical and science courses. Oh yes, the discovery of the T-square and Set-squares used in Technical Drawing was both fascinating and enlightening. It was here that I discovered my passion for engineering. At Dinthill, the emphasis was on learning and development. The school's technical focus meant that practical skills were as valued as theoretical knowledge. I learned to balance my love for sports and play with the demands of rigorous academic work. I sometimes ponder why I did not participate more actively in sports at Dinthill, especially given my love for cricket, and being a former opening batsman for the Carron Hall Primary school cricket team. Physics, Chemistry and Technical Drawing classes especially opened up new worlds of understanding where I could explore, experiment, and create.

The workshops—both metalwork and woodwork—were a favorite hub of activity for the boys. Clad in our distinctive overalls, we eagerly tackled an array of projects, ranging from basic carpentry and joinery to intricate metalwork creations. The rhythmic hum of machines, the sharp scent of sawdust mingling with the tang of machine oil, and the sense of pride in crafting something with our own hands made every session exhilarating.

Meanwhile, the home economics department was a lively and cherished space for the girls. Dressed in crisp aprons, they took on the roles of aspiring chefs, skillfully mastering a variety of fancy dishes that filled the air with mouthwatering aromas. Others found their passion in the art of dressmaking, taking pride in crafting elegant, designer garments that showcased their creativity and skill.

Beyond the workshops and kitchens, another exciting space was the commerce classroom, where some students were enthralled by the rhythmic clatter of typewriters. The opportunity to develop typing proficiency and business skills added a layer of professionalism to their education, sparking enthusiasm for future careers in business and administration.

The students specializing in agriculture actively participated in a variety of hands-on practical exercises, gaining invaluable real-world experience that complemented their classroom learning. One of their primary activities involved planting and nurturing a diverse range of crops, ensuring they understood the full growth cycle—from seed selection and soil preparation to irrigation and harvesting.

In addition to crop cultivation, the students were also deeply involved in animal husbandry. A key aspect of their training included working with the dairy cows on the school farm. They learned essential skills such as proper milking techniques, understanding the health and well-being of the animals and maintaining sanitary conditions to ensure the quality of the milk produced.

Whether it was the thrill of shaping raw materials into functional creations, the joy of preparing gourmet meals, the excitement of mastering office skills, or planting seeds and milking cows, these hands-on experiences made our school days truly unforgettable.

Another thrilling memory from this time was my deep fascination with detective adventure stories, particularly *The Hardy Boys* and *Nancy Drew* series. These books were more than just stories; they were portals into a world of mystery, suspense, and thrilling investigations that kept me on the edge of my seat. Each book was a gripping journey, filled with twists, turns, and daring escapades that made my heart race.

We would eagerly borrow copies from libraries, swap books among friends, and even purchase new additions to our growing collection. There was an unspoken challenge among us—to see who could get their hands on the most books and solve the mysteries before the final page. My ultimate goal was to complete the entire series, and though I may not have reached every single title, I came pretty close.

I distinctly remember the sheer excitement of cracking open a fresh edition, flipping through the pages with anticipation, completely engrossed in the unraveling plot. Time would disappear as I followed Frank and Joe Hardy or Nancy Drew on their daring quests, and I often found myself unable to put the book down until I reached the very last word. There were nights when I read well past my bedtime.

Looking back, those books not just entertained me but also ignited my love for reading, sharpened my imagination, and fueled my curiosity. They were a thrilling escape into a world where bravery, intelligence, and determination always triumphed.

## The Legendary Principal, Mr. C.V. Philips

From 1968 to 1972, Dinthill was under the stern yet influential leadership of Mr. C.V. Philips, a principal whose name still evokes a mix of respect and trepidation. Mr. Philips, known to us simply as CV, was a strict disciplinarian who prided himself on proper etiquette and ethics. Impeccably dressed, always in a tie and with a dignified demeanor, he governed Dinthill with an iron fist - the mere sight of him could send shivers down any student's spine.

CV implemented and enforced a rigorous dress code that reflected his commitment to discipline and order. Male students were required to wear proper colored khaki uniform with shirts tucked in, complete with maroon and gold shoulder epaulettes. Female students donned knee-length navy blue sleeveless dresses over white blouses, cinched with maroon and gold plaid belts. Everyone had to wear a round tag/pin that represented the colors of the four Houses: McNeil (blue), Easter (yellow), Wint (green), and Denham (red). I sensed some of the girls found it more desirable to wear their dresses significantly shorter rather than at knee's length – after all, this was the "mini-skirt" and "hot pants" fashion era. The violators would constantly battle with teachers, prefects and occasionally CV himself. Any deviation from this dress code was considered inexcusable and CV would not hesitate to administer punishment. His interrogations were usually followed by eloquent lectures, emphasizing the importance of adhering to the school's standards.

Detention was a common tool used by teachers and seniors to maintain discipline. It involved writing exercises, extra work on the blackboard, staying late after school, or picking up trash around the schoolyard.

One memorable incident from my first year exemplifies CV's approach. Our entire class was summoned to his office for an infraction committed by one of us, but when no one confessed, he gave us all detention. This collective punishment was a testament to his commitment to discipline and his belief in collective responsibility.

There are numerous legendary tales of students' encounters with CV resulting in a lengthy detention or reprimand or even suspension. One such story involved a graduating senior student named Herman. The morning after our graduation ceremony, Herman was spotted by CV wearing a t-shirt untucked. Summoned to CV's office, Herman received a stern rebuke: *"Herman, you have disrespected and disappointed me."* Shocked and dismayed, Herman apologized and quickly tucked in his shirt. A teacher later advised him to write a letter of apology, which he dutifully presented to CV. CV's response, *"Thank you Herman, that was the proper thing to do,"* underscored his belief in maintaining decorum and the importance of rectifying mistakes.

Despite his seemingly harsh methods, CV's dedication to his students' education was unquestionable. Under CV's tenure, the batch of '72 achieved numerous milestones. We became the first batch to graduate with over 90% of the students who enrolled in 1968 with a diploma and the first to have a formal graduation ceremony held in July. I have fond memories of the graduation ceremony held in the main administration building, where Mrs. Davidson and another dignitary handed out diplomas to us ecstatic graduates. The event was attended by our proud family and friends, adding to the celebratory atmosphere. I vividly recall wearing my newly tailored dark grey suit, white shirt, and gold tie, a tribute to the school's colors of maroon and gold. The occasion was capped by a grand graduation ball at the Alcan Bauxite Sports Club in Ewarton on another day.

The graduation ball was a night of elegance and celebration. The ladies wore stunning white gowns, while the gentlemen sported gabardine bush jackets with bell-bottom pants and stylish platform shoes. The highlight of the evening was dancing to the reggae rhythms of the Inner Circle Band, with the late Jacob Miller as the lead singer. I still remember the band strumming Al Green's *"Here I Am, Come and Take Me,"* creating an unforgettable atmosphere of joy and celebration.

The night's festivities, however, had an unexpected but humorous twist. Some of the ladies from Spanish Town were left stranded at the Sports Club when their chartered taxi failed to show up. They spent the entire night at the club and had no choice but to walk over two miles to Linstead early the next morning to catch the first taxi to Spanish Town. Imagine the strange sight of four ladies clad in white gowns, strolling down the street at dawn—a blend of elegance and resilience that perfectly captured the spirit of our time at Dinthill.

CV's tenure at Dinthill, which lasted from 1960 to 1974, was marked by a blend of strict discipline and a deep commitment to excellence. His methods, while sometimes harsh, were driven by a genuine desire to see us succeed. The lessons we learned under his leadership—respect for rules, the importance of proper conduct, and the pursuit of excellence—I believe have remained with us, shaping our lives long after we left the campus of Dinthill.

## Life on the Campus

Although I did not live on campus, I learned about the experiences and events that our batchmates went through. Life on the campus during the late 1960s to early 1970s was a rich tapestry of tradition, camaraderie, and adventure. The male student population living on campus was made up of approximately one-third of the boys in our batch. The living quarters consisted of four dormitories, each housing members of the school's four Houses: McNeil, Easter, Wint, and Denham.

These Houses were more than just living arrangements; they were the epicenters of student life, fostering a sense of community and healthy competition. Each

House had a Prefect, usually a senior student, who served as the house captain, ensuring discipline and leading house activities. The resident student body was overseen by a resident teacher, known as the Master, who maintained order and discipline, approved weekday outings, and ensured that daily schedules were followed. These schedules dictated everything from wake-up times and meals to study periods, devotions, and bedtime, creating a structured environment that balanced academics with personal development.

Two main clubs, the Student Christian Movement (SCM) and the Dinthill Literary and Social Club (DLSC), played a significant role in extracurricular life. The presidents of these clubs were typically fourth-year students who organized activities each semester, providing a platform for personal growth and social interaction. These clubs were pivotal in shaping student experiences, offering opportunities to engage in meaningful discussions, social events, and community service.

One specifically memorable event was the outbreak of Dengue Fever in 1969. One of the dormitories was transformed into a makeshift hospital to care for infected students, highlighting the close-knit nature of the community and the lengths the students would go to support one another in times of need.

Leadership roles within the student body were highly coveted. Typically, the Head Boy was chosen from among the resident students, but in 1971, both the Head Boy and Deputy Head Boy were day students, a rare deviation from tradition. Despite these changes, the resident students continued to play a crucial role in the school's leadership and daily operations.

As Batch'72, we prided ourselves on our innovation and creativity. We started the first weekly magazine called *"Inspiration,"* a publication that became a staple of campus life. We also had a *"Tuck Shop,"* operated by a fourth-year resident student, where all students could purchase snacks and lunches, providing significant comfort and convenience amidst the rigorous schedules.

The beginning of each school year brought the *"grub concert,"* an initiation tradition for residents where first-year students, or "grubs," performed entertainment acts while wearing their jackets backward. This event was both a rite of passage and a competition, with the winner receiving a surprise prize—often a sealed box containing live frogs, adding an element of humor and surprise to the tradition.

Among the many tales that circulated the campus were the legendary night raids on the orange orchard. The orchard was patrolled by two security/watchmen: the tall *"good watchie,"* who often turned a blind eye to the escapades, and the short *"bad watchie,"* who actively tried to thwart the raids. The thrill of sneaking into the orchard under the cover of darkness, the excitement of evading capture, and the solidarity in protecting each other's identities created a bond among the students that transcended the boundaries of the resident Houses.

These nighttime adventures were filled with laughter and mischief. On at least one occasion, the *"bad watchie"* was pelted with oranges while the culprits were making their escape. The secrecy surrounding these raids was paramount, with all participants sworn to protect the identities of their fellow offenders, fostering a sense of brotherhood and shared rebellion against authority.

The resident life on the Dinthill campus was a blend of strict discipline, academic rigor, and vibrant student life. The experiences shared, from the structured daily routines to the spontaneous adventures, helped to shape the boys into a resilient and close-knit community.

## The '72 Student Strike

In our final year at Dinthill, the resident students led by the Batch of '72 reached a breaking point. The conditions they had to endure had become intolerable. The food in the canteen had deteriorated to a point where it was barely edible, and the dormitory beds were furnished with old, worn-out mattresses. Despite numerous petitions to CV, no actions were taken to address the grievances.

Frustration simmered among the resident students, and a collective decision was made to escalate the situation through a *"strike"*. This was a bold move, unprecedented in the school's history, and it required both leadership and courage. The plan was simple but powerful: they would refuse to eat the canteen meals and remove the mattresses from the beds, visibly demonstrating the severity of their plight.

The strike commenced with resolute determination. Three times a day, the meals provided by the canteen were rejected as a visible and impactful act of protest. The removal of the mattresses further underscored the dissatisfaction, as the empty bed frames were a stark symbol of the neglect felt. The atmosphere on campus was tense, but there was a palpable sense of unity and purpose among the students.

The leaders of the protest were soon summoned to CV's office. It was a daunting encounter, as they were fully aware of CV's reputation for strict discipline. However, this time, they were not just students facing a principal; they were advocates for their peers, standing up for the right to better living conditions. In that meeting, the case was clearly presented detailing the issues faced and the actions that were being demanded.

To CV's credit, he acknowledged the seriousness of the situation. He agreed to meet with the Dinthill Board of Trustees to discuss the issues and concerns. The Board, after considering the plight, gave the green light to have the old mattresses replaced and an improvement in the quality of the meals. The strike had succeeded, and it was a clear victory for student activism and leadership was the byproduct. In return, the boys had also agreed to perform an extensive clean-up of the campus for the first time in celebration of Labor Day.

The success of the strike was not just a testament to determination but also a demonstration of the solidarity that existed within the Batch of '72. During the two-plus days of the strike, the day student counterparts played a crucial supportive role. They helped by bringing in meals from outside the school and provided snacks from the Tuck Shop. This collaboration between the resident and day students highlighted the strong camaraderie and mutual support that defined our batchmates. The strike of 1972 was a landmark event in the school's history.

## Mealtime on Campus

I would not do this story justice if I did not talk about an essential element of life on campus – the food. We had the wonderful opportunity of enjoying a balanced, hot lunch daily from the canteen. Day students, like me, could purchase a meal ticket from the form's assigned teacher or prefect in the morning, with the cost being substantially subsidized at just a few cents. For the resident students, canteen meals were automatically provided three times a day.

Alternatively, lunch could be acquired from the Tuck Shop, which was a buzzing center of congestion. It had available, an array of snacks, pastries, and beef patties, along with soft drinks at a minimal cost. My all-time favorite pastry, the *"tutti-frutti,"* was a pure delight. In addition, we had the incomparable *"Fudgie"* on his converted motorcycle who provided a variety of frozen treats for purchase. His ice cream sandwiches and cakes were my favorites, along with the occasional *"nutty buddy."*

Fudgie's dedication, promptness, and dependability never ceased to amaze me. He was always there, a comforting presence on campus. On bad days, Fudgie's treats served as a welcomed pacifier, providing a sweet escape from the stresses of school life. Mealtimes on campus were not just about nourishment; it was a cherished part of our daily routine, filled with fond memories of the treats and opportunities for socialization with peers.

## The Extra-Curricular Activities

One of the most vibrant aspects of life at Dinthill was the rich array of extracurricular activities. Among these, the House-system stood out as a cornerstone of student life, fostering a sense of community and healthy competition. Being a member of Easter House was a source of great pride for me. The spirited rivalry among the four houses—Easter, Wint, McNeil, and Denham—in athletics, football, netball and cricket was one of the most exciting facets of our school experience. Each year, the house competitions were a highlight, bringing students together in a spirit of camaraderie and determination. The drive to win was intense, and we trained hard to achieve our goals. These competitions were not merely about securing victories; they were also about building teamwork, resilience, and a sense of belonging. We supported each other through rigorous training and celebrated the triumphs with great enthusiasm.

The athletic competitions were especially thrilling, as they showcased the talents of some outstanding athletes who went on to represent Dinthill on national and even international stages. Maurice "TP" Clarke, a renowned sprinter, represented Jamaica in the 100M and 200M at the first CARIFTA Games in Barbados. Icoleen Simpson, an exceptional long-distance runner, dominated the 800M event at Dinthill and later represented Jamaica in the Central American and Caribbean (CAC) Games. Beverly Harrison and Roy Brown were notable for being Champion Girl and Boy, respectively, both hailing from Wint House—a remarkable achievement.

Other standout athletes included Vincent Gallimore, Lolita Tracy, Rosie Salmon, and Jennis Ramsey, whose contributions were integral to our House's success. These athletes' accomplishments not merely brought pride to their respective Houses but also inspired their peers to strive for excellence.

Cricket was another area where Dinthill excelled, especially during the years when Alvin Watkis of Batch '72 captained the team. We enjoyed consistent success against other schools, thanks to all the outstanding players including the likes of Stephen Townsend, Maroney Hamilton, Carl Lecky, Norman Narraysingh, and Alvin Watkis himself. Alvin's talent was recognized beyond Dinthill, as he was invited to cricket camp for trials for the Jamaica under-19 youth cricket team in 1970-71. This period of cricketing success brought a sense of pride and achievement to the school.

Despite our successes in athletics and cricket, Dinthill struggled mightily in football. The football team often faced heavy defeats, especially against the formidable Vere Technical High School. Scores like 6-nil in the Vere games were not uncommon, as our team frequently found itself at the mercy of Vere's superior skill players. On one memorable occasion though, we managed to secure a nil-nil draw against Vere on their home ground, only to face the wrath of their disappointed fans who jeered and threw objects at us. There was a widespread belief that Vere's success was due to their recruitment of experienced players from established football leagues around the island.

In contrast, our principal, Mr. CV Philips, was not extremely supportive of elevating sports to the same level as academic achievements. I believe he placed a higher value on scholastic excellence over sports. Despite that, the house system and extracurricular activities at Dinthill were integral in building character and a strong sense of community among the students. The bonds we formed and the experiences we shared in these activities are cherished memories that have left a lasting impact on all of us from Batch of '72.

## My Most Impactful Teachers

I must say, throughout my time at Dinthill, I had the privilege of being taught by some of the most remarkable teachers who left an indelible mark on my academic journey. One of the most transformative experiences at Dinthill was discovering my passion for art in Ms. Mills (affectionately called Granny Mills) class. Granny Mills had a unique way of making every student feel special. She had a nurturing presence that encouraged creativity and self-expression. Her art classes were a sanctuary where I could explore my artistic talents freely. She would often say, *"Art is not just about what you see, but how you see it."* This philosophy resonated with me deeply. In addition, I had inspiration earlier by a fellow Carron Hall student, Terrence "Artist" Gibson, who had a natural talent for drawing, especially recreating comic book characters.

I remember an assignment where we had to create a self-portrait or capture the likeness of someone else. My classmate, Sherneth from Form 2A, eagerly volunteered to be my subject. With careful strokes, I crafted a black-and-white portrait of her, which unexpectedly caught the admiration of Granny Mills. She loved it so much that she proudly displayed it on the wall of her classroom, turning it into a cherished piece for all to see. Under her guidance, I honed my skills in drawing and painting, finding a new medium to express myself. My love for technical drawing was also deeply influenced by the precision and creativity I learned in her art class.

Among the pantheon of distinguished educators at Dinthill, a name that stood out was Mr. Swaby, affectionately dubbed *"Avogadro"* by his students. This moniker, a nod to the renowned scientist Amedeo Avogadro, was a testament to Mr. Swaby's brilliance and his deep knowledge of Chemistry. To us, he was more than just a teacher; he was a genius who could unravel the complexities of Chemistry with ease.

Mr. Swaby was an introvert, a man who took his work very seriously and rarely, if ever, smiled. His stern demeanor and high expectations set a tone of seriousness and dedication in his classroom. Despite his reserved nature, or perhaps because of it, he commanded immense respect from all his students. He demanded excellence and instilled a rigorous academic discipline that pushed us to strive for the highest standards.

One of the hallmarks of Mr. Swaby's teaching was his skill in fostering a competitive yet supportive classroom environment. The weekly quizzes and the rigorous lab sessions were designed to push us to our limits, encouraging us to not just compete with each other but also to support one another in our quest for knowledge. This competitive spirit, tempered with camaraderie, helped build a strong sense of community among us. Each week, we were motivated to achieve perfect scores, knowing that anything less than 100% would be met with his silent disapproval. The term tests were equally challenging, reinforcing the need for thorough understanding and mastery of the subject.

The Chemistry lab under Mr. Swaby's guidance was a place of wonder and discovery. It provided us with the opportunity to witness firsthand the marvels of chemical interactions and the creation of various compounds. It was in the lab that we truly appreciated the practical applications of the theoretical concepts we learned in class.

The lab proved also to be a fertile ground for mischief. Some students, emboldened by curiosity and the thrill of experimentation, often ventured into unauthorized and unsafe experiments. One memorable prank involved the production of hydrogen sulfide ($H_2S$) gas, notorious for its foul smell reminiscent of rotten eggs. The pranksters delighted in the chaos that ensued as the stench permeated the lab, causing much laughter and disruption.

Despite the occasional mischief, Mr. Swaby's impact on our education was profound. His ability to break down complex chemical principles into simple, digestible concepts made learning Chemistry enjoyable. His dedication to his students' success and his unwavering demand for excellence instilled in us a sense of discipline and a drive to excel.

Another teacher that stood out during my third and fourth years was Mr. John Earl. As an Englishman, Mr. Earl was an intriguing and humorous character who brought his unique personality into the classroom. He taught us Woodwork, Carpentry & Joinery, and Building Construction, but his lessons extended far beyond the curriculum.

Mr. Earl had a knack for captivating his students with fascinating personal stories from his time in the British military. These accounts, reminiscent of the adventures in the James Bond movies, *"On Her Majesty's Secret Service,"* painted a vivid picture of a life filled with excitement and intrigue. His tales were not just entertaining; they were infused with a sense of history and adventure. Through his stories, we could almost see the distant lands and feel the excitement of covert operations.

His British pride was evident in his often-critical view of the United States' role in World War II. Mr. Earl never hesitated to boast about the significant contributions of his homeland, suggesting that Britain's efforts were far more impactful than those of the Americans. His critiques sparked lively discussions and debates, encouraging us to think critically.

One of the most memorable moments in Mr. Earl's class was his remark about Muhammad Ali. He once commented, *"Muhammad Ali talks too much,"* a statement that instantly stirred a reaction. Given Ali's immense stature as not just a prominent boxer but also an outspoken critic of the injustices faced by

Black Americans, Mr. Earl's comment was provocative. Ali's association with the Civil Rights Movement and his fearless stance against the Vietnam War and racial discrimination made him a hero to many of us. Mr. Earl's criticism, therefore, was met with a mix of shock and amusement. It was a bold statement, reflective of Mr. Earl's willingness to challenge popular opinions and provoke thoughts among his students.

Despite his sometimes-controversial views, Mr. Earl was deeply respected for his teaching prowess and his ability to connect with students. His classes were never dull; his humor and candidness kept us engaged and entertained. He managed to blend the technical aspects of woodwork and building construction with lessons on history, culture, and critical thinking, creating a rich and varied learning experience. I credit him for giving me the confidence to undertake numerous *"do it yourself"* (DIY) projects around the home later in my life.

## Role Models and Mentors

The students in the batches ahead of me were a constant source of inspiration, setting the bar high and challenging us to strive for excellence. Among them, the brilliant non-brother tandem of Erol D. and Erol E. Morgan stood out as shining examples of academic prowess and leadership. Their dedication to their studies was nothing short of remarkable, and their names became synonymous with success at Dinthill.

These two exceptional young men weren't just top performers in their batch—they embodied what it meant to be well-rounded scholars and leaders. Whether in the classroom, or in extracurricular activities, they consistently demonstrated a level of discipline and intellectual curiosity that was both impressive and motivating. They weren't just working toward their own success; they were paving the way for those of us who followed, proving that Dinthill students could stand shoulder to shoulder with the best and brightest anywhere.

Their success stories became part of the school's culture, shared among students as both motivation and a challenge to rise to their level. Teachers often held them up as examples, using their achievements to encourage us to push beyond our limits. The Morgan duo's ability to balance academic excellence with leadership responsibilities inspired me to aim higher in my own pursuits.

I aspired to follow in their footsteps, not just in academics but in the way they carried themselves—with confidence, integrity, and a commitment to excellence. Their achievements showed me that with hard work, perseverance, and the right mindset, anything was possible.

Looking back, I am grateful for their influence. Their legacy at Dinthill wasn't just about their personal accomplishments—it was about the example they set for future generations.

## The Crucible of Senior Year

As I advanced through the years at Dinthill, the challenges grew more intense. The workload increased, and the expectations were higher. The senior year was a crucible that tested my limits. Balancing academic work, leadership duties, and personal interests required careful time management and dedication. My academic dedication did not go unnoticed. Teachers and peers alike began to recognize my efforts and potential as I was selected for the prestigious position of Deputy Head Boy. I was fortunate and privileged to be a member of the esteem group of student leaders chosen to be "prefects". This group was led by the Head Boy, Alvin Watkis and Head Girl, Beverly Tracy.

As part of the elite prefect group, I was involved in maintaining discipline, organizing school events such as morning devotions, representing the student body in various capacities, and providing mentorship to junior students. I found immense satisfaction in guiding the junior students, helping them navigate the challenges of high school life. Whether it was offering advice on academic matters or providing support during difficult times, I tried to be a role model they could look up to. These experiences taught me the importance of service and responsibility. This role also helped me develop leadership skills that would prove invaluable in my future endeavors.

Preparing for the General Certificate of Education (GCE) examinations demanded intense focus and discipline. My dedication to my studies paid off when the results of the GCE examinations were announced. I had achieved passing grades in all my subjects except one and distinctions in several. A testament to my hard work and the support of my teachers, peers and family. These accomplishments opened doors to further educational opportunities and laid the foundation for my future career as a civil engineer. The pride I felt was shared by my parents, whose sacrifices had made this achievement possible.

## Home Life During the Dinthill Years

The day I first boarded the bus to attend Dinthill was bittersweet. I was excited for the journey ahead, yet there was a deep sense of change in the air. Leaving behind my siblings, who would miss me dearly, made the moment even more emotional. Everyone in the household understood that life as we knew it was shifting, and nothing would quite be the same again. Still, I welcomed this new chapter with open arms, eager to embrace the opportunities that awaited me at Dinthill.

This period of transition extended beyond just me—my mother was also embarking on her own transformative journey, enrolling in teacher's college. With both of us stepping into new roles, the responsibility of managing the home fell to my grandmother, Grandma Menda. My daily routine fast became structured and demanding. My mornings started at 5 AM for the long commute, and I wouldn't return home until 6 or 7 PM. Weekends were dedicated to homework, preparing my school uniform, and catching up with friends and former classmates from primary school.

However, as life moved forward, an unforeseen tragedy struck our family in 1969. Grandma Menda suffered a stroke, throwing our home into turmoil. It was an incredibly difficult time, especially for my mother, who displayed remarkable strength and resilience as she balanced her studies with the responsibilities of caring for the family. Despite the hardship, we found joy in a momentous occasion the following year—my mother's marriage to Sam Forbes in 1971. The wedding in Kingston was a extremely joyous event, marking the official union of our families. However, in our hearts, Sam had already been a father figure long before the marriage, and his presence in our lives was nothing short of a blessing.

Another pivotal moment in my life came in 1971 when my mother accepted the position of principal at Cedar Valley Primary School in St. Catherine. It was a tremendous opportunity for her, a recognition of her dedication and hard work as an educator. While I was proud and excited for her, the decision to leave Blue Gate, the first home I had ever known, was bittersweet. Moving meant saying goodbye to the familiar sights and sounds of my childhood—the rolling green hills, the friendly faces of neighbors who had become like family, and the comforting routines of life in St. Mary.

Our new home in Cedar Valley was the principal's cottage, a spacious and comfortable house that, in many ways, was an upgrade from our home in Blue Gate. The additional space was welcome, but it could not immediately replace the warmth and deep-rooted familiarity of the place I had left behind. As I adjusted to my new surroundings, I couldn't help but reminisce about the tight-knit community of my childhood—the impromptu games with friends, the simple pleasures of exploring the countryside, and raiding neighbor's fruit trees.

St. Catherine had a different rhythm compared to St. Mary. The landscape, though beautiful in its own way, lacked the lush hills and dense fruit trees I had grown up with. Instead, vast sugarcane fields stretched for miles, and sprawling orange groves dotted the terrain. The smell of ripening citrus and the distant hum of machinery from the cane fields painted a different picture of rural Jamaica—one that I had to grow accustomed to.

Fortunately, the transition was made easier by the fact that I had already been attending Dinthill since September 1968 and boarding in Linstead since 1969. I was no stranger to St. Catherine, and my growing independence helped me navigate the change. Though my heart remained tied to the memories of my early years in St. Mary, I embraced the challenges and new experiences that came with this move.

One of the first things I noticed about Cedar Valley was the strong sense of community, much like what I had experienced in Blue Gate. The people were welcoming, and I quickly made a few friends among our new neighbors. One person who stood out in my memory was Mr. Harold, a jovial man whose reliable mini-bus was the main mode of transportation between Cedar Valley and Linstead. He had an easygoing nature and was known for his safe driving, ensuring that passengers could count on him for their daily commutes. His bus made several trips per day, serving as a lifeline for the residents who needed to travel for school, work, or shopping.

As time went by, I began to settle into my new life. Cedar Valley was different, but it had its own charm. The experience of moving at such a formative age taught me valuable lessons about adaptability, and the importance of embracing change. It reinforced the idea that while places may change, the essence of home is not just in a location—it is in the people, the experiences, and the memories we carry with us.

## Graduation Day: A Family Milestone

The next major milestone for our family came in July 1972—my graduation from Dinthill Technical High School. It was a day filled with excitement, pride, and deep emotions, marking the culmination of years of hard work and perseverance. My mother and sisters were there to witness the occasion firsthand, their presence making the day even more meaningful. Seeing their faces in the audience, beaming with pride and joy, was an unforgettable moment. Their unwavering support had carried me through my journey, and this milestone was as much theirs as it was mine.

I have a vivid memory of the morning, starting with my close friend Tim and me getting dressed at the Parker's home. The anticipation was high as we carefully put on our suits, white shirts, and colorful ties, determined to look our best for this important occasion. I wore a grey suit with a gold tie—symbolic of Dinthill's maroon and gold colors—while Tim looked equally sharp in his attire. Mr.

Parker, a kind and supportive figure, was attending the ceremony and graciously offered to transport us to the school.

The graduation ceremony took place in the school auditorium, a space that had witnessed many academic milestones and assemblies over the years. It was presided over by our esteemed principal, C.V. Philips, whose leadership and dedication had guided so many of us through our educational journey. The moment I stepped onto the stage to receive my diploma, handed to me by Mrs. Davidson—one of my favorite English teachers and the vice principal—felt surreal. She had been a pillar of support throughout my time at Dinthill, and to receive my diploma from her hands made the moment even more special.

The ceremony was a well-organized and inspiring event. A distinguished keynote speaker delivered an address that left a lasting impression, urging us to step into the next phase of our lives with confidence and purpose. One of my fellow graduates delivered a heartfelt speech, expressing gratitude on behalf of the graduating class to our parents, teachers, and administrative staff. It was a moving tribute to the many individuals who had shaped our academic and personal growth.

As I sat among my classmates, I could feel the collective sense of accomplishment in the room. Every graduate beamed with pride and, perhaps, a bit of relief—after years of dedication, we had finally made it to the end of this chapter. After the ceremony, there were warm embraces, handshakes, and expressions of gratitude exchanged among students, teachers, and families. We confirmed our plans for the upcoming graduation ball, an event we all eagerly anticipated as a final celebration of our shared journey.

The memory of that day remains one of the most cherished moments in my life—a testament to perseverance, love, and shared accomplishments. It was not just about receiving a diploma; it was about the journey that had led us there, the sacrifices made, and the bright future ahead. For my family and me, this day symbolized not just my personal achievement but also the collective strength and determination that had brought us to this point.

## A Broader Perspective

In Jamaica, the late 1960s and early 1970s were years of profound political and social change. The country had gained independence from Britain in 1962, and by 1968, the sense of national identity was growing stronger. One of the most notable changes was the transition from the British currency system of *"pound, shillings, and pence"* to the Jamaican dollar and cents – the US$ = 0.77 JA$ in 1972. This shift was more than a mere change in currency; it symbolized Jamaica's growing independence and identity. Michael Manley, a charismatic leader of the People's National Party (PNP), emerged as a pivotal figure during this time. He was elected to be Prime Minister by an election held in February 1972. His vision of Democratic Socialism aimed to address the inequalities in Jamaican society and improve the lives of the poor and working-class citizens.

His policies aimed at reducing illiteracy and implementing a National Youth Service resonated deeply with me. These policies were more than political rhetoric; they were a call to action for my generation. The introduction of the National Youth Service, which encouraged graduates to serve their communities, reinforced the value of giving back. It shaped my belief that education should be a force for positive change, not just a means to personal advancement.

Between 1968 and 1972, Jamaica experienced other transformative events that would help shaped its future. The Rodney Riots erupted in October 1968 after the government barred activist and professor at UWI, Walter Rodney, leading to widespread protests. The National Lottery was introduced on December 7, 1968, followed by Jamaica joining the Caribbean Free Trade Agreement (CARIFTA) in 1969. In February 1969, Norman Manley resigned as Leader of the Opposition, and his son, Michael Manley, was elected leader of the PNP. Air Jamaica began operations on April 1, 1969, enhancing national connectivity.

Norman Manley's death on September 2, 1969, marked the end of an era. The Cross-Harbour Causeway, connecting Kingston to Portmore, was symbolically opened on January 21, 1970. On May 24, 1970, a statue of Sir Alexander Bustamante, National Hero, was unveiled. Jamaican sprinter Donald Quarrie won gold medals in the 100 and 200 meters at the 1970 Commonwealth Games, highlighting Jamaica's athletic prowess. At the 1972 Summer Olympics, Lennox Miller won a bronze medal in the 100 meters, adding to Jamaica's long history of achievements in track and field athletics.

A statue of Norman Manley, National Hero, was unveiled on July 4, 1971, and the first National Heroes Day was celebrated on October 18, 1971. Jamaica's first five National Heroes were officially honored in 1969: Sir Alexander Bustamante, Norman Manley, Paul Bogle, George William Gordon, and Marcus Garvey.

The global events of the late 1960s and early 1970s profoundly influenced my worldview. This period was marked by significant social and political movements. The civil rights movement in the United States was at its peak, fighting for racial equality and justice. The assassination of Martin Luther King Jr. in 1968 was a tragic event that galvanized activists and highlighted the urgent need for change. The Vietnam War continued to be a contentious issue, with widespread protests and opposition. The anti-war movement gained momentum, particularly among the youth, who were increasingly vocal about their desire for peace and social justice. The war's impact was felt far beyond the borders of Vietnam, influencing global politics and inspiring movements for peace and justice worldwide. Additionally, the U.N. General Assembly's support for the isolation of South Africa for its apartheid policies demonstrated a growing international commitment to human rights and racial equality. These events collectively shaped my understanding of the interconnectedness of global struggles and the importance of standing up for justice and equality. They instilled in me a sense of responsibility to contribute to positive change and to support movements that strive for a fair and equitable world.

## The Technological Revolution

The period between 1968 and 1972 was also a time of remarkable technological advancements. The space race between the United States and the Soviet Union was in full swing, capturing the world's imagination. The Apollo program, initiated by NASA, aimed to land humans on the moon and return them safely to

Earth. On July 20, 1969, the world watched in awe as Apollo 11 astronauts Neil Armstrong and Edwin "Buzz" Aldrin became the first humans to set foot on the moon. Armstrong's iconic words, "That's one small step for man, one giant leap for mankind," echoed the sentiment of human achievement and the potential of technological progress.

This era also saw significant advancements in computing technology. The development of integrated circuits and microprocessors paved the way for the personal computer revolution that would unfold in the coming decades. Companies like Intel were founded during this time, setting the stage for today's digital age. These technological advancements laid the groundwork for innovations that we now take for granted. Can you imagine this era without modern technological tools like personal computers, smartphones, the internet, and pocket calculators? Back then, we relied on multiplication tables, logarithmic tables, encyclopedias, and typewriters to perform tasks that are now accomplished with a few clicks or taps. Calculations were done manually or with the aid of slide rules, and research involved extensive use of library resources rather than quick online searches. Typing documents required meticulous effort on a typewriter, with no easy way to edit or format text as we do today. The absence of instant communication meant letters and landline phones were the primary means of staying in touch. Reflecting on these older technological tools' highlights how transformative the late 1960s and early 1970s were in helping not merely to revolutionize computing but also fundamentally changed the way we live, work, and interact with the world today.

## The Musical Evolution

Music was a powerful force in shaping the cultural landscape of the late 1960s and early 1970s. In Jamaica, reggae music was emerging as a defining genre. Artists like Bob Marley & The Wailers, Jimmy Cliff, and Toots and the Maytals were gaining international recognition. Reggae's infectious rhythms and socially conscious lyrics resonated with audiences worldwide, spreading messages of peace, love, and resistance.

Bob Marley's rise to fame during this period was especially significant. His music, blending reggae with elements of ska and rocksteady, carried powerful messages of unity and resistance. Bob Marley & The Wailers recorded the album "Catch A Fire" between May and October 1972. Songs like "Stir It Up," "Soul Rebel," and "Trenchtown Rock" became anthems for a generation seeking change.

On the international stage, artists like The Jackson Five, Al Green, Stylistics, Chi-Lites, The Temptations, Stevie Wonder and others were having tremendous influence on the local culture. I was always fascinated and relished the infusion of American R&B "soul music" into the Jamaican airwaves, parties and club scenes.

## The Arts and Cultural Movements

The arts flourished during this period, reflecting the social and political changes of the time. In Jamaica, the cultural renaissance was marked by a renewed interest in African heritage and identity. The Rastafari movement, with its emphasis on African roots and spirituality, influenced not just music but also visual arts, literature, and fashion.

Sports played a significant role in uniting people and providing a sense of national pride. In Jamaica, the achievements of athletes like Donald Quarrie, who would later become an Olympic gold medalist at the 1976 Games, were a source of inspiration. Quarrie's success in sprinting showcased Jamaica's potential on the global stage.

As I reflect on this period, I am struck by the resilience and creativity of the people who lived through these times. Their contributions to politics, technology, music, and the arts continue to shape our world today.

## Returning as a Teacher After Graduation

Graduating in 1972 was a bittersweet moment. It marked the end of an era but also the beginning of a new chapter in my life. I felt a deep sense of gratitude for the education and experiences I had received at Dinthill. The decision to return to Dinthill as a teacher was driven by a strong desire to give back to the school that had given me so much. I believed this would also be consistent with Manley's National Youth Service initiative.

Mr. Earl's departure in 1972 gave me the unique opportunity to step into his former position as a teacher. I was fortunate to receive tremendous encouragement and support from CV Philips and Mr. Lawson. Mr. Lawson, a peer of my father from the Dinthill Agricultural School era, was the manager of the metalwork and woodwork shops. He played a crucial role in my transition into teaching. His support was unquestionable, providing me with the broad latitude to operate the workshop however I saw fit. This autonomy allowed me to experiment and implement new ideas, fostering a creative and productive learning environment for my students.

One specifically fond memory from this time was pursuing a hobby of mine—assembling and testing audio amplifiers. I shared this passion with fellow teacher and past student, Palmore Robinson. Palmore, also a graduate from Batch '72, was performing similar functions in the metalwork shop. His expertise and access to milling sheets of metal in the workshop was crucial to the process of building the chassis for the amplifiers. Our collaboration on the amplifier project was not just enjoyable but also a testament to the strong bonds formed during our time at Dinthill.

Teaching the 3rd- and 4th-year students in woodwork, building construction, and technical drawing was a fulfilling experience. It was an opportunity to share my knowledge and passion with a new generation of students. Seeing their progress and enthusiasm reminded me of my own journey.

I had the opportunity to better prepare myself and my students for the GCE "O level" exam in Building Construction. Previously, no Dinthill student had ever passed this subject, and I had failed it in 1972. In 1973, however, I succeeded in passing the subject, along with a couple of my students, including my good friend Leon Traille.

I spent one year as a teacher before attending the College of Arts, Science and Technology (CAST, now the University of Technology) to study Structural

Engineering. My friend and former student, Leon, and I were ecstatic to be classmates at CAST. This was the next steppingstone to the next chapter in my life.

## Lifelong Learning

Reflecting on my journey to Dinthill, it wasn't merely a commute; it was a transformative passage from boyhood to young adulthood. Those years were defined by growth, challenges, and accomplishments that laid the bedrock for my future endeavors. The spark for learning ignited at Dinthill has continued to fuel my quest for knowledge and skill development throughout my life. The memories of that time—the camaraderie with peers and the guidance of mentors—remain cherished chapters in my life's narrative. I am profoundly grateful for the experiences and opportunities that have shaped my path.

The legacy of my Dinthill days transcends academic achievements; it encompasses profound life lessons. I learned the resilience needed to persevere through challenges, the adaptability required in diverse environments, and the importance of leadership and its impact on personal and community growth. Above all, the transformative power of education and the ethos of giving back were indelibly impressed upon me. These principles have not just guided my career but have also enriched my personal life journey, shaping the way I contribute to my community and beyond.

## Lasting Friendships and Alumni Connections

The friendships I formed at Dinthill were some of the most enduring and meaningful relationships of my life. My fellow prefects and batchmates were not just friends but a support system that extended well beyond our school years. Many of us have stayed connected and actively participate in the Dinthill Technical High School Alumni Associations in the USA, Canada, UK and Jamaica.

These connections have kept the spirit of Dinthill alive, no matter where we are in the world. The shared memories, the challenges we overcame, and the successes we celebrated together created a bond that has stood the test of time. The Alumni Associations have become a platform for us to continue contributing to the school's legacy, supporting current students, maintaining the strong sense of community that Dinthill instilled in us while upholding the motto "***Facta Non Verba***"—from the Latin phrase, meaning *"Deeds not just Words"*.

In 2012, I experienced the thrill of attending my very first high school reunion, hosted by the Dinthill Alumni Association in Fort Lauderdale, Florida. This special event marked the 40th anniversary for the batch of 1972—a gathering that drew classmates from across the globe. Over three unforgettable days in March 2012, we celebrated with sheer joy, culminating in a spectacular dinner ball where we were honored with commemorative badges. Reconnecting with classmates after 40 years sparked an incredible camaraderie that made the occasion truly extraordinary.

Since that memorable reunion, I've eagerly returned to Fort Lauderdale for numerous annual alumni events at the same venue, each one filled with equal excitement and enjoyment.

Fast forward to 2022, we gathered once more—this time back at Dinthill itself in Jamaica to celebrate our 50th anniversary. The festivities spanned four unforgettable days in July, highlighted by a grand dinner, heartfelt presentations, and special recognitions for our former teachers. Holding the event in Jamaica allowed even more of our batchmates, now living on the island, to join in the festivities.

For me, the highlight was a nostalgic picnic at the former cottage of our principal, where we indulged in delicious food, drinks, and danced to the iconic music of our era. It was an event brimming with cherished memories and the enduring bonds of friendship that have defined our journey from school days to today.

# Chapter 4

# A Taste of College

## Attending CAST

I n 1973, after completing my studies at Dinthill, I took a significant step forward by enrolling in the College of Arts, Science and Technology (CAST), now known as the University of Technology (UTech). This opportunity was made possible through the free education policy introduced by the Michael Manley government at the time. Enrolling at CAST marked a major milestone in my life, ushering in a new phase of personal and academic growth. The transition from high school to college was both exhilarating and intimidating. At Dinthill, we had been nurtured in a structured environment where teachers closely guided us through our academic journey. However, CAST presented a different reality—one that required a greater level of independence and self-discipline.

Attending CAST also meant relocating to Kingston, a significant change from the familiarity of Linstead. For my first year, I boarded with my step-uncle, Fitzy Forbes, and his wife, Inez, at their home in Duhaney Park. The neighborhood was a well-planned but densely populated residential area with a maze of interconnected streets. Unlike the relatively quiet and predictable pace of Linstead, Kingston was bustling with energy—a city constantly in motion.

The daily commute to CAST fast became one of my biggest adjustments. Public transportation was provided by the Jamaica Omnibus Service (JOS), but navigating the crowded buses was a daily challenge. Each morning, I took a bus from Duhaney Park to Half Way Tree, one of Kingston's busiest commercial hubs, where I had to transfer to another bus heading to Papine, near CAST. The sheer volume of people in the city was overwhelming at first. The sight of thousands of commuters rushing in and out of buses, taxis, and private cars was unlike anything I had experienced before. Half-Way Tree, in particular, was a hive of activity, packed with shops, offices, and an endless flow of pedestrians moving purposefully in all directions.

One morning, I had an unforgettable introduction to Kingston's notorious public transportation hustle. It was pouring rain, and the thought of standing at the bus stop, getting drenched while waiting for a JOS bus, was far from appealing. That's when I decided to take a chance on one of the infamous *"robot"* taxis—unregistered mini-buses that operated illegally but were a common alternative for those desperate to get to their destination swiftly. The moment I squeezed into the already packed vehicle, I knew I was in for an adventure.

As fate would have it, the driver was in a hurry, weaving through traffic and speeding up Washington Boulevard when suddenly—sirens! A police officer signaled for the bus to pull over. The mood inside shifted from mild discomfort to full-blown anxiety. We all knew what was coming. The officer took one look at the driver, who was operating without a legitimate taxi license, and ordered everyone out. The rain was still coming down hard, and within seconds, we were left stranded on the side of the road, soaked to the bone as we scrambled to find another ride. The cop, in his no-nonsense tone, made it clear: using robot taxis was at our own risk. This was a harsh but common reality of city life. Yet despite the inconvenience, people—myself included—continued to take the gamble when needed.

This transition from the more relaxed pace of life in Linstead to the fast-moving urban environment of Kingston was an eye-opening experience. It forced me to adapt speedily, developing resilience and time management skills that would serve me well throughout my academic and professional journey. Despite the challenges, I embraced the new opportunities that came with this phase of life, eager to make the most of the education and experiences that lay ahead.

## The New Home in Portland

In addition, 1973 marked a major transition for my family as we moved into our newly built home in Windsor Castle, located in the parish of Portland. This was an exciting and long-awaited milestone yet adapting to a new environment and community presented its own set of challenges. The move also meant the expansion of our household, as two of Sam's children—his daughter Babbette and son Eddie—joined us. With this, we had frankly become one big, happy family, sharing the joys of living in a modern home equipped with all the latest amenities of the time. I was proud of the fact that I was a source of inspiration and support for my siblings who went on to attend high school themselves.

The house itself was not just a place to live—it was a testament to craftsmanship, community, and the determination to build something lasting. Designed and constructed by Sam's good friend Barry Ramsey, a highly skilled builder from our previous home district of Blue Gate, it stood as a remarkable achievement. Barry was not just a builder; he was a visionary, bringing architectural designs to life with a meticulous attention to detail that set him apart. His crew, a group of hardworking young men, including Stanley and Randell, also from Blue Gate, dedicated themselves wholeheartedly to the project. They often camped out at the site for weeks at a time, working tirelessly from dawn until dusk to ensure every wall, beam, and finish was executed to perfection.

Watching Barry and his team pour their sweat, skill, and dedication into the construction of the house was a profound experience for me. Every nail hammered, every wall raised, and every detail refined was a lesson in the art and science of construction. It deepened my admiration for his craft and further fueled my passion for Structural Engineering, reinforcing my desire to design and build structures that were both functional and enduring.

The house was designed in a contemporary architectural style, featuring a pitched roof, a spacious veranda, a carport, and glass louver windows that allowed for excellent ventilation—an essential feature for Jamaica's tropical climate. It was a perfect blend of form and function, balancing aesthetic appeal with practical considerations for comfort and efficiency.

One of the standout features of the house was the large carport, spacious enough to accommodate two small cars or Sam's mini-bus, making it a highly functional addition to the home. Another practical yet vital feature was the elevated emergency water storage tank, an idea I had personally conceived to counter the frequent interruptions in public water supply. Barry not just embraced the concept but executed it flawlessly, ensuring that the household always had a reliable backup source of water. In the front yard, two Julee mango trees were planted, that would eventually bear the juicy fruit in the next few years. I would enjoy the fruits years later when I visited from the U.S.

The house was more than just a structure; it became a place filled with cherished memories and personal moments of reflection. One of my favorite pastimes was playing cricket in the empty carport. I would bowl a rubber ball against the wall, pretending it was a skilled batsman I was challenging. In my mind, I was honing my skills as a spin bowler, imagining match-winning performances on the cricket field. Though I never pursued spin bowling in an actual game, these moments became a form of stress relief, offering a break from the pressures of school and life.

Moving into this home was not just about having a new place to live—it was about the pride of seeing a vision come to life, the appreciation of hard work, and the realization of what could be accomplished with determination and skill. It was a place that inspired me, not just in my personal growth but also in shaping my future aspirations.

Windsor Castle sat on the border between St. Mary and Portland, the latter being further east. The relocation meant that my younger siblings had to adjust to new schools in Portland, while my mother took up a position at Windsor Castle Primary, where she served as an assistant headmaster. The commute from Windsor Castle to Kingston was an adventure in itself. To get to Kingston, one had to travel through Annotto Bay, a coastal town, before navigating the infamous Junction Road. This winding, narrow road hugged the Wag Water

River and featured some nerve-wracking deep drop-offs, making it both a scenic and perilous journey. Along the way, travelers would pass Castleton Botanical Gardens, a well-known attraction famous for its lush tropical flora.

The commute reminded me of my earlier days traveling to and from Dinthill, especially when passing through the Devil's Race Course in St. Catherine. However, the Windsor Castle-to-Kingston journey was much longer—about 36 miles (58 km)—and the country buses were often packed with passengers, their luggage, and the occasional farm produce. Despite the challenges, I made the trip home from Kingston occasionally on weekends and during holiday recesses from college, cherishing the opportunity to reconnect with family and the familiar comforts of home.

One of the more fascinating aspects of living in Windsor Castle was the railway service that passed through the district. The train from Kingston in the evenings had a scheduled stop there enroute to Port Antonio, offering a unique and scenic travel experience. Unlike road travel, which followed established highways, the train journey provided a different perspective of Jamaica's countryside, weaving through mountains, passing through tunnels, and cutting across dense woodlands and small rural towns. The rhythmic motion of the train, the occasional whistling as it approached a station, and the breathtaking views made for an unforgettable experience. Sadly, the railway service was discontinued in the late 1990s, bringing an end to what had been a convenient and picturesque mode of transportation.

Windsor Castle sat close to the sea, with the shimmering blue waters visible from our front yard, just about a mile away. The landscape differed significantly from the lush banana fields of St. Mary or the expansive rural areas of St. Catherine. Here, the terrain was relatively flat, with houses built closer together and open vacant lands scattered throughout. Along the coastline, a vast stretch of wetlands and swamps added to the area's natural character. Fishing was a way of life for many locals, and the easy access to the sea allowed them to set out in small boats, returning with fresh catches to feed their families or sell in local shops and along the streets.

Beyond Annotto Bay, within St. Mary, lay the expansive Gray's Inn Sugar Estate, a major hub of sugar cane production in its heyday. The surrounding lands were dominated by vast sugar plantations, feeding the operations of Gray's Inn Sugar Factory, which played a vital role in the region's economy. However, in later years, with the decline of Jamaica's sugar industry, the factory was shut down, and the once-thriving estates underwent significant transformation. Today, much of the land that once flourished with sugar cane has been repurposed or left idle, marking the end of an era for a once-booming industry.

Despite the changes, Windsor Castle held a special charm of its own. It was a place where we built new memories, embraced new experiences, and adapted to the rhythms of life in Portland. The move had not merely brought our family closer together but had also set the stage for new adventures in this vibrant and evolving community.

## The CAST Campus

Stepping onto the campus of CAST for the first time felt like entering an entirely new world—one unlike anything I had experienced before. The campus was expansive, with multiple multi-story buildings lining the main access road, interspersed with parking lots designated for students, faculty, and visitors. The sheer size and structure of the institution immediately signaled that I had moved beyond the familiar confines of high school into a more complex and demanding environment. Nestled next to the vibrant hub of Papine and directly across from the prestigious University of the West Indies (UWI) in Mona Heights, CAST enjoys a prime location. But the real showstopper lies at the rear of the campus, where the breathtaking Blue Mountains rise majestically in the distance, painting a stunning backdrop that never fails to inspire.

A mix of excitement and nervous anticipation filled me as I took in my surroundings. This was the next stage of my journey, but it also felt somewhat overwhelming. Unlike Dinthill, where friendships had been firmly established and routines were predictable, CAST was a vast, unfamiliar territory where I initially felt like just another face in the crowd. However, that sense of isolation began to fade when I started recognizing familiar faces. A wave of relief washed over me when I reconnected with Leon Traille, Richy Brown, and Erol Boyd—former Dinthill students who, like me, were embarking on the Structural Engineering program. Knowing I wasn't alone in this new chapter made the transition easier.

The registration process itself was another stark reminder that I was no longer in high school. At Dinthill, course selection was largely predetermined, but at CAST, students had to take a more active role in shaping their academic paths. Before I could officially enter the Structural Engineering program, my application had to be reviewed and approved by the Department Head—a level of scrutiny and responsibility that underscored the seriousness of this next step. It was clear that this journey would require greater independence, self-discipline, and determination, but I was eager to rise to the challenge for the next three years of my life.

The facilities at CAST were outstanding. The structural engineering laboratories were well-equipped with state-of-the-art technology and tools, enabling us to gain essential hands-on experience that was crucial for comprehending theoretical concepts. My experience in land surveying around the campus was extremely memorable. We used advanced equipment such as theodolites to measure angles and distances accurately, which helped in mapping out the terrain and creating detailed site plans. We also used planimeters to measure areas.

These practical sessions were both educational and engaging, providing a necessary break from traditional lectures and offering insight into the realities of working as engineers. During these sessions, we not just applied our classroom knowledge but also learned how to troubleshoot real-world problems, communicate effectively with team members, and manage time efficiently.

We engaged in designing a variety of projects, ranging from simple structures like single-story residential buildings to complex multi-stories buildings and bridges. This was all accomplished by hand calculations with the aid of *"slide rules"* as digital calculators and computer software were not yet widely available to us. Furthermore, performing quantity surveys (QS) tasks allowed us to estimate building costs by calculating the quantities of materials needed and understanding budget constraints. This comprehensive approach ensured that we were well-prepared for the demands of the engineering profession.

I remember one of our lecturers, Mr. Williams, once said, *"An architect can design a building that resembles a masterpiece artwork, but it takes a structural engineer to ensure it stands."*

Daily meals on campus offered two main options. Students could either purchase lunch from various eateries around the center of Papine or enjoy a hot meal at the campus cafeteria known as "Farquharson Hall". Farquharson Hall, opened in 1965 and named after the first chairman of the College Council, The Honorable Donald Farquharson, served as a central hub for campus life at CAST. I was especially impressed with the quality and variety of meals provided in the cafeteria, which also had the added benefit of convenience. By my third year, when I became a resident student, I had the advantage of three daily meals included in the cost of boarding. This arrangement not just ensured that I had nutritious meals but also created a space to bond with friends and classmates over shared experiences. Overall, dining in Farquharson Hall was a pleasant and memorable part of campus life. Beyond its primary function as a dining facility, the hall doubled as an auditorium, hosting various events, including graduation ceremonies.

## The CAST Principal

Dr. Alfred Sangster, who was at the helm of the institution, was characterized by his gentle demeanor combined with a firm commitment to discipline and excellence. In 1970, Dr. Sangster accepted the position of Principal at CAST marking the beginning of a transformative era. During his tenure, he oversaw significant growth in student enrollment, the introduction of innovative academic programs, and the establishment of new departments such as Architecture, Computing, and Technical Teacher Training. His visionary leadership was instrumental in transitioning CAST into the University of Technology, Jamaica (UTech) in 1995.

Dr. Sangster's contributions to education and national development earned him numerous accolades, including the Order of Jamaica (OJ) for distinguished service. He was also awarded honorary doctorates from the University of the West Indies and the University of Technology. Beyond his professional achievements, he served as chairman of various private and public boards, demonstrating his unwavering commitment to nation-building.

Dr. Sangster passed away on January 27, 2025, at the age of 95, leaving behind a legacy of educational excellence and visionary leadership.

## Events that Shaped My Life while at CAST

My first year at CAST went smoothly from an academic standpoint, as I successfully completed all my courses. However, the daily commute from Duhaney Park to campus proved to be exhausting. The long hours spent navigating the crowded JOS buses left little time for extracurricular activities or socializing on campus after classes. Despite this challenge, I made the most of my time outside of school, reconnecting with an old childhood neighbor from Blue Gate, Leroy, who lived with his mother in Duhaney Park.

Leroy was an outgoing and charismatic guy, deeply immersed in Kingston's vibrant party scene. He had a passion for disco music and dancing, and before long, I found myself tagging along on his weekend adventures. Together, we explored the lively house party culture of the 1970s, attending gatherings not solely in Duhaney Park but also in other areas across Kingston. These were legendary nights filled with pulsating music, flashing lights, and a carefree atmosphere that provided the perfect counterbalance to the intensity of schoolwork.

Fashion was just as important as the music. Like many young men of the era, we took pride in our style—rocking trendy bell-bottom pants, platform shoes, and well-groomed afros that made us feel like we had stepped straight out of a fashion magazine. The soundtrack to those unforgettable nights featured some of the biggest disco hits of the time, including *Rock the Boat* by The Hues Corporation, *Rock Your Baby* by George McCrae, *Kung Fu Fighting* by Carl Douglas, and

*Never Can Say Goodbye* by Gloria Gaynor. Then there was Barry White with a string of hits between 1973 and 76. These songs weren't just music; they were the pulse of an era, uniting people in joy and liberation. I remember the buzz around Bruce Lee's 'Enter the Dragon' release in 1973, a time when Kung Fu movies and dance music shaped pop culture and on the streets the lyrics was – *"Everybody was Kung Fu Fighting, it was Fast as Lightening"*

Those weekends of dancing, laughter, and youthful exuberance provided a much-needed escape from the academic pressures of CAST. They allowed me to experience a different side of Kingston—one filled with energy, culture, and a strong sense of camaraderie. Looking back, those moments weren't just about having fun; they were about embracing life, making connections, and creating lifetime memories.

I have fond memories of living with Fitzy and Inez, whose warm hospitality made me felt right at home. They welcomed me into their household with open arms, creating a comfortable and supportive environment during my time in Kingston. Fitzy, in particular, was a passionate fan of Muhammad Ali, and his enthusiasm for boxing was infectious. Whenever there was a big fight on TV, he would become animated, cheering and analyzing every move with great excitement. Watching those matches together became a special bonding experience, filled with lively discussions and shared admiration for Ali's skill and charisma in the ring. Those moments added a sense of familiarity and enjoyment to my time in their home, making my transition to Kingston all the more memorable.

During the summer of 1974, I had the opportunity to stay with my grandfather, Cyril Toomer and his wife, Myrtle, at his home in Hughenden, Kingston. Unlike the compact and densely populated neighborhood of Duhaney Park, Hughenden featured larger homes with more spacious yards, giving the area a more open and serene feel. My grandfather's house was designed to accommodate two separate families, with one section rented out while he occupied the other. This was his retirement home, a place where he had settled into a quieter life after years of hard work.

That summer was a special time for me, as it allowed me to bond with him in a way I hadn't before. Grandpa Cyril was full of wisdom, and I cherished our conversations—his stories of the past, his life experiences, and the valuable advice he shared. Whether we were sitting on the veranda enjoying the cool evening breeze or sharing meals together, those moments left a lasting impression on me.

Staying in Hughenden also gave me the chance to reconnect with my uncle Lindo and his family. I spent quality time with his wife, Lorna, and my two cousins, strengthening our family ties. The atmosphere was relaxed and enjoyable, a welcome break from the daily hustle of school and city life. That summer was not just a time of rest but one of meaningful connections, laughter, and cherished memories.

In September 1974, I began my second year at CAST and moved into a boarding house run by Ms. Brown on Old Hope Road, just a short walk from the college. I didn't miss the hectic JOS bus commute one bit. Ms. Brown managed a home that accommodated six CAST students while also caring for her large family. She was a warm and nurturing woman who ensured we were always comfortable and had an environment conducive to studying. Her older daughters were incredibly industrious, assisting her with daily household tasks. She had a tradition of gathering everyone in a circle around the large dining table for morning devotion before breakfast.

Living there allowed me to engage more in extracurricular activities on campus, and despite our different fields of study, the other students and I formed strong friendships. One of my fondest memories was our early morning jogging sessions. At 4:30 AM, we would challenge ourselves to run beyond the steep hills of Papine, testing our endurance by seeing how far we could push toward the Blue Mountains. These runs were not just about physical fitness but also a test of willpower. They helped clear our minds and prepared us mentally for the day ahead in class.

Our location at Ms. Brown also gave us easy access to the beautiful Hope Gardens, a peaceful retreat surrounded by lush botanical landscapes. It fast became one of my favorite hideaways—a perfect spot for studying and unwinding in nature's tranquility.

## The Yamaha Adventure: A Ride of Terror and Thrill

Another unforgettable memory was when Erol bought himself a sleek, roaring Yamaha motorcycle. The moment he brought it home, it was as if he had acquired a prized stallion—untamed and full of power. He was determined to master the machine, and every chance he got, he would take it to the parking lots on campus to practice. We would gather around, watching him cautiously maneuver at first, then gradually growing more confident with each ride. The tentative start-and-stop motions soon gave way to smooth acceleration, controlled turns, and eventually, an air of effortless command over the bike.

Then came the day he decided he was ready for the real road. His eyes gleamed with excitement as he announced his plan to ride down to Half Way Tree. I don't know what possessed me, but without thinking, I volunteered to ride shotgun. Maybe it was the thrill of the moment, the rush of adventure—or maybe I just didn't want to miss out on what promised to be an epic experience.

As soon as we merged onto the streets of Kingston, weaving through the bustling traffic, my heart pounded like a jackhammer. The cars, buses, and pedestrians seemed to close in from all sides, a chaotic blur as we darted between them. Every sharp turn, every sudden acceleration sent a jolt of fear through me, but I forced myself to play it cool. I couldn't let Erol see my terror—I had to hold on, grit my teeth, and act as if this wild ride was all part of the plan.

Deep down, I knew I had made a mistake. I was clinging to the back of a speeding motorcycle, in the middle of unpredictable Kingston traffic, **without a helmet!** My mind screamed at me about the risk, but it was too late to turn back. I stole a glance at Erol—calm, focused, completely in his element. If he had any doubts, he didn't show them.

The minutes stretched into what felt like an eternity before, at last, we made it back safely. As soon as we pulled to a stop, I felt an overwhelming sense of relief flood through me. I had survived. The thrill was real, but so was the sheer terror. That day cemented one thing in my mind—I was **not** cut out for motorcycles.

To this day, I have never been tempted to ride one again. That experience left an indelible mark on me. I often think back and shudder at how reckless we had been—especially with me riding without a helmet. Maybe Erol had one, but I certainly did not. It was a risk I would never take again, and looking back, I am just grateful that our adventure didn't end in disaster.

## The Second-year Social Activities

During my second year at CAST, I began to explore more of the vibrant social life that the campus and surrounding areas had to offer. One of the most anticipated and unforgettable events was the annual "Barn Dance". This beloved tradition was a highlight of the year, a celebration of Jamaican culture, music, and community. The dance featured some of the top reggae bands of the time, including iconic names like Third World and Fab-5. Their rhythms reverberated through the air, setting the stage for an unforgettable night of music, movement, and connection.

The Barn Dance wasn't just an event; it was an experience that drew students from various institutions all over Jamaica—teachers' colleges, nursing schools, and even UWI. It was one of those rare occasions when the usual barriers between academic disciplines and campuses disappeared, replaced by an infectious sense of unity. People from all walks of life came together, dancing, laughing, and celebrating the rich cultural heritage that bound us together. As students, it was a much-needed break from the relentless pressure of coursework and exams.

The music—pure reggae—was the heartbeat of the night. The pulsating bass and energetic beats of Third World and Fab-5 seemed to pull everyone onto the dance floor, where people let go of their daily stresses. The air was filled with laughter and excitement as students reveled in the freedom to unwind. It was an opportunity to connect with old friends and meet new ones, building relationships that went beyond the classroom. Those nights were about more than just the music—they were about the camaraderie, the unity, and the shared joy of being young, alive, and part of something bigger than ourselves.

Outside of the dance halls, I also found myself exploring other interests that enriched my life during this time. One unexpected yet rewarding activity I picked up was martial arts. Classes were offered right on campus, and I decided to give it a try. At first, it was simply a curiosity, a way to challenge myself outside of academics. But soon, it became a valuable outlet for focus and discipline. The movements, the techniques, and the mental sharpness required felt like a perfect counterbalance to the intellectual demands of my studies. It wasn't just physical; it was also about developing inner strength, resilience, and a deeper understanding of control.

I will never forget the electric atmosphere of October 30, 1974—the night the world stood still for *The Rumble in the Jungle*. Muhammad Ali faced off against the seemingly unstoppable George Foreman in Kinshasa, Zaire, for the heavyweight crown. It was the fight of the century, and I had the privilege of witnessing it live via satellite at the Carib Theatre, one of the grandest venues in Kingston.

The place was jam-packed, a sea of anxious yet hopeful faces. The tension was palpable, as if the very walls of the theater vibrated with nervous anticipation. Foreman, the undefeated powerhouse, was the clear favorite, and many believed Ali was stepping into a lion's den. But those who really knew Ali—his brilliance, his unbreakable spirit—held onto hope. The crowd leaned forward, hanging onto every second, most of us rooting for *The Greatest* to defy the odds once again.

As the fight began, Foreman came out swinging, unleashing his infamous sledgehammer punches. The entire theater gasped with each brutal blow, but Ali didn't crumble. Instead, he danced, dodged, and then did something shocking—he leaned against the ropes, allowing Foreman to pound away. Some in the theater groaned, fearing the worst, while others murmured in confusion. Was Ali trapped? Was this the end?

But then, as the rounds progressed, realization dawned—Ali had a plan. He was absorbing Foreman's fury, letting the bigger man exhaust himself in a flurry of wasted energy. The legendary *rope-a-dope* strategy was unfolding right before our eyes, and the tide was turning. With each passing minute, Foreman's punches lost steam, his movements became sluggish, and Ali, ever the master tactician, saw his moment.

Then came the eighth round—the climax of a masterclass in strategy and resilience. In a sudden explosion of speed and precision, Ali unleashed a devastating combination. Foreman staggered, his legs wobbled, and then—*boom!*—he crashed to the canvas. For a split second, the entire theater fell silent, as if time itself had stopped.

And then, chaos. Jubilation. Euphoria.

The Carib Theatre erupted in sheer pandemonium. Strangers embraced, fists pumped the air, cheers shook the walls. We had just witnessed history—Muhammad Ali had *done it*! Against all odds, he had reclaimed the heavyweight crown, cementing his status as the greatest boxer of all time. That night wasn't just about a fight. It was about resilience, intelligence, and the triumph of will over brute strength. And I was there to witness it.

All in all, my time at CAST wasn't just about textbooks and lectures—it was about learning to appreciate the fullness of life, from the rhythms of reggae at the Barn Dance to the discipline of martial arts. These experiences shaped my social life and helped me develop a greater appreciation for the vibrant, multifaceted culture that Jamaica offered.

## Second-year Milestone Achieved

At the end of my second year at CAST, I reached a significant academic milestone—completing all the courses required in Structural Engineering for a certificate. The journey had been rigorous, filled with long hours of studying, practical assignments, and endless problem-solving, but the sense of accomplishment when I received my certificate during the annual graduation ceremony was immeasurable. I was elated, not just because of the achievement itself but also because it marked a pivotal moment in my academic journey.

As I stood there during the ceremony, a wave of pride and satisfaction washed over me. It wasn't just about the certificate—it was a testament to the hard work and dedication that had carried me through countless challenges. I had made it through the second year, but I knew the journey wasn't over. This was just a stepping stone. The bigger prize, the ultimate goal of earning my diploma in Structural Engineering, was still ahead, and that fueled my motivation to press on into the third year with even more focus and determination.

Despite the drive to continue pushing forward, I took a moment to really embrace the occasion. I couldn't have made it this far without the support of my peers and the guidance of my lecturers. As I walked across the stage to receive my certificate, I saw the faces of friends and mentors who had been there with me through thick and thin. Their encouragement, their feedback, and their shared experiences had all played a part in shaping the path I was on. I made sure to take the time to thank those who had helped me get to this point—my lecturers who provided not just academic instruction, but also wisdom and encouragement, and my fellow students, with whom I shared many late-night study sessions and challenges.

As the ceremony wrapped up and the celebrations began, I felt a renewed sense of purpose. I knew the third year would demand even more of me, but I was ready. The sense of accomplishment from completing the second year, paired with the knowledge that I had the support of a great community, propelled me into the next phase of my studies with excitement and determination. It wasn't just about achieving a diploma—it was about continuing to grow, both as an engineer and as an individual, and I was eager to see what the future held.

## Third and Final Year at CAST

My third year at CAST started in September 1975, with me able to secure living accommodation on campus since senior students were given priority. My dormitory room was located on the second floor overlooking the athletic playing field at the time, with the picturesque view of the mountains in the background. I would soon realize the advantages of this location having a front row, unimpeded view of track and field events and soccer matches as the balcony provided this opportunity. My classmate friends were very appreciative of this opportunity.

A significant part of my journey at CAST involved forging connections and interacting with other students to help hone in my teamwork skills. Among the key companions were Leon, Lance, Noel, and Erol, and together we formed the "Olympics" study group, aptly named for our late-night study sessions symbolizing our commitment to hard work and endurance.

The "Olympics " all-night study challenge group was a memorable part of my college journey. Our group aimed to motivate each other to maintain focus and excel academically through intense overnight study sessions. This camaraderie not just helped me academically but also fostered deep bonds of friendship that extended beyond our studies. Nights spent discussing theories and quizzing each other turned into some of the fondest memories of my time at CAST.

Our camaraderie extended far beyond academics, spilling into a vibrant social and cultural life. We eagerly attended events together, often making our way to the Carib and Regal theaters in Cross Roads to catch the latest Kung Fu movies. Our adventures didn't stop there—we explored social gatherings at other colleges, including UWI, always seeking new experiences.

One unforgettable night stands out: the live telecast of the legendary 1975 Muhammad Ali vs. Joe Frazier fight at the National Stadium. Dubbed the "*Thrilla in Manila*," this epic showdown was a nationwide sensational event. The stadium was packed to the brim, buzzing with energy as fans, including us, passionately rooted for Ali. Every jab and punch was met with thunderous cheers, the atmosphere electric with excitement. The fight was brutal, with both fighters pushing their physical limits in the sweltering heat. Ali emerged victorious after Frazier's corner stopped the fight before the 15th round. The crowd erupted in an explosion of joy, the deafening roar echoing into the night. The event was watched by millions worldwide and solidified Ali's legacy as one of the greatest boxers of all time.

As the adrenaline settled, reality hit—getting a taxi or bus was impossible amid the throng of ecstatic fans. So, with no other option, we embraced the moment and embarked on a four-mile (6.6 km) trek back to Papine, blending into a steady stream of fellow spectators. Thankfully, our early morning fitness routines paid off, turning what could have been an exhausting journey into yet another memorable adventure.

Sports were also an integral part of college life, offering both participation and entertainment through events like athletics champs, football (soccer), cricket and badminton. Early morning jogs up the hills of Papine and evening games of badminton and volleyball under the lights provided great opportunities for physical fitness and relaxation. Joining sports activities helped me stay physically active and provided a healthy outlet for stress. Furthermore, participating in these activities allowed me to develop teamwork skills, discipline, and a sense of fair play. I distinctly recall two exceptional athletes who proudly represented CAST in track and field championships, leaving an unforgettable legacy—lightning-fast sprinter Anthony Davis and the relentless mid-distance runner Tony Belcher. My favorite football player on the CAST team was the electrifying and relentless Noel (Bram) King, who commanded the center-back position with skill and tenacity. He was not merely a standout on the field but also one of my closest friends and a key member of our tight-knit "Olympics" study group.

Bram was really one of a kind, always bringing energy and joy to those around him. He loved entertaining and having fun, and I fondly remember his spot-on impressions of Bob Marley performing on stage—complete with his attempt to dress like the reggae icon. It became a running joke, with others often calling out, *"Hail up, Bob!"* whenever they saw him. He certainly added color and amusement to our days, making every moment livelier and more memorable.

The campus boasted a highly active and engaged student union, deeply involved in social and political activism. Beyond advocating for student concerns, the union also played a key role in supporting the efforts of Dr. Trevor Munroe, who was at the forefront of political activism during that time.

In the early 1970s, Dr. Trevor Munroe was a prominent lecturer and political activist in Jamaica, deeply involved in leftist movements and advocating for social and economic change. A Rhodes Scholar, he earned his doctorate in political science from Oxford University and returned to Jamaica to lecture at UWI.

During this period, Munroe was a leading figure in the Workers' Liberation League (WLL), a Marxist-Leninist organization that later evolved into the Workers Party of Jamaica (WPJ). He was vocal in championing the rights of workers and the poor, promoting socialist ideals in a time of political and economic upheaval in Jamaica. His activism aligned with the broader socialist policies of the Michael Manley-led People's National Party (PNP), which sought to reduce inequality and strengthen ties with socialist states.

Munroe was known for his dynamic public speaking, university lectures, and engagement in national discourse, often challenging the status quo and pushing for radical reforms. His influence extended into media and grassroots organizing, making him a significant intellectual and activist voice in Jamaica's leftist movement of the 1970s.

The faculty at CAST played a significant role in shaping our education. Our professors were not just teachers; they were mentors who guided us through the complexities of structural engineering. Their expertise and passion for the subject were evident in their teaching. They encouraged us to ask questions, challenge assumptions, and think creatively. Two professors, specifically Mr. Williams and Mr. Spencer, the department head, left lasting impressions on me. They often shared stories from their professional experiences, illustrating how theoretical concepts are applied in real-world scenarios. These anecdotes made the lessons more relatable and inspired many of us in many ways professionally.

## A Day of Triumph: CAST Graduation, June 1976

That day in June 1976 began with an unusual blend of nervous anticipation and euphoria—an awareness that we were about to experience one of the most memorable days of our lives. Graduation day had finally arrived. The morning felt different, electric with excitement. We had breakfast earlier than usual, our usual banter tinged with a sense of expectation. As the hours ticked by, the other boys gathered in my dorm apartment, meticulously preparing their outfits, making sure they looked their absolute best for the grand occasion later that evening.

At the time, *Bush jackets*—a style popularized by Prime Minister Michael Manley—were the formal wear of choice, paired with stylish bell-bottom gabardine pants. The look was sharp, sophisticated, and symbolic of the era. I carefully laid my outfit on the bed, ensuring every crease was perfectly ironed out. Presentation mattered. It was a day of prestige, a culmination of years of relentless effort, and every detail had to be just right. Grooming was also essential—afro hairstyles had to be neatly trimmed and shaped to perfection, a task we took upon ourselves using nothing but a pair of scissors and mirrors.

As the evening approached, we made our way to the ceremony, a grand event attended by friends, family, faculty, and fellow students. My mother was there, her presence making the moment all the more special. Dr. Sangster, who was the principal at CAST, delivered the opening remarks, setting the tone for the night. This was followed by an inspiring keynote address, a speech filled with wisdom and encouragement, reminding us of the journey we had taken and the limitless possibilities that lay ahead.

Then came the moment we had all been waiting for—the presentation of the certificates and diplomas. A wave of excitement surged through the hall as each graduate was called to the stage. When my name was announced, I felt a surge of pride and exhilaration. As I walked up to the podium to receive my diploma, I could hear the enthusiastic cheers of my classmates, their voices rising above the applause. The most spirited cheers came from my "Olympics" study group, the friends with whom I had shared endless nights of studying, problem-solving, and pushing each other to excel. We had supported each other through the challenges, and now, we celebrated each other's success with unrestrained joy.

This was more than just a ceremony; it was the culmination of a long, grueling, yet deeply rewarding journey. The sense of achievement was overwhelming. We had made it. Every late-night study session, every tough exam, every ounce of effort had led to this defining moment.

But the celebration wasn't over yet. That night, the atmosphere shifted from formal to festive as the graduation dance transformed the venue into a place of pure jubilation. We danced, laughed, and embraced the moment, fully aware that this was the closing chapter of our CAST journey.

## Achieving a Childhood Dream in Structural Engineering

For me, majoring in structural engineering had been a natural choice. Even as a child, I had been fascinated by the built environment—the towering structures, intricate bridges, and the sheer ingenuity behind their construction. I spent countless hours playing with construction toys, meticulously piecing together miniature buildings, bridges, and towers, driven by an innate curiosity about how things were built and what made them stand strong.

This early fascination grew into a passion as I arrived at CAST. The program was rigorous, each course designed to build upon the last, increasing in complexity and depth. I immersed myself in the principles of structural design, materials science, and construction techniques, each subject unlocking new dimensions of understanding.

By the time I graduated, I felt prepared, armed with the knowledge and skills to step into the professional world. This was just the beginning. The foundation had been laid, and I was ready to take on the challenges that awaited in the field of structural engineering. The journey that started with childhood curiosity had now become a professional pursuit—one that I was eager to embark upon with confidence and determination.

# Chapter 5

## Life Immediately After CAST

### Stepping Into the Professional World

G raduating with honors in 1976 was a moment of immense pride for both me and my family. It was the culmination of years of dedication, late-night studies, and perseverance. However, the joy of receiving my diploma was quickly met with the sobering reality of stepping into the workforce. The job market was competitive, and while I was eager to apply my knowledge, I knew that securing the right opportunity would require patience and persistence. Fortunately, my education at CAST had provided me with a strong foundation in structural engineering, giving me the technical skills and problem-solving abilities to stand out among other candidates.

After exploring several options, I secured a position as a junior project manager with the Ministry of Works, a pivotal step in my professional journey. This role was more than just a job—it was the doorway into the real-world applications of engineering and project management. I was stepping into the intricate world of large-scale infrastructure projects, where engineering theories met practical challenges, and where every decision had tangible, lasting impacts on the country's development.

### Building Jamaica's Infrastructure

Working for the Ministry of Works proved to be an invaluable experience. As a junior project manager, I was entrusted with responsibilities that were both demanding and rewarding. I was actively involved in major highway projects, critical to Jamaica's infrastructure growth. These projects were complex undertakings, requiring coordination between multiple engineering design firms, construction contractors, financial stakeholders, and government officials. They operated on tight deadlines, with significant budgets and immense public interest.

My primary assignment was working on the May Pen Bypass Highway and a connecting road to Lionel Town, a project funded by the World Bank for the Jamaican government. This endeavor introduced me to a diverse team, including overseas engineering consultants, who brought international expertise to the table. Working alongside them expanded my understanding of global best practices in engineering and project management.

Each day presented new challenges. I was responsible for overseeing construction activities, ensuring work was executed according to plan, and liaising with contractors to maintain quality and safety standards. I fast became adept at reading blueprints, understanding how each structural element fit into the broader project, and making necessary adjustments on-site when unforeseen field conditions arose. Construction, I learned, was never as straightforward as it appeared on paper—adaptability was key.

## Mastering Leadership and Communication

One of the biggest hurdles I faced was not just technical—it was managing people. Construction projects brought together a diverse workforce—engineers, architects, surveyors, heavy equipment operators, and laborers—all with varying skills, backgrounds, and perspectives. Coordinating such a vast team required effective leadership, patience, and strong communication.

I swiftly realized that clear and precise communication was vital to ensuring that everyone remained aligned with the project's objectives. Miscommunication could lead to costly delays, errors, or even safety hazards. I learned to listen actively, provide clear instructions, and mediate conflicts between workers and supervisors. Whether it was addressing a contractor's concerns, negotiating changes in scope, or resolving disputes on-site, these experiences shaped me into a stronger leader and problem-solver.

## Lessons Learned

The Ministry of Works was my first real exposure to the world of civil engineering beyond the classroom. It tested my skills, expanded my knowledge, and taught me the importance of adaptability and teamwork in large-scale projects. I walked away with not just technical expertise but a deeper appreciation for the human element in engineering—understanding that success wasn't just about blueprints and calculations, but also about collaboration, leadership, and resilience.

That first job set the tone for my career ahead. It fueled my passion for infrastructure development and gave me the confidence to take on even bigger challenges. I didn't know it then, but these early experiences would serve as the foundation for a lifelong journey in engineering, project management, and leadership.

Social networking significantly contributed to my professional development. After work, colleagues frequently convened for happy hours or other social events in a relaxed setting. These gatherings provided opportunities to build relationships, share knowledge, and discuss pressing job issues. Networking allowed me to stay informed about developments in the field and organization. During this period, I had an exceptional interaction with my immediate supervisor, Karl (Marts) Martin, which marked the commencement of a strong and enduring friendship.

## My Friend Martin (Marts)

Marts was a confident, knowledgeable, and tactful member of the team, always stepping in when needed to resolve disputes between lower staff and management. We could always count on him to be our advocate, skillfully and assertively addressing any issue at hand. His guidance and mentorship were invaluable to me.

I remember how, whenever I voiced complaints about work or personal matters, Marts would respond in his reassuring tone, *"Then Rose, what are you gonna do?"*—a simple yet powerful reminder to focus on solutions rather than just the problem.

Beyond work, we shared many social outings, but my most memorable experience with him was attending an international Test Cricket match at Sabina Park in April 1977, where the West Indies played Pakistan. Cricket has always been more than just a sport in the Caribbean—it is a cultural phenomenon, a unifying force, and a source of immense national pride. Experiencing a Test match at Sabina Park, one of the most iconic cricket venues in the region, was a dream come true.

We certainly picked the perfect match to witness firsthand. The West Indies, known for their dominant and flamboyant style of cricket, delivered an electrifying performance, ultimately securing a resounding 140-run victory over Pakistan. This win not just energized the passionate home crowd but also clinched the five-match series 2-1 in favor of the West Indies. The atmosphere inside Sabina Park was electric, filled with the rhythmic beats of drums, the blaring of horns, and the lively chatter of thousands of enthusiastic fans who had gathered to witness their team in action.

I distinctly remember that day being scorching hot, with the blazing Kingston sun beating down relentlessly on the stadium. My skin felt like it was on fire, but the excitement of the match and the energy of the crowd made the discomfort fade into the background. Everywhere I looked, fans were dancing, and shouting encouragement to their beloved West Indies cricketers. The passion was palpable, and the roar of the crowd every time a West Indies batsman struck a boundary, or a bowler took a wicket was deafening.

Being there in person, feeling the vibrations of the crowd's cheers, and witnessing the skill and athleticism of the players up close was a surreal experience. Watching the West Indies team, which boasted legendary cricketers, was an unforgettable privilege. The bowlers, known for their aggressive pace and precision, dismantled the Pakistani batting lineup with a combination of raw pace and strategic brilliance. The batsmen, playing with flair and confidence, thrilled the spectators with powerful strokes and majestic shots.

This match was especially special for me because it was my first time seeing a Test match live at Sabina Park. Though I had followed cricket on the radio and television for years, being in the stadium brought an entirely new level of excitement. There was something magical about the camaraderie among the fans, the rhythmic clapping, and the shared sense of pride that came with supporting the West Indies team. It was a day when everything aligned—the home team played exceptionally well, the atmosphere was electrifying, and I was there to witness it.

As the final wicket fell and the West Indies sealed their victory, the stadium erupted into joyous celebration. Strangers hugged each other, flags waved higher, and the sound of drums filled the air. Leaving the stadium that day, I felt an immense sense of satisfaction, not just because of the thrilling match but also because I had been a part of something really special—a moment of collective joy and triumph that would forever remain etched in my memory.

Looking back, I am grateful to have shared this moment with my good friend Marts, creating a memory that still brings a smile to my face decades later.

Marts was also a dedicated soccer player, often joining his peer group for pickup games on Sunday mornings. It was his way of keeping fit and relaxation.

His professionalism and encouragement played a crucial role in my decision to further my studies. He went above and beyond, even helping transport me to the embassy and ensuring I had everything needed for my migration to the U.S.

I was deeply saddened by his untimely passing in September 2023.

The experience gained from working on highway projects was instrumental in shaping my career. It gave me a deep appreciation for the importance of infrastructure in national development. Highways are the arteries of a country, facilitating trade, movement, and economic growth. Being part of such significant projects instilled a sense of pride and responsibility in me. I realized that my work had a tangible impact on people's lives, improving connectivity and accessibility across different areas.

After spending a year with the Ministry of Works, I decided to further my education abroad in pursuit of a bachelor's degree. This journey led me to apply and successfully gain admission to Howard University in Washington, DC, in 1977.

## Major Jamaican and Global Events (1973-1977)

### The 1973 Oil Crisis and Yom Kippur War

One of the most significant global economic events of the decade, the 1973 Oil Crisis, was triggered by the Yom Kippur War. After the United States and other Western nations supported Israel in its conflict against Egypt and Syria, the Organization of Arab Petroleum Exporting Countries (OAPEC) retaliated by imposing an oil embargo. This action led to a drastic increase in oil prices, quadrupling the cost of crude oil and causing widespread economic turmoil worldwide. Countries dependent on imported oil faced inflation, recession, and energy rationing, forcing governments to implement energy-saving measures. The crisis highlighted the world's dependence on Middle Eastern oil and led to long-term shifts in energy policies, including increased investment in alternative energy sources.

The Yom Kippur War was a conflict between Israel and a coalition of Arab states, primarily Egypt and Syria, that began on October 6, 1973. Launching a surprise attack on the Jewish holiday of Yom Kippur, Egyptian and Syrian forces initially made significant territorial gains. However, Israel, with support from the United States, managed to turn the tide and push back the Arab forces. The war had lasting geopolitical consequences, leading to a shift in U.S.-Middle East relations and setting the stage for the Camp David Accords in 1978.

## Watergate Scandal and Nixon's Resignation (1974)

The Watergate Scandal was a political crisis in the United States that began with a break-in at the Democratic National Committee headquarters in 1972 and culminated in the resignation of President Richard Nixon on August 8, 1974. Investigations revealed that Nixon's administration had attempted to cover up its involvement in the break-in. The scandal led to unprecedented political turmoil in the U.S., exposing corruption at the highest levels of government. Facing likely impeachment, Nixon became the first U.S. president to resign, handing over the presidency to Vice President Gerald Ford.

## The Fall of Saigon and the End of the Vietnam War (1975)

The Vietnam War, one of the most controversial conflicts of the 20th century, ended on April 30, 1975, with the fall of Saigon to North Vietnamese forces. The U.S. withdrawal in 1973 left South Vietnam vulnerable, and after a series of military defeats, the South Vietnamese government collapsed. The world watched dramatic scenes of U.S. helicopters evacuating American personnel and South Vietnamese allies from the U.S. embassy in Saigon. The war's end marked the reunification of Vietnam under communist rule and had lasting effects on U.S. foreign policy, leading to a period of military caution known as the "Vietnam Syndrome."

## U.S. Celebrated the Bicentennial (July 4, 1976)

The United States celebrated its 200th anniversary of independence with grand nationwide festivities. Parades, fireworks, and special events were held across the country, with major celebrations in Washington, D.C., New York, and Philadelphia. The event was a moment of national pride, bringing together a country still recovering from the Vietnam War and Watergate scandal.

## The US Presidential Election (1976)

The 1976 United States presidential election was a significant event in American politics. It saw Jimmy Carter, a Democrat and former Governor of Georgia, defeat the incumbent President Gerald Ford, a Republican who had assumed office after Richard Nixon's resignation in 1974. Carter's victory marked a shift in the political landscape, emphasizing his outsider status and promise of restoring trust in government following the Watergate scandal. The election was closely contested, reflecting the nation's mood amid economic challenges and concerns over foreign policy, especially in the aftermath of the Vietnam War and during the Cold War era.

## The Ethiopian Revolution (1974-1977)

Ethiopia underwent a period of political upheaval that began with the overthrow of Emperor Haile Selassie in 1974. The military junta known as the Derg took power, leading to a brutal period of purges and violence. The revolution resulted in the establishment of a socialist state but also triggered widespread famine and conflict, leading to a humanitarian crisis.

## Apple Inc. Founded (1976)

In 1976, Steve Jobs and Steve Wozniak co-founded Apple Inc., introducing their first personal computer, the Apple I. This marked the beginning of the personal computing revolution, which would eventually change the way people interact with technology worldwide.

## Michael Manley's Government

Michael Manley's socialist government during this period was a transformative period in Jamaica's history. His bold policies aimed at reducing economic inequality and promoting national self-sufficiency left a lasting impact. However, the era was also marked by economic difficulties, political violence, and strained international relations. Manley's government implemented sweeping reforms aimed at improving the lives of the working class and reducing foreign dependency. Manley's legacy remains a subject of debate—admired for his vision of social justice but criticized for the economic and political turmoil that accompanied his leadership. Ultimately, his tenure reshaped Jamaica's socio-political landscape and set the stage for future policy directions.

## Formation of the National Housing Trust (1976)

One of Manley's key initiatives was the creation of the National Housing Trust (NHT) in 1976. The NHT was established to provide affordable housing for working-class Jamaicans by offering low-interest loans for home ownership. This was part of Manley's broader effort to improve living conditions and promote social equity.

## Political Violence and the 1976 State of Emergency

As the political rivalry between the People's National Party (PNP) and the Jamaica Labour Party (JLP) intensified, the country experienced increasing violence. Political gangs clashed in urban areas, leading to numerous deaths. In response, the government declared a state of emergency in 1976 ahead of the general elections. This allowed authorities to detain opposition figures and enforce curfews in an attempt to control the unrest. Despite the tensions, Manley's PNP won the election, securing another term in office.

## The Rise of Reggae on the Global Stage

Between 1973 and 1977, Bob Marley transformed from a rising Jamaican artist to a global musical and cultural icon. This period was critical in the evolution of reggae music, as Marley's influence expanded beyond Jamaica, bringing the genre to international audiences. His music, infused with themes of resistance, social justice, and Rastafarian spirituality, resonated worldwide. During these years, Marley released some of his most iconic albums, survived an assassination attempt, and played a pivotal role in Jamaican politics and global popular culture.

In 1973, The Wailers released *Burnin'*, an album that featured one of Marley's most enduring songs, "Get Up, Stand Up." The album also included "I Shot the Sheriff," which was later recorded by Eric Clapton in 1974, significantly boosting Marley's recognition in mainstream music circles. The exposure helped introduce reggae to a broader audience, solidifying its place in global music culture.

However, by 1974, internal conflicts led to Peter Tosh and Bunny Wailer leaving the group, prompting Marley to continue under the name "Bob Marley and The Wailers." He recruited the I-Threes, a female vocal trio consisting of Rita Marley, Marcia Griffiths, and Judy Mowatt, to provide harmonies, further shaping the band's signature sound.

Released in 1974, *Natty Dread* was the first album credited to Bob Marley and The Wailers. Songs like "No Woman, No Cry" became anthems of resilience, and the album marked the beginning of Marley's evolution into a global protest figure. The song "Revolution" also reflected his growing political consciousness.

By 1976, Marley's *Rastaman Vibration* had reached international audiences, bringing reggae and Rastafarian culture to the mainstream. Jamaica's music scene became a cultural export that resonated with global movements for social justice and change.

In 1977, Marley recorded *Exodus*, an album that would define his legacy. *Exodus* featured a mix of politically charged songs like "Exodus" and "Jamming" alongside deeply spiritual and uplifting tracks such as "Three Little Birds" and "One Love." The album was a commercial success and remained on the UK album charts for over a year. Marley's music also became a symbol of resistance and unity.

By the end of 1977, Marley had achieved worldwide recognition, setting the stage for his continued influence until his untimely passing in 1981. His music continues to inspire generations, reinforcing messages of love, struggle, and resilience.

## The 1976 Carifesta in Jamaica

Jamaica hosted the Caribbean Festival of Arts (Carifesta) in 1976, bringing together artists, musicians, and performers from across the Caribbean. The event celebrated Caribbean identity and cultural heritage, further cementing Jamaica's influence in the region's artistic landscape.

## The Impacts of Local and Global Events Summarized

Between 1973 and 1977, both Jamaica and the world at large experienced profound transformations. Globally, economic crises, political upheavals, and cultural revolutions reshaped societies. The oil crisis of 1973 sent shockwaves through the global economy, triggering inflation and recessions in many nations. The Cold War remained a defining force in international politics, with tensions escalating between the United States and the Soviet Union. Additionally, movements advocating for civil rights, gender equality, and decolonization were gaining traction, bringing significant social changes across continents.

Meanwhile, Jamaica was undergoing its own period of turbulence and transformation. The country faced political tension between the two dominant parties—the People's National Party (PNP) led by Michael Manley and the Jamaica Labour Party (JLP) led by Edward Seaga. Economic struggles, fueled by inflation and unemployment, created unrest among the population. Despite these challenges, the island was experiencing a cultural renaissance, with reggae music becoming an international phenomenon and sports figures like Don Quarrie and the West Indies cricket team bringing global recognition to Jamaica.

These years were pivotal in shaping the future trajectory of the island nation and the broader global landscape. It was against this backdrop that I made the life-altering decision to migrate to the United States in pursuit of higher education. As I embarked on this journey, I was uncertain of what lay ahead, yet eager to embrace the opportunities and challenges that awaited me.

# Chapter 6

# The American Dream

## The Beginning of my US Journey

On August 17, 1977, at the age of 22, I embarked on a transformative journey to the United States, leaving behind the familiar comforts of Jamaica. This decision was both exhilarating and daunting, driven by a determination to pursue higher education and seize new opportunities. My destination was Howard University in Washington, D.C., a prestigious institution renowned for its rich history and commitment to excellence.

The path to this new chapter was fraught with challenges, especially during the process of obtaining a student visa from the U.S. Embassy in Kingston, Jamaica. My initial attempt was marred by anxiety and unforeseen hurdles. Due to the high volume of applicants, I found myself having to spend the night in a line of hopeful individuals along the sidewalk outside the embassy. Without provisions for sleep or food, I quickly adapted by connecting with others around me, sharing our stories and aspirations. Many were seeking visitor visas, and I was surprised to find no exceptions made for student visa applicants. We would share snacks among ourselves and took turns getting short naps on pieces of cardboard boxes. This camaraderie provided some comfort amidst the uncertainty.

This was a period when many Jamaicans were emigrating to the U.S. due to political and economic upheaval in the mid-1970s. People lined up overnight to be among the first 100 candidates the embassy would allow to enter each day. After enduring the overnight wait, I finally met with an immigration officer, just to be informed that I needed additional documentation, resulting in a visa denial. However, I was given an appointment to return about a week later. This time, I was allowed to enter without standing in the overnight line. To my delight, the immigration officer showed more understanding and compassion for my situation and did not even require the additional documentation previously requested. I was granted the visa, filling me with excitement for the journey ahead.

As the Air Jamaica airplane descended toward Baltimore Washington International (BWI) Airport, a whirlwind of emotions gripped me. My heart pounded with anticipation, a mixture of exhilaration and uncertainty coursing through my veins. This was it—the moment I had dreamed of, yet now that it was happening, reality felt almost too overwhelming to grasp. The familiar world I had known in Jamaica was behind me, and ahead lay the unknown, an unfamiliar land filled with endless possibilities and daunting challenges.

As I stepped off the aircraft, the air felt different, almost electric. The hum of activity around me—passengers hurriedly making their way through the terminal, the crisp voice of airport announcements echoing overhead, the sight of uniformed personnel guiding travelers—created an atmosphere unlike anything I had ever experienced. This was not just another journey; this was the beginning of a new life. I was in America, a place I had only read about and seen in movies. Now, I was here, standing on its soil, feeling its energy, absorbing its vastness.

Despite the excitement, a pang of anxiety tugged at me. I was alone in a foreign country, navigating an airport I had never set foot in before. Every moment felt like a test of resilience. The formalities of Immigration and Customs loomed ahead, and as I approached the officers, I steeled myself for the scrutiny. Questions were asked, documents examined, and finally, I was given the signal to proceed. A deep breath escaped my lips—I had cleared the first hurdle.

Pushing my way through the bustling terminal, I felt an odd sense of displacement, like an islander cast into an ocean of unfamiliarity. Then, out of the corner of my eye, I spotted something that sent a wave of relief crashing over me—familiar faces in an unfamiliar land. There they were, my step-aunt

Philaberta, whom I would come to know simply as Aunt Phil, and her husband, Les. Their eyes lit up as they waved enthusiastically, beckoning me toward them.

At that moment, the emotional weight of the journey hit me. A lump formed in my throat, but I swallowed it down, forcing myself to stay composed. As I reached them, I felt the warmth of their embrace, a comfort that reassured me that I was not entirely alone in this new world. I imagined my family back home exhaling in relief, knowing I had made it safely and was now in good hands.

Yet, even with the warmth of their welcome, I couldn't ignore the daunting reality before me. This was no vacation; this was the start of something life-changing. The road ahead was uncharted, and the stakes were high. However, one thing provided me with unwavering determination—the prospect of attending Howard University in Washington, D.C. The very name carried prestige, a promise of growth, learning, and transformation. It was where I would refine my skills, expand my knowledge, and carve out a future that once existed solely in my imagination.

Adding to my sense of security was the knowledge that I would be staying with Aunt Phil and Les in their home in Takoma Park, Maryland. Situated just a short distance—about 5.6 miles—from Howard University. Their home offered a sanctuary, a place where I could find my footing as I adjusted to this new chapter of my life. Aunt Phil, the sister of my stepfather, Sam Forbes, exuded kindness and understanding. I knew that in their home, I would have not just shelter but guidance and support as I transitioned into this new reality.

As we made our way out of the airport and into the crisp evening air, my mind raced with thoughts of what lay ahead. The roads, the towering buildings, the fast-moving cars—all of it was a stark contrast to the world I had left behind. But amidst the flurry of emotions—excitement, fear, hope—I felt a deep resolve settle within me. This was my moment. This was my chance to embrace the unknown, to step boldly into the future, to rise to the challenge of a new life in a new land.

With Aunt Phil and Les by my side, I took my first steps into this American dream, ready to embrace whatever lay ahead.

## My First Home in America

My aunt Phil's house was located in Takoma Park, MD, close to Langley Park. Takoma Park has a vibrant and electric vibe, known for its tree-lined streets, historic homes, and a strong sense of community. My aunt Phil and her husband Les, originally from Jamaica, had settled in this part of Maryland for many years. The neighborhood itself offered a blend of charming shops, local cafes, and a variety of restaurants. Known for its arts scene, with galleries and cultural events adding to its unique charm, Takoma Park combines suburban tranquility with urban amenities, making it a beloved spot for both residents and visitors. We were within walking distance of Langley Park center located at the intersection of New Hampshire Avenue and University Boulevard. A few miles east along University Boulevard, you would find the University of Maryland, College Park campus.

From the moment I arrived, my new family embraced me with open arms, making the transition into this new chapter of my life seamless and welcoming. The space I had was perfect—not just a place to rest, but a sanctuary where I could focus on my studies while still enjoying moments of relaxation. Les, an avid American football fan, wasted no time introducing me to the game, eager to recruit me as a supporter of his beloved Baltimore Colts (who later became the Indianapolis Colts) and Washington Redskins (now the Commanders). It wasn't long before I found myself caught up in the excitement of the sport and the National Football League (NFL), cheering alongside him on game days.

This was also my first taste of baseball—another American staple. I still remember watching the powerhouse New York Yankees dominate the sport, led by none other than the legendary Reggie Jackson, aptly nicknamed "Mr. October." Witnessing his heroics on the field made baseball an easy sport to appreciate. Les also introduced me to televised NBA games. His favorite team at the time was the Washington Bullets (now called the Wizards), who won the championship trophy in 1978. That's when I became a basketball fan myself. Les was always enthusiastic about sharing the history of sports and his favorite teams with me.

Watching sports, sitcoms, news, and movies on TV fast became a favorite pastime. I was amazed by the array of TV stations available in color, numbering more than six at the time, well before cable TV became widespread. Back in Jamaica, we just had one TV station, the Jamaica Broadcasting Company (JBC), and our TVs were primarily black and white. Listening to the radio also became a cherished way to relax. The abundance of FM stations here seemed limitless compared to Jamaica, which had just two FM stations at the time. My first major purchase was a "boom box," a combination radio and cassette tape player. I still remember WHUR FM 96.3 as my first favorite radio station, owned by Howard University and still thriving today.

I can still hear the smooth, soulful sounds of popular R&B pouring from the radio, filling the air with timeless melodies. Classics like *"Love Ballad"* by L.T.D., featuring the rich vocals of Jeffrey Osborne, first captivated audiences in 1976. The Commodores delivered a string of unforgettable hits, including *"Sweet Love," "Just to Be Close to You," "Three Times a Lady," "Easy,"* and the infectious groove of *"Brick House."* Various hits from the incomparable Earth Wind & Fire. Heatwave's heartfelt ballad *"Always and Forever"* became a staple of romantic slow dances, while Funkadelic's *"One Nation Under a Groove"* brought an electrifying blend of funk and social consciousness to the airwaves. These songs weren't just music; they were the soundtrack of an era, weaving their way into memories that still feel as fresh as ever.

I distinctly recall my early explorations of downtown Washington, D.C., particularly along the bustling F Street NW corridor, where the energy of the city was palpable. Occasionally, I would venture into the historic streets of Georgetown, soaking in its unique charm and vibrant atmosphere. As time passed and I gained mobility with my own car, my shopping excursions expanded beyond the city. I found myself frequenting popular shopping destinations in Maryland, such as Silver Spring, Wheaton, and Prince George's Plaza, each offering its own distinct retail experience. Eventually, Tysons Corner in Virginia became another favorite, with its expansive selection of stores and modern appeal. These outings were more than just shopping trips—they were opportunities to explore new neighborhoods, experience the changing landscapes, and embrace the freedom that came with having my own vehicle.

Mealtimes in my new home became an adventure of their own. Adjusting to American cuisine was no small feat, but it was an experience filled with curiosity and discovery. One meal, in particular, stands out—my first Thanksgiving dinner. I'll never forget sitting at the table, staring at the massive turkey, wondering how it would compare to the flavors I was accustomed to. That first bite was an unforgettable moment, marking my introduction to a tradition that was entirely new yet deeply cherished in this household.

Christmas brought its own set of wonders. The dazzling lights, the festive shopping, the beautifully decorated Christmas tree—it all felt like something out of a movie. The holiday season was a spectacle, filled with new traditions and experiences that left a lasting impression.

Yet, what honestly made Aunt Phil and Les' home special was the sense of community. Their house was always alive with warmth and laughter, as neighbors and fellow Jamaicans frequently dropped by, filling the space with stories, music, and the comforting familiarity of home.

And then, there was the thrill of driving. Sitting behind the wheel of Aunt Phil's or Les' car was an exhilarating experience. The open roads, the faster pace, the sheer vastness of everything—it was both exciting and nerve-wracking. The biggest challenge? Adjusting to driving on the right-hand side of the road instead of the left, as we did in Jamaica. It felt unnatural at first, but with time and practice, I adapted, adding yet another layer to my growing list of new experiences in this fascinating land.

I would go on to spend the next five years living here, embracing every challenge, and every unforgettable moment. This home, this family, and this community became my foundation in America, shaping my journey in ways I never could have imagined.

I also had the good fortune of having an older brother, Everton Rose, who had been living in Washington, DC, for quite some time before my arrival. I was happy to reconnect with him, as our lives had taken different paths after he migrated to live with his mother. Everton was the eldest of my father's children, and though we had not grown up together, our bond as brothers remained strong.

When I arrived in Washington, he welcomed me with open arms, eager to fulfill his big brother role. His warmth and generosity made my transition to life in the United States much easier. In him, I found not just a sibling but also a mentor, someone who had already navigated many of the challenges I was about to face. He offered invaluable guidance and support, helping me adjust to the culture, the climate, and the expectations of a new country. Whether it was offering advice on driving, sharing insights on life in America, or simply being a comforting presence, Everton was always there for me.

His unwavering support reassured me during times of uncertainty, and I always knew that, no matter what, I could count on him. Having him in my corner gave me an added sense of stability and belonging in an unfamiliar environment. Looking back, I remain deeply grateful for the role he played in my journey, for his kindness, and for the brotherly love he showed me from the moment we reunited.

## My First Out of State Adventure

Sometime during my first year in the U.S., I embarked on an adventure—my first Greyhound bus trip to Hartford, Connecticut, to visit my uncle Clarence, better known as Manny. Uncle Manny was my dad's brother; someone I had only met once before when he visited Jamaica around 1967 or 1968. The journey felt daunting at first, but it fast turned into an exhilarating, exhausting, and suspense-filled experience—one I would never forget.

This was my first trip outside Maryland, and along the way, I got my very first glimpse of New York City. As the bus approached the city, I could feel the excitement building. Stepping off for my transfer, I was instantly swept up in the electrifying energy of the "Big Apple." The towering skyscrapers, the relentless motion of people hurrying in every direction, the blaring horns, and the dazzling lights—it was overwhelming yet exhilarating. It felt as though I had stepped into the middle of a blockbuster movie, except this was real, and I was living it!

The city's incredible architecture left me in awe. The soaring buildings, each seemingly taller and more magnificent than the last, stood as monuments to human ingenuity. As we traveled along I-95, the grand bridges, stretching effortlessly across the waterways, and the network of tunnels amazed me. Watching the subway trains rumbling overhead and disappearing into the city's depths added to the sense of New York's vastness and complexity. It was a world unlike any I had ever known.

However, I couldn't help but feel a tinge of disappointment at the extensive display of graffiti that covered many surfaces. It seemed to be everywhere—on bridges, walls, and even subway cars—marking the city with an unmistakable and chaotic signature. Despite this, the sheer vibrancy and dynamic spirit of New York overshadowed the negatives.

Over time, the city became a familiar place to me. What started as a fleeting first encounter soon turned into a routine destination, as I found myself returning often to visit friends and relatives—this time by car. Each visit offered new experiences, fresh discoveries, and a deeper appreciation for the city that never sleeps.

Arriving in Hartford was equally thrilling, filled with anticipation of exploring a new city and reconnecting with family. Uncle Manny and his family welcomed me warmly, making me feel right at home. He took me on a tour of the city, and I even got to witness a live game of "Jai-Alai," a fast-paced sport played in an enclosed court where fans eagerly placed bets. It was my first and last time seeing the sport, but the experience added to the uniqueness of my visit.

My time in Hartford was truly special—I cherished the opportunity to bond with my uncle and his family, creating memories that would last a lifetime. Sadly, Uncle Manny passed away in July 1992, but the moments we shared remain etched in my heart forever.

## My return to Jamaica

My first trip back to Jamaica after moving to the United States was during the summer of 1978, while on break from school. It was a long-awaited homecoming, and the excitement of returning filled me with a deep sense of joy. The moment I stepped off the plane, the warm island breeze and the familiar scent of the Caribbean air immediately took me back to my childhood. Seeing my family and old friends again after being away for a seemly long year, was nothing short of exhilarating. There was an unspoken warmth in those reunions, a deep connection that time and distance had not diminished.

Everyone was eager to hear about my experiences in the U.S., especially my time at Howard University. Questions flew from every direction—what was life like in Washington, D.C.? How different was it from Jamaica? How was school, and did I plan on staying in America permanently? Sharing my journey was both exciting and humbling, as I realized how much I had grown and adapted to a new culture while still holding on to my Jamaican roots.

Beyond the reunions and conversations, I found myself appreciating Jamaica in ways I never had before. The beauty of the beaches, the vibrancy of the culture, and the incredible flavors of the food all seemed richer, more meaningful. I indulged in fresh mangoes, sweet guineps, juicy otaheite apples, and plates of ackee and saltfish with fried dumplings, cornmeal porridge, savoring every bite as if rediscovering them for the first time. It dawned on me that these simple pleasures—things I had once taken for granted—were now treasures that I deeply missed while living abroad.

That summer trip was just the beginning. Over the years, I made many more visits back to Jamaica, each one bringing its own moments of reflection and reconnection. No matter how far life took me, those visits reaffirmed that Jamaica would always be home.

## Meeting Bob Marley

On one of my trips back to Jamaica between 1978 and 1979, I had an unforgettable, almost surreal experience at the Kingston airport. As I made my way through customs, I suddenly found myself face-to-face with *The Man*—the legendary Bob Marley. Time seemed to slow as I stood there, staring at the global icon whose music had become the heartbeat of a generation.

What struck me most wasn't just his powerful presence, but how incredibly humble, approachable, and down-to-earth he was. Here was a man who had captivated the world with his powerful messages of love and unity, yet he carried himself with a quiet grace. Seizing the moment, I reached out, shook his hand, and muttered, *"Hail up, Bob. Keep spreading your positive vibes."* He flashed a warm smile, his eyes filled with wisdom and kindness.

I have vivid memory of the time in 1980, Bob was on his final tour, unknowingly to us, battling the illness that would take him from us too soon in 1981. I had even purchased tickets for his scheduled performance in Washington, DC—a concert he would never get to perform. Though fate denied me the chance to witness his magic on stage, that brief encounter in Kingston remains etched in my memory.

To this day, I carry the weight of that moment—the energy of his presence, the sincerity of his spirit, and the everlasting impact of his music. Bob Marley wasn't just a musician; he was a movement, a force of nature. And for a fleeting moment in time, our paths crossed.

# Chapter 7

# Attending University

## Howard University: A Historic Campus

Nestled in the heart of Washington, D.C., Howard University stands as a beacon of academic excellence, cultural heritage, and social progress. Established in 1867, the university has played a pivotal role in the education and empowerment of African Americans, producing leaders across various fields. Its campus, spanning over 250 acres, is a blend of historic landmarks and modern infrastructure, fostering an environment that inspires both intellectual and personal growth.

Howard University is located at 2400 Sixth Street NW, Washington, D.C. The campus is bordered by major streets including Georgia Avenue NW, Sherman Avenue NW, and Florida Avenue NW, providing easy access within the city. Howard's proximity to key institutions enhances its significance; it is situated near the Washington Hospital Center, Howard University Hospital, Children's National Hospital, and Catholic University of America. These neighboring institutions contribute to a dynamic academic and healthcare ecosystem, offering students opportunities for research, internships, and collaboration.

## Architectural and Historical Landmarks

Howard's campus boasts a rich architectural landscape, with buildings that reflect its storied past and commitment to the future. The Founders Library, with its stately clock tower, is an iconic symbol of the university and houses extensive archives, including rare manuscripts and historical records. It serves as a vital resource for students and scholars exploring African American history and culture.

Another landmark, Cramton Auditorium, is a major venue for lectures, concerts, and cultural events. Over the years, it has hosted prominent speakers, musicians, and political leaders, reinforcing Howard's role as a hub for discourse and artistic expression. Meanwhile, the Andrew Rankin Memorial Chapel provides a spiritual center for students, offering services, discussions, and a place for reflection.

## The Heart of Student Life: The Yard

At the core of Howard's campus is The Yard, an expansive green space where students gather, socialize, and celebrate traditions. It is the site of major university events, including homecoming festivities, step shows, and social activism. The Yard serves as an essential part of campus culture, fostering a sense of unity and belonging among students and alumni alike.

## The Blackburn Student Center

The Armour J. Blackburn Center at Howard University has a rich history rooted in the university's commitment to African American culture, education, and community. Named after Armour J. Blackburn, a prominent alumnus and benefactor of Howard University, the center serves as a focal point for cultural and social activities on campus. It was established to provide a space for students to celebrate their heritage, engage in academic and social events, and foster a sense of community.

Opened in the spring of 1979, the Blackburn Center fast became a hub of campus life, hosting concerts, lectures, student organization meetings, and cultural events. Its architecture and design reflect both modern aesthetics and cultural symbolism, emphasizing its importance as a gathering place for the university community. I have fond memories of the center's opening just weeks before my graduation, experiencing the excitement of exploring its new and vibrant spaces. The breathtaking view of the McMillan Reservoir and the distant Children's Hospital added to the refreshing and inspiring atmosphere, making it a truly unforgettable moment.

Over the years, the Blackburn Center has evolved to meet the changing needs of Howard University students while remaining a symbol of pride and unity. It continues to play a vital role in promoting diversity, inclusion, and academic excellence at Howard University.

## Academic and Research Facilities

Howard University is home to cutting-edge academic and research facilities that support its diverse programs. The Engineering and Science Hall is a state-of-the-art complex designed to enhance STEM education, offering laboratories, innovation hubs, and collaborative workspaces. Similarly, the School of Business and Howard University School of Law are recognized for producing top professionals in their respective fields, with rigorous programs that emphasize leadership, ethics, and social justice.

## Howard University Hospital and Medical Programs

A key component of the campus is the Howard University Hospital, which not just serves the surrounding community but also provides essential training for medical students. The hospital has been at the forefront of medical advancements and is integral to Howard's mission of service and education in healthcare.

## A Campus Steeped in Legacy and Progress

Beyond its physical spaces, Howard University embodies a profound legacy of activism, scholarship, and cultural influence. Located just minutes from the U.S. Capitol and White House, the university has been a driving force in shaping policies, movements, and leadership in the United States. The vibrant, diverse student body continues to uphold the institution's traditions while pushing forward new ideas and innovations.

Howard University's campus is more than just a collection of buildings—it is a living, evolving testament to excellence and resilience. Whether through its historic landmarks, bustling student life, or pioneering academic programs, Howard remains a place where generations of students find inspiration and purpose.

## My Pursuits at Howard

At Howard University, I pursued a Bachelor of Science in Civil Engineering, a discipline that perfectly blended my passion for science with my ambition to create meaningful, real-world solutions. Arriving on campus in September 1977, I was fortunate to reconnect with several former students from CAST in Jamaica. Among them was my good friend and former classmate, Leon Traille, a member of the "Olympics" study group at CAST, who had enrolled at Howard a year earlier. His guidance proved invaluable. He not just clarified the intricacies of the registration process but also escorted me to different department offices to ensure all was in order. Additionally, he assisted in choosing mandatory courses and generously provided textbooks he had previously used for some of those courses.

A crucial part of my enrollment involved transferring course credits from my studies at CAST. Fortunately, I was awarded enough credits to bypass the first two years of coursework, allowing me to enter at the junior level (third year). This accelerated my academic journey significantly, positioning me to complete my degree within two years—a major advantage that streamlined my path toward graduation.

Adjusting to this new environment was a challenge—not just academically in the School of Engineering, but also in adapting to the climate and culture. Having never experienced life in America before, I was uncertain about what to expect, especially when it came to the changing seasons. Fortunately, my step-aunt and uncle were there to guide me through my first fall, advising me on the proper clothing, including a warm jacket and other cold-weather essentials.

I distinctly recall the first time I felt the crisp chill of autumn. Dressed in my usual tropical attire, I was comfortable throughout the day—until dusk fell, bringing with it a sudden, biting cold unlike anything I had ever encountered in Jamaica. Shivering, I hurried home, wrapped my hands around a mug of hot cocoa, and found myself longing for the familiar warmth of home. The very next day, I made my way to a garment store in the Langley Park Center and purchased my first winter jacket. It wasn't the most stylish or the warmest, but at that moment, it was a necessary shield against the biting cold. For a while, it did its job, offering at least some protection from the elements.

As the season wore on and the chill deepened, I upgraded to a classic London Fog tan-colored trench coat. Unlike my first purchase, this coat provided both warmth and a touch of sophistication, making those harsh winter months far more bearable.

Commuting to Howard University required taking the Metro Bus from Langley Park, then transferring to another bus on Georgia Avenue that dropped me off near the campus. I was immediately struck by the punctuality and efficiency of the bus system, a stark contrast to the often unpredictable public transportation back in Jamaica. However, my first semester presented significant challenges, not just in terms of coordinating the bus schedules but also enduring the brutal winter weather while waiting at bus stops. Having grown up in the tropics, I had no prior experience with cold temperatures, and those early months were a rude awakening to the realities of winter.

There were countless moments when I longed for the warmth of Jamaica, especially during those early mornings and late evenings standing in the freezing wind. The first snowfall was a mesmerizing sight, a picturesque transformation of the city into a winter wonderland. But beyond its beauty, it fast became a harsh reality. Shoveling snow from the walkways and driveway at home was an exhausting chore, and simply navigating the campus and making my way to the bus stops became an ordeal. Slipping on icy sidewalks and trudging through snow-covered streets added to the daily struggle.

However, the true test came in February 1979, when Washington, DC, was hit by a historic blizzard that dumped up to 23 inches of snow, paralyzing the city for days. Temperatures plummeted to frigid levels, and everything came to a standstill. I found myself stranded at Howard, unable to make the commute back home. With no other option, I sought refuge at my friend Leon's dormitory, Meridian Hill, located on 16th Street, NW. The experience of being snowed in was surreal—what had once been an abstract concept in books and movies was now my lived reality. That blizzard cemented my understanding of winter in a way no prior cold day ever could.

By the summer of 1978, I was able to purchase my first car, which significantly improved my commute to Howard and made getting around town much more convenient. Excited by this newfound mobility, I immediately embarked on an adventurous road trip to New York City. It was a bold and daring move, navigating the heavy traffic along I-95 and maneuvering through the chaotic streets of New York—an experience that instantly brought back memories of the wild traffic in Kingston.

The coursework at Howard University was rigorous, demanding both a solid theoretical foundation and practical application. Balancing these aspects required dedication and resilience, but I was fortunate to have professors who were not merely experts in their respective fields but also deeply invested in their students' success. From my first semester onward, a few lecturers in the engineering school left a lasting impression on me—Dr. Johnson, Dr. Abron-Robinson, Dr. Noel, Dr. Sample, and Dr. Hwang. Their teaching extended beyond the classroom; they provided mentorship, encouragement, and a genuine sense of devotion to ensuring that I—and all their students—thrived in a challenging academic environment.

## Choosing My Major: Water Resources Engineering

Arriving at Howard University as a junior meant that I had to make some critical decisions about my academic path. Since I had already completed foundational coursework in engineering, it was time to declare a major and focus my studies in a specific area. Fortunately, I had the guidance of some incredible professors, one of whom was Dr. Johnson, a highly respected faculty member who would later become the Chairman of the Civil Engineering School. Dr. Johnson took a keen interest in my academic progress and recognizing my aptitude and interest in water systems encouraged me to consider a specialization in water resources engineering.

At the time, the field of water resources engineering was gaining national significance, thanks to increased federal investment in research and infrastructure. The Civil Engineering School at Howard was particularly well-positioned in this regard, benefiting from substantial federal grants that supported research in various aspects of water resources, especially in wastewater treatment. This area was rapidly evolving due to growing environmental concerns and newly enacted regulations.

One of the most pivotal legislative actions influencing the field was the passage of the Clean Water Act of 1972, a landmark environmental law aimed at reducing water pollution and improving the quality of the nation's waterways. With the stricter wastewater treatment regulations that followed, municipalities across the United States faced mounting pressure to upgrade their treatment facilities and implement new technologies to comply with federal mandates. This surge in regulatory requirements created a high demand for skilled engineers who could design and oversee these systems, making wastewater engineering an exciting and promising career path. The opportunity to contribute to solving real-world environmental challenges was compelling, and I was eager to be part of the movement.

Beyond wastewater treatment, another critical area of water resources engineering was flood protection and management. In response to devastating floods that had impacted various parts of the country, the U.S. government had instituted the National Flood Insurance Program (NFIP) to help protect communities from the financial burden of flood damage. Initially administered by the Department of Housing and Urban Development (HUD), the program focused on developing floodplain maps and conducting hydraulic and hydrologic studies to assess flood risks for eligible communities. These studies were essential in determining which areas required flood protection measures and in setting insurance rates based on potential flood hazards.

I found this aspect of water resources engineering extremely fascinating. Flooding was a global issue, and the idea of applying engineering principles to mitigate its impact on communities resonated with me. As I learned more about floodplain mapping, stormwater management, and urban drainage design, I saw a direct connection between these concepts and the experiences I had growing up in Jamaica, where heavy rains often led to severe flooding and infrastructural challenges.

## Gaining Practical Experience: A Job with HUD

One of the most defining moments of my senior year came when Dr. Hwang, another esteemed professor in the Civil Engineering Department, helped me secure a part-time job with HUD working on the National Flood Insurance Program. This was an invaluable opportunity—not only did it provide financial support, but it also allowed me to apply the theoretical knowledge I had gained in class to real-world problems.

My primary role at HUD involved quality control for floodplain mapping projects. This meant reviewing flood studies, assessing hydrologic and hydraulic data, and ensuring that the maps being developed accurately reflected flood risks in designated communities. I found the work incredibly rewarding, as it gave me a firsthand look at how government agencies and engineers collaborated to create safer, more resilient communities.

One of the key takeaways from this experience was understanding the real-world impact of engineering decisions. It became clear that floodplain maps were not just technical documents; they directly influenced public policy, insurance rates, land-use planning, and disaster preparedness. Homeowners, developers, and local governments relied on these studies to make critical decisions about property development and flood mitigation strategies. Working on this project also provided an early glimpse into interdisciplinary collaboration. This broadened my perspective on the field of engineering, reinforcing that technical expertise alone was not enough—effective engineers also needed strong communication skills and an ability to work across disciplines.

## The Impact of Part-time Work Experience on My Career

The experience at HUD proved to be a turning point in my career. While I had entered Howard with a broad interest in civil engineering, my exposure to water resources, floodplain management, and stormwater engineering helped me refine my focus. I became specifically drawn to stormwater management, which deals with controlling rainwater runoff in urban areas to reduce flooding, erosion, and water pollution.

Urbanization was rapidly changing the landscape of cities, and as more land was developed, the challenge of managing stormwater became more complex. Traditional drainage systems often failed to cope with extreme weather events, leading to increased flooding, water contamination, and infrastructure damage. Recognizing the importance of these issues, I saw an opportunity to specialize in designing sustainable stormwater solutions that could both protect the environment and enhance urban resilience.

Looking back, I credit Dr. Johnson and Dr. Hwang for steering me toward this path. Their mentorship and encouragement not just influenced my academic choices but also instilled in me a sense of purpose in my work. Their dedication to student success and impactful research demonstrated what it meant to be an engineer who not merely solved problems but also made a meaningful difference in society.

Beyond my core engineering courses, I had the opportunity to take electives that broadened my perspective and enriched my university experience. Sociology was very fascinating, as it explored human societies, cultural norms, and the social forces that shape them. The curriculum provided an insightful exposure to African heritage and its deep connections to political and economic movements, especially the civil rights struggles both in the U.S. and globally. Intro to Music offered a refreshing exploration of different musical traditions, deepening my appreciation for various art forms. But perhaps the most enjoyable elective for me was Badminton, which became a much-needed escape from the rigors of engineering coursework. I built a great rapport with my instructor, and we often played games after class, which helped me unwind and stay active.

## The Extracurricular Activities & Special Connections

Howard University was more than just academics— extracurricular events at Howard primarily revolved around sports and the fall Homecoming, with football playing a major role as the Howard "Bisons" fiercely competed in college league games. This gave me the opportunity to experience American football up close at Howard Stadium. However, I was most thrilled by the soccer matches, where the team, made up mostly of exceptional Caribbean and African players, showcased remarkable talent.

It was a thriving community with a dynamic campus life that fostered personal growth and leadership development. Among the many student organizations, the Caribbean Student Association (CSA) stood out as a home away from home for me. The CSA brought together students from across the Caribbean, providing a strong support system and organizing numerous cultural and social events. While parties were certainly a part of the experience, the CSA also played a significant role in activism, leading protests and demonstrations on issues affecting both the Caribbean and the broader Black diaspora.

One of the most remarkable aspects of Howard was the diversity of its student body, with students hailing from various U.S. states and countries worldwide. I found myself particularly drawn to fellow students from the Caribbean and Africa, forging lasting friendships that enriched my time at the university. I fondly recall my close friendships with Noel from Trinidad, Kofi from Ghana, and Sadia from Guyana. There was a large contingent of Jamaican friends, and I recall crossing paths with several of them from my time at CAST, including Leon, Neville, Tony, Peter, Sylvester, Lance, and Delroy.

I had the privilege of witnessing and celebrating the joyous unions of three dear friends and fellow students at the Howard University Chapel.

The first was the wedding of Kofi and his beautiful bride. Then, in May 1980, my Jamaican friend and fellow CAST alumnus, Peter Turner, married Maria, whom he met at Howard. Their union marked the beginning of a lifelong friendship that endured until Peter's untimely passing in September 2020. Peter had a gentle spirit, always wearing a warm smile that made everyone around him feel at ease and welcomed. I remember him at CAST, a year ahead of me, standing out as one of the most outstanding students, someone everyone looked up to emulate. During my first year at Howard, he was also my graduate teaching assistant for the fluid mechanics lab, a role in which he offered both guidance and support. His memory remains with me always.

The third wedding I attended was very special, as I had the honor of serving as best man for my best friend, Leon Traille, when he married his lovely wife, Monica, whom he also met at Howard. Their wedding took place in mid-1980 at the chapel, making it yet another cherished moment in my time at Howard.

I have also maintained a lasting friendship with Tony Belcher, a former CAST student who pursued Electrical Engineering at Howard University, ever since our time there.

These connections I made not just provided camaraderie but also deepened my appreciation for the shared histories and cultural ties that bound us together. Howard was more than an academic institution—it was a mosaic of experiences that shaped my worldview and helped my growth.

## My Introduction to Tennis

My introduction to tennis began during my time at Howard University, sparked by a growing fascination with the professional game. I found myself captivated by legendary players like Arthur Ashe, Jimmy Connors, Chris Evert, Bjorn Borg, and John McEnroe, watching their matches with admiration. Their skill, strategy, and athleticism intrigued me, and I became eager to experience the game firsthand.

One day, after a badminton class, a fellow student invited me to try tennis. Eager to give it a shot, we grabbed some wooden rackets—standard at the time—and headed to the courts at Banneker Recreation Center. I naively assumed that my badminton experience would translate well to tennis, expecting a smooth transition between the two sports. However, I quickly realized how wrong I was.

Tennis required an entirely different approach—different strokes, footwork, and a unique sense of timing. My initial attempts were far from graceful; I sent ball after ball soaring over the fencing, completely misjudging the power and control needed. Despite the early struggles, I gradually started to adjust, learning how to keep the ball within the court. With each practice session, my coordination improved, and I began to appreciate the game's rhythm and technique.

This modest introduction to tennis was the start of something that would grow into a lasting passion. Though I never pursued it competitively, the sport became a cherished pastime, one that I would enjoy playing purely for fun in the years that followed. Tennis not just provided great exercise but also became a social outlet, allowing me to connect with friends over friendly matches and spirited rallies. Looking back, I am grateful for that first invitation to the court—it opened the door to a sport that would bring me enjoyment for years to come.

## Completion of Year One

By the end of my first year in June 1978, I achieved a significant milestone by earning a place on the Dean's List. This accomplishment was especially rewarding because it made me eligible for financial assistance from the university, easing the burden of tuition for the upcoming Fall semester. Beyond the academic recognition, this achievement had a profound impact on my confidence, reaffirming my ability to excel in a rigorous engineering program.

In addition to this honor, I was fortunate to secure a part-time assistant position in the computer lab. This role provided a unique opportunity to not just assist fellow students with their programming assignments but also to gain hands-on experience with the intricate operations and maintenance of an IBM 360 mainframe computer system. At the time, mainframe computing was the backbone of complex data processing in engineering and scientific research, making this exposure incredibly valuable.

Working in the lab allowed me to develop technical proficiency, problem-solving skills, and a deeper appreciation for the role of computer science in engineering. I quickly realized how computational tools could streamline complex calculations, optimize designs, and solve engineering challenges more efficiently. Additionally, the position enhanced my leadership and communication skills, as I often had to guide students, troubleshoot issues, and ensure smooth operations within the lab.

This experience sparked a growing interest in computing, which would later prove instrumental in my career. It was a pivotal moment that broadened my perspective on how emerging technologies could revolutionize the engineering field, paving the way for future advancements in computer-aided design, modeling, and data analysis.

## A Day to Remember: Graduation, May 1979

Graduation day in May 1979 was one of the most exhilarating and defining moments of my life. It was a day filled with joy, gratitude, and reflection, a culmination of years of hard work, perseverance, and the unwavering support of family, friends, mentors, and peers. The journey to that moment had been anything but easy, but standing there in my cap and gown, ready to receive my degree, I felt an overwhelming sense of accomplishment.

The road to graduation had been paved with challenges and triumphs, from navigating a new academic environment to overcoming the sometimes harsh winters of Washington, D.C. I had faced rigorous coursework, sleepless nights preparing for exams, and the pressures of excelling in a highly competitive field. Yet, in that moment, all the struggles seemed worth it. I had made it. More importantly, I had made my family and my countrymen proud.

### The Commencement Ceremony: A Grand Spectacle

The day of the commencement ceremony was filled with excitement. The anticipation in the air was palpable as the graduating class gathered near Burr

Gymnasium, preparing for the formal march onto the playing field. It was a sea of black gowns and caps, each student adorned with stoles that represented the colors of their respective schools and colleges or the degrees they had earned. The sight was breathtaking—a true testament to the diverse and accomplished student body at Howard University.

As we proceeded onto the field, I took a deep breath, absorbing the magnitude of the moment. The ceremony was grand and dignified, with proud families and friends seated in the stands, beaming with joy. The keynote speaker took the stage and delivered a speech filled with wisdom and encouragement, reminding us that our journey was just beginning. But the most memorable part of the ceremony for me was the address by Howard University's President, Dr. James Cheek. His inspirational message struck a deep chord, reinforcing the ideals of leadership, service, and the responsibility that came with our education.

I recall looking around at my fellow graduates—some I had studied alongside, some I had formed lasting friendships with, and others who had faced their own personal battles to make it to this day. The pride on their faces mirrored my own. This was a victory for all of us.

What made this ceremony even more meaningful was the presence of my Aunt Phil and her husband, Les. They had been a pillar of support for me throughout my time in the United States, offering not merely a place to stay but also encouragement, warmth, and guidance. Having them witness this monumental milestone in my life was incredibly significant. Their pride in my achievement was evident, and it meant the world to me that they were there to celebrate with me.

Later that day, I attended the Honors Awards Ceremony for engineering graduates, which was held in the School of Engineering auditorium. This event was more intimate, celebrating the academic achievements and contributions of students within our discipline. It was a special moment to be recognized among my peers, knowing that the hours spent in classrooms, laboratories, and study groups had all led to this point. As an added bonus, I graduated among the top five students in my class of over 30 civil engineering majors.

## A Moment of Reflection

As the day came to a close, I took a moment to reflect on my journey. From my early days at Dinthill Technical High School to my time at Howard University, I had come a long way. There were moments of doubt and uncertainty, but through it all, I had persisted. My success was not mine alone—it was a testament to the love and support of those who had guided me along the way.

Graduating with a degree in Civil Engineering was not just a personal triumph; it was a responsibility. I now had the tools and knowledge to make a real impact in my field, and I was eager to embark on the next chapter of my journey.

That day, as I held my diploma in my hands, I felt an immense sense of pride, gratitude, and excitement for what lay ahead.

## Pursuing a Master's Degree in Civil Engineering

After graduating with my Bachelor of Science in Civil Engineering from Howard University in May 1979, I made the pivotal decision to continue my studies and pursue a Master of Science in Civil Engineering. I had developed a deep interest in water resources engineering, especially in the areas of stormwater management and flood protection, and I saw the master's program as an opportunity to expand my knowledge and expertise.

## Graduate Teaching Assistantship and Early Research

I was fortunate to receive a Graduate Teaching Assistant (GTA) position, which provided both financial support and valuable academic experience. As a GTA, I conducted hydraulics laboratory sessions, assisted undergraduate students with coursework, and contributed to ongoing research projects within the engineering department. This role not just deepened my understanding of fundamental engineering concepts but also helped me develop essential skills in teaching, mentoring, and problem-solving.

By the end of 1980, I had successfully completed all my required coursework, which included advanced topics in hydrology, fluid mechanics, numerical modeling, and hydraulics. With the coursework behind me, I shifted my focus to my master's thesis research, which would become one of the most demanding yet rewarding projects of my academic career.

## Master's Thesis: A Real-world Stormwater Challenge

My thesis research was centered around a critical issue in stormwater management: "Comparing the Differences Between Flood Flow Frequencies and Rainfall Frequencies for Small Rural Watersheds." This topic had real-world implications, as understanding the relationship between storm intensity and flood response was crucial for designing effective flood control infrastructure, stormwater systems, and urban drainage planning.

Under the expert guidance of both Dr. Hwang and Dr. Tseng, my thesis advisors, I embarked on a comprehensive research study that required extensive data collection and hydrologic analysis. The core of my work involved gathering historical rainfall and streamflow data from several well-established hydrological stations across the eastern United States. These datasets were essential for understanding how rainfall patterns translated into flood events, a subject that was becoming increasingly important due to the evolving federal flood management policies and the need for accurate flood risk assessment models.

One of the most challenging aspects of the research was obtaining high-quality, long-term historical data. At the time, accessing detailed rainfall and streamflow records was not as straightforward as it is today, requiring significant effort to locate, compile, and verify datasets from multiple government agencies and research institutions. Despite these challenges, my determination and perseverance kept me moving forward.

## A Complex but Rewarding Modeling Tasks

A crucial part of my research involved developing and executing hydrologic and hydraulic models to simulate storm events and flood responses. These models helped analyze the statistical relationships between rainfall frequency and resulting flood magnitudes, providing valuable insights into the predictability and variability of stormwater behavior.

The process of building these models was both technically demanding and intellectually stimulating. It required extensive computational work, data analysis, and validation of the models against real-world flood events. I found myself constantly refining my approach, adjusting input parameters, and troubleshooting inconsistencies in the simulations. Though the work was at times frustrating, the challenge fueled my passion for engineering problem-solving. Each breakthrough brought a new level of understanding and confidence, reinforcing my belief in the practical impact of engineering research.

## Balancing Graduate Research with My First Professional Job

As I delved deeper into my thesis research, a new opportunity arose that marked the beginning of my professional engineering career. In 1981, I secured another part-time job with an engineering consulting firm in Fairfax, Virginia. This firm was one of three "Technical Contractors" responsible for preparing and reviewing Flood Insurance Studies and Flood Maps under the National Flood Insurance Program (NFIP), which was still administered by the U.S. Department of Housing and Urban Development (HUD) at the time.

My prior experience working with HUD's Flood Insurance Program during my undergraduate years gave me a significant advantage in this new role. I was already familiar with the floodplain mapping process, the regulatory framework, and the hydrologic and hydraulic analysis methods used to determine flood risk for communities across the United States. This allowed me to transition into my new responsibilities with confidence, and I swiftly became an integral part of the team.

During this time, I obtained permanent resident status, commonly known as a "Green Card," which allowed me to secure a full-time position.

However, balancing a demanding full-time job with my ongoing master's research was no easy feat. My days were filled with engineering work and meetings, while my nights and weekends were dedicated to analyzing data, running models, and writing my thesis. The workload was intense, and there were times when I felt overwhelmed, but my strong work ethic, discipline, and passion for the field kept me going.

## Completing My Master's Degree: A Hard-Earned Achievement

After years of rigorous research, analysis, and writing, I completed my master's thesis and successfully defended it in 1984. The defense process was nerve-wracking, as I had to present my findings to a panel of esteemed faculty members, answer challenging questions, and justify my methodology and conclusions. However, the countless hours of preparation paid off, and I was able to demonstrate a deep understanding of my research.

With the successful defense of my thesis, I officially earned my Master of Science in Civil Engineering and graduated in December 1984. The feeling of relief, pride, and accomplishment was indescribable. It had been a long and challenging journey, but I had not just deepened my expertise in water resources engineering but also laid the foundation for a successful career in the field.

## A Pivotal Chapter in My Career

Looking back, my decision to pursue a master's degree at Howard University was one of the most pivotal choices of my life. The experience equipped me with advanced technical knowledge, exposed me to cutting-edge research, and provided invaluable professional opportunities. My work with hydrologic and hydraulic models, my understanding of flood risk management, and my experience juggling academia and industry work all played a crucial role in shaping my career path in water resources and environmental engineering.

The challenges I faced during my master's program—whether it was navigating complex research, balancing work and studies, or defending my thesis—helped instill in me a resilience and determination that would serve me well throughout my professional life. With my master's degree in hand, I was now fully prepared to embark on the next chapter of my career, ready to make meaningful contributions to the field of water resources engineering.

## Broader Lessons from My Time at Howard

Beyond the technical skills I gained, my experiences at Howard University taught me several invaluable lessons:

**The Importance of Mentorship** – Having mentors like Dr. Johnson and Dr. Hwang made all the difference in my journey. Their guidance helped me navigate complex career decisions and exposed me to opportunities I might not have discovered on my own.

**The Value of Hands-On Experience** – Working at HUD reinforced the idea that classroom learning is just part of an engineer's education. Practical exposure is essential in bridging the gap between theory and real-world applications.

**Engineering as a Tool for Social Good** – My work in flood management showed me that engineering isn't just about designing structures—it's about protecting communities, improving public safety, and shaping policies that affect people's daily lives.

**The Need for Adaptability** – The fields of water resources and environmental engineering were rapidly evolving in response to new regulations and emerging challenges. This experience taught me that staying current with industry developments and being adaptable were key to long-term success.

## The World from 1978 - 84: A Story of Change and Conflict

As the sun set on the 1970s, the world stood at a crossroads. In the United States, President Jimmy Carter worked tirelessly to bring peace between Israel and Egypt. After intense negotiations at Camp David, the two nations signed a historic agreement, marking the first time an Arab country recognized Israel. In 1978 a new leader emerged—Pope John Paul II. Unlike his predecessors, he was not Italian but Polish, and his very presence sent ripples through Eastern Europe, inspiring millions living under communist rule.

Meanwhile, in 1979, in Iran, unrest boiled over. The Shah, long supported by the U.S., fled as revolutionaries led by Ayatollah Khomeini took control. The Islamic Republic was born, and soon after, American diplomats in Tehran found themselves hostages, a crisis that would haunt Carter's presidency. Not far away, another superpower made a bold move. The Soviet Union, fearing instability on its borders, invaded Afghanistan. What seemed like a quick intervention turned into a grueling war, as Afghan rebels, armed with U.S. support, resisted fiercely.

Back in the United States, 1980 became a turning point. A former Hollywood actor, Ronald Reagan, won the presidency in a landslide. His vision was clear—cut taxes, rebuild the military, and take a hard stance against communism. While Reagan celebrated his victory, two nations in the Middle East plunged into war. Iraq, led by Saddam Hussein, launched an attack on Iran, sparking an eight-year conflict filled with brutal trench warfare and chemical weapons.

Then, in 1981, the world held its breath. Just months into office, Reagan was shot outside a Washington hotel. Miraculously, he survived, and his popularity soared. At the same time, NASA made history, launching the first reusable space shuttle, Columbia, marking the dawn of a new era in space exploration. But beneath the excitement of scientific progress, a silent threat loomed. Doctors in the U.S. identified a mysterious illness attacking the immune system—what would soon become known as AIDS.

By 1982, war broke out in an unlikely place—the remote Falkland Islands. Argentina, claiming ownership, invaded, but Britain, under Prime Minister Margaret Thatcher, responded with military force. After fierce battles, the British emerged victorious, solidifying Thatcher's leadership. Meanwhile, the Lebanese Civil War spiraled further into chaos. Israel launched an invasion to drive out the PLO, drawing the U.S. and other nations into the conflict.

Despite years of persistent activism, protests, and marches advocating for a federal holiday to honor Dr. Martin Luther King Jr., one of the most pivotal moments in this movement occurred in 1983. For over a decade following Dr. King's assassination in 1968, civil rights leaders, politicians, and grassroots organizers had been pushing for national recognition of his legacy. However, opposition remained strong, specifically from conservative lawmakers who questioned the need for a holiday dedicated to a single individual.

In response to this resistance, the King Center, led by Coretta Scott King, organized a massive March on Washington on August 27, 1983. This event, modeled after the historic 1963 March on Washington for Jobs and Freedom where Dr. King delivered his famous *I Have a Dream* speech, drew an overwhelming crowd of more than 500,000 people from across the nation. Civil rights activists, labor unions, politicians, and ordinary citizens flooded the streets of Washington, D.C., demanding that Congress pass legislation to establish a national holiday in Dr. King's honor.

The march was a powerful demonstration of unity and determination, featuring speeches from prominent figures such as Coretta Scott King, Jesse Jackson, and Democratic leaders in Congress. Their calls for justice resonated deeply, amplifying public pressure on lawmakers. Soon after, the House of Representatives passed the King Holiday Bill, and on November 2, 1983, President Ronald Reagan signed it into law, officially designating the third Monday of January as Martin Luther King Jr. Day.

The 1983 march not just served as a turning point in securing the holiday but also reaffirmed Dr. King's lasting impact on American society. The first official Martin Luther King Jr. Day was observed on January 20, 1986, marking a historic victory for the civil rights movement and a tribute to Dr. King's enduring fight for justice and equality.

As 1983 dawned, Cold War tensions hit new heights. The U.S. deployed missiles in Europe, and the Soviet Union responded aggressively. That same year, a Korean passenger jet strayed into Soviet airspace and was shot down, killing hundreds. The world teetered on the edge of conflict. In the Caribbean, the U.S. launched an invasion of Grenada, removing a Marxist government under the guise of protecting American students.

Then came 1984, a year marked by both triumph and tragedy. In India, Prime Minister Indira Gandhi was assassinated by her own Sikh bodyguards, igniting violent riots across the nation. In the U.S., Los Angeles hosted the Summer Olympics, but the Soviet Union and its allies boycotted in retaliation for the American-led boycott of the 1980 Moscow Games.

As the world moved toward the mid-1980s, one thing was clear: the era was defined by bold leadership, ideological clashes, and technological progress. The events of these years would shape the future in ways few could have predicted.

These events shaped global politics, economics, and society, influencing the Cold War, the Middle East, and technological advancements.

## The Arts and Black Music in the U.S. (1978-1984)

Between 1978 and 1984, Black music and the arts in the United States underwent a transformative period, blending old traditions with new innovations. Disco reached its peak and then rapidly declined, making way for the emergence of hip-hop, the continued evolution of R&B, and the dominance of funk and soul. Meanwhile, visual arts, literature, and theater reflected the social and political movements of the time, often centering themes of Black identity, struggle, and celebration.

## The Rise and Fall of Disco (1978-1980)

By 1978, disco had reached its golden age, driven by Black and Latino communities, as well as LGBTQ+ culture. Songs like Chic's "Le Freak" (1978) and Sister Sledge's "We Are Family" (1979) dominated the charts. Donna Summer, known as the "Queen of Disco," ruled with hits like "Last Dance" and "Hot Stuff" (1979). However, by 1980, backlash against disco grew, particularly among rock fans and mainstream America, culminating in the infamous "Disco

Demolition Night" in 1979 at Comiskey Park in Chicago, where anti-disco sentiment turned into a riot.

## The Birth of Hip-Hop (1979-1984)

Amid disco's decline, hip-hop was emerging from the Bronx as a revolutionary force. In 1979, The Sugarhill Gang released *Rapper's Delight*, the first commercially successful rap song, introducing hip-hop to mainstream audiences. Soon after, Grandmaster Flash and the Furious Five elevated the genre with *The Message* (1982), a socially conscious track about urban life struggles. Hip-hop was still underground but rapidly gaining attention, setting the stage for its explosion in the late 1980s.

## Funk, Soul, and R&B Dominate the Charts

The early 1980s saw a golden era for funk and R&B. Prince blended rock, funk, and new wave with his 1982 album *1999*, and by 1984, he had reached superstardom with *Purple Rain*, an album and film that showcased his unique musical genius. Meanwhile, Rick James brought a grittier, streetwise funk with *Super Freak* (1981), while Earth, Wind & Fire, Maze featuring Frankie Beverly, and Cameo continued to add their influences on the music scene.

R&B remained strong, with artists like Luther Vandross, whose smooth voice defined the era, and Anita Baker, who was emerging as a key figure in the quiet storm subgenre.

## Michael Jackson: The King of Pop (1982-1984)

In 1982, Michael Jackson changed the music industry forever with *Thriller*. With hits like "Billie Jean," "Beat It," and "Thriller," the album became the best-selling of all time. His performance at Motown 25 in 1983, where he debuted the moonwalk, cemented his status as the biggest pop star in the world. His success broke racial barriers on MTV, forcing the network to play more Black artists.

## Black Artists in Theater, Literature, and Visual Arts

Theater thrived with productions like "Dreamgirls" (1981), loosely based on The Supremes, which brought Black music and storytelling to Broadway. Writers like Toni Morrison gained prominence, with her novel *Song of Solomon* (1977) and *Tar Baby* (1981) exploring Black identity and heritage. Meanwhile, visual artists like Jean-Michel Basquiat used graffiti-influenced art to comment on race and class in urban America.

From the disco craze to the rise of hip-hop, and from Prince's genre-blending mastery to Michael Jackson's unparalleled success, 1978-1984 was a defining period for Black music and the arts. This era not just shaped contemporary pop culture but also laid the foundation for the future of hip-hop, R&B, and visual storytelling.

## Major Changes Taking Place in Jamaica 1978-84

Between 1978 and 1984, Jamaica underwent a period of significant transformation, marked by intense political rivalries, economic shifts, and cultural milestones that would shape the country's modern trajectory. These years saw a blend of hope, turmoil, and resilience as Jamaicans navigated a landscape of political violence, international economic pressures, and the evolution of their world-renowned music industry.

## Political Landscape: From Violence to Change

By the late 1970s, Jamaica was in the grip of severe political violence, fueled by deep divisions between the ruling People's National Party (PNP), led by Michael Manley, and the opposition Jamaica Labour Party (JLP), headed by Edward Seaga. The battle for political control extended beyond parliament and into the streets, where armed gangs affiliated with both parties engaged in deadly confrontations. The situation had grown so dire that Kingston's inner-city communities became war zones, with civilians caught in the crossfire.

Amid this crisis, 1978 saw a remarkable moment of unity when political gang leaders, encouraged by influential figures, including reggae artists, agreed to a peace treaty. This truce was symbolized in one of the most iconic events in Jamaican history—the *"One Love Peace Concert"* held at the National Stadium on April 22, 1978. The event featured a historic moment when Bob Marley, the nation's most revered cultural figure, called Michael Manley and Edward Seaga on stage, bringing them together in a symbolic handshake before a cheering crowd. Though the gesture was largely symbolic, it underscored the power of music in Jamaica's socio-political fabric.

However, peace was short-lived. As the 1980 general elections approached, violence escalated once more. The 1980 election campaign became one of the bloodiest in Jamaica's history, with more than 800 people killed in politically motivated attacks. The result was a decisive victory for the JLP's Edward Seaga, who unseated Manley in a landslide. With Seaga at the helm, Jamaica's political and economic policies took a sharp turn towards the West, in particular under the influence of then-U.S. President Ronald Reagan.

In 1983, Seaga called a *snap election*, a controversial move that was boycotted by the PNP, citing concerns over electoral reforms. This led to the JLP winning all 60 parliamentary seats, effectively creating a one-party government—an unprecedented event in Jamaica's democratic history.

## Economic Struggles and IMF Policies

Economically, Jamaica was facing major hardships. Under Manley, the country had turned to the International Monetary Fund (IMF) for financial assistance, which came with strict austerity measures that were unpopular among the working class. Upon assuming power, Seaga deepened Jamaica's ties with the United States, securing financial aid and investment support. His administration pursued a free-market economic approach, promoting privatization and foreign investment in an effort to stabilize the struggling economy. However, despite these efforts, unemployment remained high, and inflation continued to challenge ordinary Jamaicans.

One of the hardest-hit industries was bauxite and alumina, a sector that had once been a backbone of the Jamaican economy. By the early 1980s, declining global demand caused production to slow, leading to widespread layoffs and economic hardship, especially in communities dependent on mining jobs.

## Cultural Shifts: The Evolution of Jamaican Music

Despite political and economic turmoil, Jamaica's cultural identity remained strong, particularly in the realm of music. Reggae had gained global recognition by the late 1970s, thanks in large part to Bob Marley and the Wailers. However, the most heartbreaking cultural event of the period came on May 11, 1981, when Marley succumbed to cancer at the age of 36. His death marked the end of an era but also solidified his status as a global icon. His funeral, attended by thousands, was a testament to his profound impact on Jamaica and the world.

Meanwhile, dancehall music was emerging as the new dominant sound in Jamaica. Artists like Yellowman, Barrington Levy, and Eek-A-Mouse brought a more rhythm-heavy, deejay-led style of music that resonated with younger audiences. The rise of Reggae Sunsplash, an annual music festival that started in 1978, further showcased Jamaica's rich musical heritage and helped introduce new talent to the world stage.

## Natural Disasters and Resilience

Jamaica also faced natural challenges during this period. In 1980, Hurricane Allen, one of the strongest storms to threaten the island in years, swept through, causing widespread damage to homes, farms, and infrastructure. The devastation just added to the economic strain, especially in rural communities reliant on agriculture.

## The Road Ahead

By 1984, Jamaica had transformed in many ways. The political landscape had shifted dramatically under Seaga's leadership, the economy was still grappling with the challenges of global market fluctuations, and dancehall had begun to take its place as the country's leading musical genre. However, through it all, the resilience of the Jamaican people remained evident. They continued to shape their own destiny, finding strength in their culture, music, and unwavering national pride.

## A Foundation for the Future

My decision to major in water resources engineering at Howard, set the foundation for my future career. The knowledge and skills I gained at Howard, coupled with my experience working on federal flood programs, positioned me for a rewarding career in environmental and infrastructure engineering.

As I moved forward, I carried with me not just technical expertise but also a deep appreciation for the role of engineers in shaping the built environment and protecting natural resources. The journey that began with my first engineering classes at Howard had now evolved into a clear professional calling—one that I would continue to pursue with passion and purpose in the years to come.

This new phase of my professional journey has brought immense fulfillment, seamlessly blending my analytical expertise, meticulous attention to detail, and deep-seated commitment to helping others realize their aspirations. As I reflect on the path I have traveled—from the vibrant landscapes of Jamaica to the halls of Howard University and the impactful engineering projects across the United States—I recognize that the values and lessons ingrained in me during my formative years continue to serve as my guiding principles.

The resilience, curiosity, and relentless pursuit of excellence that shaped my early years remain the foundation of my personal and professional life. Each experience, challenge, and triumph has been a stepping stone, contributing to a career and a life enriched by purpose, growth, and meaningful contributions. I am profoundly grateful for the opportunities that have shaped me, and I embrace each new chapter with the same dedication and passion that have driven me from the very beginning.

# Chapter 8

# The Start of a Professional Career

## My New Home & Friendships

U pon completing my studies, I decided to make the Washington, D.C. area my home, drawn by its rich history, cultural diversity, and significant political importance. It was an ideal place to begin and build my career in civil engineering. In 1981, I moved out of my Aunt Phil's home and settled into an apartment in Wheaton, MD, a suburban area close to Washington, D.C. This move marked a new chapter of independence and professional growth.

In Wheaton, I had the good fortune of living in the same apartment complex as Leon, a close friend and fellow graduate of both CAST and Howard University. Like me, Leon was embarking on his professional career, and our shared experiences from our university days created a strong bond as we navigated the challenges of early professional life. Our friendship provided invaluable support and camaraderie during this formative period.

While in Wheaton, Leon started a family, embracing the responsibilities of both career and home life. In 1985, he relocated to Atlanta, marking a new chapter in his journey. Despite the distance, we remained closely connected, frequently speaking by phone and serving as sounding boards for each other as we tackled work-related challenges.

Tragically, Leon passed away in 1988—a loss that was both sudden and devastating for me and his family. His untimely departure left a void that could never really be filled. In his memory, I continue to care for the Monstera (Swiss Cheese) houseplant he gifted me before his move to Atlanta. It remains a living tribute to our friendship, a reminder of the bond we shared, and a symbol of the enduring impact he had on my life.

Adjacent to our complex lived Bert Davy, originally from St. Vincent, who fast became a part of our social circle. Bert and I bonded over our Caribbean roots and shared experiences in adapting to life in the D.C. area. One of our favorite pastimes was playing tennis. Our matches were a thrilling mix of competition and camaraderie, providing both an intense workout and a chance to unwind with good company. He had a ferocious forehand, always looking for an opportunity to unleash it and target my weaker backhand. But I refused to go down easily—sprinting, diving, and stretching for every ball, determined to keep the rally alive. My relentless hustle on the court soon earned me the nickname *"Speedy,"* a tribute to my sheer determination to chase down every shot, even when the odds were stacked against me!

These social interactions added a sense of community to my life in Wheaton, making it feel more like home despite being far from Jamaica.

I met Bert in 1985 while we were both working for the same firm in Fairfax, Virginia. He was a skilled Structural Engineer and a warm, sociable individual who enjoyed bringing people together. With a family of his own, Bert loved to entertain, often hosting lively house parties and picnics that became the highlight of our social gatherings.

I still fondly remember the vibrant atmosphere at his events—the irresistible aroma of spicy Caribbean dishes filling the air, the rhythmic pulse of Soca music blasting from his sound system, and the energy of friends and family dancing the night away. Those were truly joyful times that I will always cherish.

Eventually, Bert moved from Wheaton to Bowie, Maryland, where he transitioned into academia, becoming a lecturer at Morgan State University.

Sadly, his journey was cut short by his untimely passing around 2012. His warmth, generosity, and love for life left a lasting impression on everyone who knew him, and his memory continues to live on in the hearts of those he touched.

In 1983, I moved to Gaithersburg, Maryland, after purchasing my first single-family home—an achievement that filled me with pride and marked a major milestone in my personal and professional life. Owning a home was more than just having a place to live; it was a transformative experience that taught me the responsibilities of home ownership, from maintaining a house to making thoughtful improvements. It was also a testament to the hard work and dedication I had put into my career up to that point.

With a background in engineering and hands-on training from my days at Dinthill, I was well-equipped to handle various aspects of home maintenance and do-it-yourself projects. I found satisfaction in putting my skills to practical use—whether it was small repairs, landscaping, or making enhancements to the house. Having the ability to take care of my own home instilled in me a sense of self-reliance and deepened my appreciation for craftsmanship and structural integrity.

The neighborhood in Gaithersburg was part of a newly built subdivision, consisting of many recently constructed homes. While the modern infrastructure and fresh start were appealing, the area also presented unique challenges. The land was relatively undeveloped, requiring new homeowners to establish lawns, plant trees, and shrubs. I fast learned that maintaining a lush green lawn required patience, effort, and an understanding of soil conditions and climate. It was a slow but rewarding process to see the transformation of the outdoor spaces over time.

Gaithersburg was a highly sought-after location in Montgomery County at the time, attracting a diverse mix of professionals and families. Living there provided a sense of community and stability, and I took pride in being part of a neighborhood where homeowners were also building their lives and creating lasting memories. The friendships and connections I formed during this period enriched my experience and made my time there even more meaningful.

Although I spent just four years in Gaithersburg, the lessons I learned from home ownership—both practical and personal—have stayed with me for a lifetime. It reinforced the value of investment, the importance of maintaining a home, and the satisfaction of shaping a living space to reflect my own efforts and personality.

## Launching my Professional Career

Reflecting on my college years at Howard University, where I pursued both my bachelor's and master's degrees in Civil Engineering, I recalled how those years laid the foundation for my professional career. While still a student, I seized opportunities to gain practical experience, whether through part-time roles at HUD, working in the computer lab, or working with engineering consulting firms. These experiences were invaluable, providing me with hands-on skills and the confidence necessary to transition into full-time professional work after graduation.

In 1982, I secured a pivotal role as an Engineering Planner with the Washington Suburban Sanitary Commission (WSSC), a prominent water and sewerage municipality in Laurel, Maryland. This position was demanding yet rewarding, involving responsibilities such as overseeing field staff, designing and implementing new systems, and ensuring the maintenance of existing infrastructure. The role also required occasional 24-hour emergency response duty, underscoring the critical nature of the work in public utilities.

Managing field crews posed its challenges, but it also brought me a deep sense of satisfaction in knowing that my efforts contributed to improving operational efficiency and the quality of services delivered to the community. This role, along with my prior experiences, equipped me with the breadth of knowledge and practical insights needed to pursue professional licensure.

One assignment that stood out for me was when my supervisor tasked me with designing a sturdier steel plate cover capable of withstanding heavy truck traffic. This challenge allowed me to draw upon my structural engineering training from CAST, and I was able to develop an effective and acceptable design. Successfully completing that project reinforced my confidence in applying my technical skills to real-world engineering problems.

However, the demands of the job, in particular the 24-hour emergency duties, were becoming increasingly taxing—especially during the harsh winter months. One incident remains vivid in my memory: I was called out for an emergency response at 3:00 AM and had to travel nearly 50 miles from Gaithersburg to Fort Washington. Driving through the freezing cold in the dead of night, I found myself questioning whether this was the career path I frankly wanted to continue. That moment of realization was a turning point, signaling that it was time for me to explore new opportunities better suited to my long-term goals and aspirations.

I then requested a transfer to another division within the company, where my primary responsibilities shifted to planning capital infrastructure improvements and analyzing the capacities of existing systems. This new role provided a greater sense of fulfillment, as I felt I was making a more meaningful impact on the community. The projects often involved direct engagement with the public, affected homeowners, and various stakeholders, adding a valuable human element to the technical work.

My supervisor, Ted Graham, was an exceptional mentor and a highly skilled professional. He had a keen understanding of the public and political considerations that influenced our projects, and he took the time to meticulously explain their significance. His guidance was invaluable, helping me navigate the complexities of infrastructure planning beyond just the engineering aspects.

Over time, Ted and I developed a deep sense of trust and mutual respect. His mentorship not just enhanced my professional growth but also solidified a working relationship that extended beyond my tenure at the company. Even after I left in 1985, our paths crossed again in different capacities, reaffirming the strong professional bond we had built during those formative years.

During my time at WSSC, I developed a close friendship and professional relationship with Granville, a fellow Jamaican and colleague who was also a good friend of Marts. Our connection went back to around 1979 when Marts introduced us during one of his visits to the U.S. By the time we worked together, we already had a solid foundation. From the outset, we bonded effortlessly, forming a strong support network both at work and socially.

Having Granville as a colleague was incredibly reassuring, especially given his extensive knowledge of water systems. As a civil engineer trained at the UWI campus in Trinidad and later at the University of Maryland, he brought a wealth of expertise and insight, which made collaborating with him both rewarding and educational. We often exchanged perspectives on the job, tackling challenges together and deepening our understanding of the field.

Beyond work, our friendship flourished through shared experiences, discussions, and mutual encouragement. His guidance and camaraderie were invaluable, and our bond has remained strong long after our time at WSSC. I continue to appreciate and value his support and wisdom, just as I did back then.

In early 1984, I achieved a significant milestone by obtaining my Professional Engineering (PE) license in the state of Maryland, followed shortly by becoming licensed in the Commonwealth of Virginia. These licenses not just validated my expertise and competence in civil engineering but also opened doors to greater opportunities and responsibilities in my field. To this day, my licenses remain active, a testament to the ongoing commitment to maintaining professional standards and contributing effectively to the engineering community.

## My Job with Dewberry

In 1985, I had the opportunity to join Dewberry (formerly known as Dewberry and Davis), a prestigious and well-established engineering firm based in Fairfax, Virginia. By this point, I was a licensed Professional Engineer (PE), and having this credential made it significantly easier for me to step into a role with greater responsibility and higher compensation compared to my previous position at WSSC. At Dewberry, I felt that my diverse background and range of experiences were valued, and I was brought on as a Senior Design Engineer within their Land Development Group. This position offered a unique opportunity to apply a wide range of engineering disciplines, especially those critical for designing both residential and commercial developments.

In this role, I took on a variety of responsibilities, each of which played a key part in the successful delivery of large-scale projects. I was tasked with preparing site and subdivision plans, which required a deep understanding of lot layouts, roadway designs, and the planning of stormwater drainage systems. I applied Best Management Practices (BMP) to manage drainage and sediment/erosion control, ensuring that the projects adhered to environmental standards. My work in this area was essential for creating sustainable development projects that balanced land use with environmental responsibility.

Another significant area of focus was highway drainage design. I led the design of major drainage systems for highway projects, ensuring that flood flows and runoff were properly managed in compliance with federal and local regulations. This work required both technical expertise and the ability to consider long-term environmental and infrastructural needs.

In addition to drainage and infrastructure work, I was also heavily involved in the design of water supply and sanitary sewer systems for various developments. This aspect of my job required a solid understanding of utility networks and their integration into the overall development plans. Another major responsibility I took on was developing floodplain studies that supported flood risk assessments, a crucial element for developers seeking to comply with FEMA regulations and protect the safety of future residents.

On the financial side, I was responsible for preparing project cost estimates, developing proposals, and setting budgets for the projects I worked on. This aspect of my role allowed me to apply my engineering expertise to ensure that projects remained within financial constraints while still meeting design goals and regulatory standards. Additionally, I contributed to the business side of the firm by conducting proposals and budget planning to ensure that our projects were both financially viable and aligned with Dewberry's objectives.

Another rewarding aspect of my position was the opportunity to lead training courses for land development engineers, sharing my knowledge and providing mentorship. This not just helped to develop the technical skills of junior engineers but also contributed to fostering a collaborative and supportive team environment. Alongside my technical duties, I also served as chairman of the Personal Computer Software Evaluation Committee, overseeing the selection of new software tools to improve the firm's engineering design and workflow processes. This role allowed me to explore emerging technologies and ensure that Dewberry stayed on the cutting edge of engineering software.

Furthermore, I was actively involved in the review of FEMA's Flood Insurance Studies, contributing to national discussions on floodplain management and flood insurance policies. This broadened my view of how local engineering projects align with national disaster preparedness and risk management frameworks. I was able to apply my experience from the part-time work during my time at Howard University.

During my time at Dewberry, I developed a deep interest in designing stormwater management facilities. At the same time, I was eager to explore the capabilities of the rapidly emerging IBM Personal Computer (PC) to enhance the efficiency of the design process. Using my creativity and technical knowledge, I developed a PC program to assist in stormwater management facility design. This program would later evolve into a private software package, which I named the "Integrated Stormwater Management (ISWM) Program."

I took the initiative to market ISWM outside of Dewberry, achieving some success with clients both in Virginia and in the Caribbean. As a gesture of goodwill, I donated a free copy of the program to the Fairfax County Government's land development review agency, where it became a valuable tool for checking designs submitted for permits. However, as PC technology rapidly advanced and operating systems shifted from DOS to Microsoft Windows, the program quickly became outdated. In 1990, while attempting to upgrade ISWM to a Windows-compatible version, I accepted a position with the Department of Public Works at Fairfax County Government, and the momentum to continue the program's development faded.

Overall, my time at Dewberry was a pivotal period in my career, as it expanded my technical knowledge, honed my project management skills, and reinforced my leadership abilities within civil and environmental engineering. The exposure to a wide range of projects, along with the responsibility of managing both design and financial aspects, deepened my understanding of large-scale land development. Additionally, working alongside such a talented team and being entrusted with key roles in diverse projects was an invaluable experience that has shaped my professional journey.

## Becoming A US Citizen

I was ecstatic when I was sworn in as a citizen of the United States of America in April 1987. It was definitely one of the biggest highlights of my life. I vividly remember attending the swearing-in ceremony at a courthouse in Baltimore, Maryland. My family was overjoyed, and we celebrated this milestone with close friends and relatives. Being a citizen meant I could sponsor my mother and stepfather, who had longed to retire in America and be close to me. The sponsorship was successful, and they migrated as permanent residents in 1988. From there, the rest is history. Later on, my mother sponsored her remaining daughters and their children to live in the US. I was also proud to participate as a first-time voter in the 1988 Presidential Elections.

## Home in Reston, Virginia

During 1987, I made a significant life change by moving to Fairfax, Virginia, primarily to reduce the grueling commute to my job at Dewberry, in Fairfax. Prior to the move, I had been living in Gaithersburg, Maryland, which is located about 35 miles away. My daily commute involved traveling along the I-495 Beltway and I-270, two of the most congested highways in the Washington, D.C., metropolitan area. Rush hour traffic was especially brutal, often turning what should have been a 45-minute drive into a journey of an hour and a half or more. The Washington Metro area has long been recognized for its high levels of traffic congestion, ranking among the worst in the country. The unpredictability of traffic, coupled with the stress of navigating crowded roadways, made the commute increasingly unbearable. After months of frustration, I decided that moving closer to work was the best solution to improve my quality of life.

Fairfax provided a convenient location that drastically reduced my commute, allowing me to spend less time on the road and more time on activities I valued. However, as time passed and I became more familiar with the surrounding areas, I developed a deep appreciation for Reston, Virginia, a planned community located just a short drive from Dewberry. Reston was established in the 1960s with a vision of balancing urban development with natural beauty, an approach that resonated with me. Its design incorporated clusters of residential neighborhoods surrounded by preserved green spaces, extensive bike and pedestrian trails, and a strong sense of community. The idea of living in an environment that prioritized nature while still offering modern conveniences appealed to me greatly.

In 1989, I was fortunate enough to purchase a home in Reston. The property was situated in one of the many residential clusters that make the community unique. Each cluster in Reston has its own distinct architectural style, contributing to the neighborhood's charm and variety. One of the most striking features of Reston is its dedication to maintaining green spaces. Trees, parks, and wooded areas are integrated seamlessly into the design, ensuring that even in developed residential areas, nature remains a dominant presence. The Washington Old Dominion (W&OD) Trail, a famous multi-use trail that was built from an abandoned railroad line, runs through Reston, offering residents a scenic route for biking, jogging, and walking. The trail extends from Washington, D.C., west past the Town of Leesburg, providing a direct connection to nature and outdoor recreation. The presence of this trail added to my appreciation for Reston, as it encouraged an active lifestyle while preserving the town's historical roots.

The Reston Association, the governing body responsible for managing many aspects of the community, plays a crucial role in maintaining amenities such as swimming pools, tennis courts, and community centers. These facilities contribute to the high quality of life enjoyed by Reston residents, fostering a sense of belonging and shared responsibility for the environment. Additionally, each individual residential cluster has its own Homeowners Association (HOA), which enforces architectural standards and maintenance requirements. This system ensures that the community remains visually appealing and environmentally sustainable. I quickly discovered that my neighbors were deeply invested in preserving the beauty and integrity of the area. Residents actively participated in environmental initiatives, voiced concerns about developments that might negatively impact the landscape and embraced sustainable living practices. This collective environmental consciousness reinforced my decision to move to Reston, as it aligned with my own appreciation for well-planned, ecologically responsible communities.

A key highlight of the Reston development is the Town Center, offering a delightful destination for a variety of activities. The first retail store in Reston Town Center opened in 1990 when the initial phase of the development was completed. This phase introduced a mix of retail shops, cinema, restaurants, office buildings, and the Pavilion, which became a central gathering space. Over the years, Reston Town Center has expanded into a major commercial and residential hub in Northern Virginia.

After settling into my new home, I encountered a common but troublesome issue—drainage problems in the front yard. The house's downspouts were not properly directing rainwater away from the foundation, leading to unwanted ponding and erosion near the concrete walkway and stoop at the front entrance. Over time, the accumulation of water in this area had begun to compromise the structural integrity of the walkway, creating a persistent maintenance concern. As an engineer, I recognized that this was not a problem that could be easily resolved by simply regrading the landscape. The surrounding area's natural topography did not provide a sufficient slope to allow water to drain away effectively.

Determined to find a lasting solution, I devised an alternative drainage system that would address the issue at its source. My plan involved digging a deep trench to create a subsurface drainage system. The trench would be filled with gravel and house a perforated plastic pipe connected to the downspouts. This design would allow rainwater to be collected and dispersed into the ground, preventing further erosion and ponding near the foundation.

Executing the plan required significant physical labor. Digging the trench by hand proved to be a demanding task, but I was committed to seeing the project through. I carefully excavated the area, ensuring that the trench was deep enough to accommodate the gravel and piping system. Once the trench was in place, I laid down a layer of gravel to facilitate drainage, then positioned the perforated pipe along the bottom. The pipe was securely connected to the downspouts, directing water into the trench. Additional gravel was placed around the pipe to promote water dispersion, and a final layer of soil and sod was added to restore the landscape's appearance.

The project was both a test of endurance and a demonstration of my engineering expertise in a real-world application. Upon completion, I was pleased to see that the system functioned exactly as intended. Rainwater from the downspouts was efficiently redirected into the gravel trench, where it gradually percolated into the ground rather than accumulating near the foundation. The solution proved to be highly effective, holding up for the entire 14 years that I owned the property.

Beyond solving a practical issue, this experience reinforced my appreciation for problem-solving and hands-on projects. It reminded me of the satisfaction that comes with applying engineering principles to everyday challenges. While the project demanded considerable effort, the sense of accomplishment I felt upon completing it was well worth the investment. Moreover, the success of this solution highlighted the importance of proactive home maintenance. Many homeowners face similar drainage issues but may not recognize the long-term implications of unresolved water accumulation near their homes. Left unaddressed, such issues can lead to foundation damage, mold growth, and costly repairs. My experience in Reston emphasized the value of understanding and addressing these challenges early on, preventing larger problems down the line.

I was always impressed by the abundance of amenities available in Reston. I enjoyed playing tennis on the numerous courts, swimming in the well-maintained pools, and cycling along the scenic trails—all of which made living there really special. I called Reston home until 1995 when I moved to the neighboring town of Herndon, though I retained ownership of the property until 2003.

My time living in Reston remains one of the most memorable chapters of my life. The community's commitment to environmental stewardship, thoughtful urban planning, and resident engagement created an atmosphere that was both welcoming and inspiring. While I eventually moved on from Reston, the lessons I learned and the experiences I gained during my years there continue to shape my perspective on sustainable living, problem-solving, and the importance of investing in well-planned communities. Looking back, I can confidently say that choosing to move to Reston was one of the best decisions I ever made, not just for the convenience it provided but also for the sense of connection I felt with both the environment and the people who shared it with me.

## One of My Biggest Moments of Joy

One of the happiest and proudest moments during my time in Reston occurred in May 1992 with the birth of my son, Wynton. Judith and I, who had married in 1990, eagerly anticipating Wynton's arrival. From a young age, he showed a keen interest in soccer after watching the World Cup '98 and idolizing Ronaldo, the legendary Brazilian striker. This sparked his passion for the sport, which he pursued competitively from the age of six through high school graduation. Along his soccer journey, Wynton honed his tactical skills and displayed remarkable tenacity, standing out among his peers and coaches.

At just ten years old, Wynton joined a respected team that toured Italy for a prestigious soccer tournament, facing off against aggressive Italian players with equal determination and skill. A few years later, he had the opportunity to attend a summer soccer camp hosted by Manchester United, further enriching his experience in the sport. Wynton excelled on several top travel teams in Northern Virginia, consistently proving himself as one of the standout players. During his senior year of high school, he was named captain of the varsity team for his exceptional leadership and recognized as one of the team's top goal scorers.

Wynton's passion for soccer was boundless—he didn't just play the game; he lived and breathed it. He immersed himself in everything related to the sport, following major soccer leagues across the globe with a near-encyclopedic knowledge. He could rattle off team statistics, discuss tactical formations, and analyze match performances with remarkable insight. Tracking the progress of his favorite teams and players became second nature to him, and he would often spend hours studying the bios and career trajectories of top athletes, drawing inspiration from their dedication and skill.

But Wynton's interests weren't confined to the soccer field. His love for music and art ran just as deep. For several years, he pursued music lessons, honing his craft with patience and discipline. What started as a creative outlet eventually became a defining aspect of his life, shaping his artistic journey. The melodies and rhythms he studied laid the foundation for his own music career, as he began writing, composing, and recording original songs. Music became a powerful form of expression for him, blending seamlessly with his other passions. Wynton has created several highly admired pieces of fine art, which are displayed in my home and the homes of several family members.

In addition to his pursuits in sports, art and music, Wynton strived for academic success. He attended universities in both Virginia and France, where he thrived in diverse learning environments. While studying in France, he fully embraced the culture and language, rapidly achieving fluency in French. His time abroad not just broadened his worldview but also enriched his ability to connect with people from different backgrounds.

During his years in France, Wynton fully embraced the local culture and built meaningful connections with the people around him. He actively engaged with the community on multiple levels, immersing himself in the daily rhythms of life. One of his greatest joys was joining local soccer leagues, where he played recreational matches with men from various countries who, like him, had made France their temporary or permanent home. These games were more than just sport—they were a way to bond, break language barriers, and create friendships that extended beyond the field.

A constant companion throughout his time in France was his beloved pet dog, Philly. Having made the journey from the United States with him, Philly was not just a pet but a source of unwavering companionship and comfort. The bond they shared was undeniable, and Philly fast became an integral part of Wynton's life abroad. Whether accompanying him on long walks through the charming streets, lounging beside him during quiet evenings, or simply providing a sense of home in a foreign land, Philly was his pride and joy.

However, when Wynton made the difficult decision to return to the United States in 2015, circumstances did not allow Philly to make the journey back with him. It was a heartbreaking moment, but he found solace in knowing that Philly was left in the care of a loving and compassionate family. This family, who had also been an important part of his life in France, welcomed Philly with open arms, ensuring that his faithful companion would continue to be cherished and well cared for. Though parting was bittersweet, Wynton took comfort in knowing that Philly would remain in a home filled with love and warmth, just as he had always known.

His life as a child and young man brought immense joy to all who knew him, leaving a lasting impact through his talents and character.

# Chapter 9

## My Career with Fairfax County

### Commencement of Public Service

I n 1990, I was offered an opportunity to work with the Fairfax County Government. Fairfax County, Virginia, is a suburban county in Northern Virginia, just west of Washington, D.C. Covering approximately 406 square miles, it is the most populous jurisdiction in the state, with over 1.1 million residents. Known for its high median household income, it is one of the most affluent counties in the United States. The county is a major economic hub, home to numerous federal agencies, technology companies, and corporate headquarters. It boasts excellent schools, extensive parks, and cultural attractions, including George Washington's Mount Vernon and Tysons, one of the largest business and shopping districts in the region.

I worked in Department of Public Works (DPW) as an Assistant Branch Chief in the Planning and Design Division. This was a terrific opportunity to work with a well-regarded governmental organization. The teams within DPW were all committed to making a positive impact in the community and had to be constantly aware of the political climate and the need to satisfy the Board of Supervisors (BOS), the county's governing body. I was recruited for this position by John Koenig, who was the Division's Director at the time. Both John and my immediate supervisor, Harbans Matharoo, were pleased to have me on board and became excellent mentors. They respected and valued my expertise, fostering an environment where I could thrive and succeed. John's consistent inspiration and encouragement to work out in the gym were greatly valued. Even following his retirement in 1999, we maintained a good friendship.

In my role, I managed a team of five engineers and project managers, overseeing the design and construction of capital improvement projects that ranged in complexity and budgetary value. Additionally, I represented the department on the Engineers and Surveyors Institute (ESI) subcommittees for CADD Standards and Metric Conversion Standards and conducted training classes at ESI. The ESI was a collaborative group consisting of industry engineers, consultants, and county staff, dedicated to fostering the exchange of expertise and ideas. Its primary goal was to enhance and streamline the development plan approval process across the county, ensuring greater efficiency and improved outcomes.

After my first five years with DPW, I was promoted to Branch Chief within the Planning and Design Division. In this leadership role, I was responsible for overseeing a team of ten professionals, ensuring efficient operations and the successful execution of various engineering initiatives. My primary responsibilities included managing the resolution and documentation of drainage complaints from residents, coordinating project implementation budgets and schedules, and overseeing the planning and design of critical infrastructure projects. These projects encompassed stormwater management systems, sanitary sewer expansion, and improvements for failing septic systems—key elements in maintaining and enhancing public health and environmental sustainability.

A significant aspect of my role was spearheading the implementation of large-scale stormwater management retrofit projects, which aimed to modernize aging infrastructure and improve resilience against flooding. Additionally, I managed the Drafting Section, which played a pivotal role in preparing engineering plans and plats for Capital Improvement Projects (CIP). Our team utilized Computer-Aided Design and Drafting (CADD) technology to enhance precision and efficiency in project planning and execution.

As the digital age rapidly gained momentum in the early 1990s, the engineering industry underwent a transformative shift, steadily adopting cutting-edge digital applications that would soon become standard practice. I found myself at the forefront of this technological revolution, playing a key role in integrating digital solutions into DPW's operations. One of my most impactful contributions was leading the development of a county-wide storm sewer inventory, compiling digital maps and associated databases to streamline infrastructure management. This initiative not just improved record-keeping and accessibility but also supported collaboration with other agencies in digital design plan preparation.

Recognizing the increasing importance of computer-aided design, I took the lead in planning and implementing the first technical applications computer LAN system in the county. This system was specifically designed to support AutoCAD on the Microsoft Windows platform, marking a pivotal advancement in workplace automation. At that time, personal computers (PCs) were just beginning to be integrated into professional environments, and our department established a dedicated workstation area to provide staff with access to these emerging digital tools.

Beyond this, my efforts extended to the implementation of CADD design applications and the development of the department's first computer automation plan. These initiatives laid the groundwork for the eventual adoption of Geographic Information Systems (GIS), a technology that has since become indispensable for engineers and planners. By championing the integration of GIS, I helped establish a foundation for data-driven decision-making, significantly enhancing the department's ability to manage infrastructure projects efficiently and effectively.

## Moving to Herndon, Virginia

In 1995, I made the significant move from Reston to the Town of Herndon, a small yet historically rich town in Fairfax County. Herndon, covering just 4.2 square miles, had a population of nearly 20,000 at the time. Located merely a few miles from Washington Dulles International Airport, it was well-positioned along major transportation routes, including the Dulles Toll Road (VA-267) and the Fairfax County Parkway (Route 286). The town's convenient location provided easy access to Washington, D.C., and other major employment hubs in Northern Virginia.

Herndon has a deep-rooted history dating back to the mid-19th century when it was established as a stop on the Alexandria, Loudoun & Hampshire Railroad, later becoming part of the Washington & Old Dominion (W&OD) Railroad. The town was named after William Lewis Herndon, a naval explorer known for his heroism in the sinking of the SS Central America in 1857. With its origins as a rural farming community, Herndon grew rapidly in the late 20th century due to the expansion of the Dulles Corridor and Northern Virginia's booming technology sector. By the 1990s, the town had evolved into a thriving suburban community with a mix of historic charm and modern conveniences.

I was fortunate to purchase a newly built house in a subdivision within the Four Seasons homeowners' association. Moving into a brand-new home came with both excitement and challenges, particularly caring for the new landscape and lawn. My do-it-yourself skills were put to the test as I took on various home improvement projects. The house was equipped with all the modern amenities of the time, making it a comfortable and inviting space.

While my commute to work was now slightly longer—about 13 miles, mostly along Route 286—it was still manageable, especially compared to the congested roads I had dealt with in previous years. One unique aspect of my property was its rear view of a large stormwater management facility. Designed to temporarily hold rainwater and allow pollutants to settle before the runoff continued downstream, this facility would fill up after heavy rains and then drain completely within a couple of days. As someone with a background in civil and environmental engineering, I found it fascinating to observe the effectiveness of this system in action.

Though Herndon lacked the extensive green spaces and preserved woodlands of Reston, it had its own distinct character and charm. The community featured well-maintained public parks, recreational areas, and amenities such as swimming pools and tennis courts. Additionally, I had easy access to the W&OD Trail, a 45-mile-long paved path built on the former railway line. I often took advantage of this scenic trail, occasionally riding my bike between Herndon and Leesburg, enjoying the mix of suburban and rural landscapes along the way.

Over the years, my house has undergone several upgrades, reflecting both changes in my lifestyle and advancements in home design and technology. The most significant transformation took place in 2005 when I embarked on an ambitious project to convert my unfinished basement into a fully livable space. With a clear vision in mind, I meticulously planned the layout using AutoCAD, incorporating an entertainment room, home gym, den, bathroom, and wet bar.

This project became even more meaningful with the help of my brother, Everton. Together, we took on the challenge of framing out the space, installing wall coverings, ceilings, plumbing fixtures, and painting. Everton's contributions extended far beyond his building skills—he also provided essential resources, including his pickup truck for transporting materials and a variety of power tools that made the work more efficient. One of the most memorable moments was when we needed to install drainpipes for the shower and bar sink. Everton brought a jackhammer, skillfully breaking through the concrete floor so we could lay the pipes before resetting the section. His ingenuity and hands-on expertise were invaluable, and he even taught me a technique that significantly strengthened our framing—using screws instead of nails for a more secure connection.

Today, my basement stands as a testament to our hard work, determination, and the deep bond we share as brothers. Every element of that space reflects the sweat and dedication we poured into making it a reality.

Beyond the upgrades, my house remains my cherished home—a place of comfort, stability, and connection. Herndon has grown significantly since I first moved here, yet it has managed to retain its small-town charm, historic character, and welcoming atmosphere. These enduring qualities have made it a truly special place to call home.

## A Jamaican Gone Skiing?

One of my most exhilarating and unforgettable experiences during my time at Fairfax came in the early '90s when some of my coworkers persuaded me to join them on their annual skiing adventure. At first, I laughed and said, *"Do you guys realize there was no snow in Jamaica where I grew up?"* The very idea of skiing seemed almost comical to me, given my tropical upbringing. But deep down, I was intrigued. It was an entirely new challenge—something I had never even considered attempting. And if there was one thing I prided myself on, it was my willingness to take on new challenges.

Determined to be as prepared as possible, I started doing my homework. I read up on skiing basics, trying to wrap my mind around concepts like *carving, snowplowing,* and *balancing on two thin pieces of fiberglass while hurtling down a mountain.* My next step was a visit to a sports shop specializing in ski gear. Walking in, I was immediately captivated by the sleek, high-tech outfits, the variety of goggles, gloves, and other accessories designed to keep skiers warm and protected. The whole experience felt like stepping into a different world.

The more I explored, the more excited I became. I could feel my anticipation building with every new piece of equipment I examined. When I finally walked out of the store, I had invested a significant amount in purchasing the necessary attire—ski pants, a warm yet flexible jacket, insulated gloves, goggles, and everything else I would need for my first adventure on the slopes. At that moment, there was no turning back. I was *all in.*

## The Big Day Arrives

The weekend of our trip to The Wisp ski resort in Maryland arrived, bringing with it a mix of excitement and nerves. As we drove towards the resort, I stared out at the vast, snow-covered landscape, a far cry from the sunny beaches I was used to. My heart pounded with anticipation.

That first morning, my introduction to skiing began with a lesson on the essential equipment. We rented skis, boots, and poles, and I quickly learned that just putting the boots on was a workout in itself. The rigid, heavy design made walking feel like I was wearing concrete blocks on my feet. But the real challenge was yet to come.

## Learning the Ropes

My first real test was getting onto the ski lift. Watching others do it effortlessly, I assumed it would be easy—until it was my turn. I awkwardly shuffled forward, nearly lost my balance, and barely managed to plop myself onto the moving seat in time. As the lift carried us higher and higher up the mountain, I looked down at the slopes below—tiny figures gliding smoothly across the snow, making it look effortless. *Would I be able to do that?*

As we reached the beginner's area and exited the lift (somewhat ungracefully), we spent the next hour learning the basics—how to keep our balance, how to slow down, and most importantly, how to fall *properly*. Because, as I fast discovered, falling was inevitable. I spent a good portion of that first hour picking myself up from the snow, brushing off the cold, and trying again.

## The Next Big Challenge

After a while, I started to get the hang of it. My confidence grew, and I decided I was ready for the next step—the intermediate slope. My coworkers encouraged me, assuring me I could handle it. So, fueled by a mix of excitement and overconfidence, I took the lift to the top of the intermediate run.

As soon as I stepped off and looked down the slope, my heart nearly stopped. This was *way* steeper than I had imagined. And there was no turning back—the only way down was to *ski*.

With my coworkers cheering me on, I took a deep breath, pushed off, and started my descent. The first few moments felt exhilarating—I was actually skiing! But that confidence quickly faded as I picked up speed. My brain screamed, *Slow down! Turn! Do something!* but my legs had other ideas. I wobbled, lost control, and before I knew it—*boom!* I was face-down in the snow.

Laughing, my friends helped me up, and I continued down the slope in stages, punctuated by a series of falls. Each time, I got up, adjusted my stance, and tried again. By the time I finally reached the bottom, I was exhausted, sore, and covered in snow—but I had *done it.*

## The Celebration

The foot of the slope was the lodge that became a party scene—music playing, people celebrating, high-fives all around. I was met with cheers and congratulations from my friends, who knew exactly what I had just gone through. The energy was contagious, and despite the struggle, I felt an overwhelming sense of triumph. I had conquered my fear, embraced the challenge, and discovered a whole new world of adventure.

That first ski trip sparked a love for the sport, and I went on to hit the slopes at least four more times before finally deciding to retire my skis. It was a bucket list item checked off with pride, an experience I would never forget.

Now, whenever someone mentions how they were looking forward to seeing snow in our neighborhood, I always say with a smile, *"Snow is only beautiful when you're skiing in it—not when you have to shovel it!"*

## The Y2K Hysteria

I have a vivid and amusing memory of the final days of 1999—when the world seemed gripped by Y2K hysteria. Everywhere you turned, there were dire predictions of chaos: power grids failing, banks losing records, airplanes falling from the sky, and, worst of all, vending machines refusing to dispense snacks. The idea that computers, which had dutifully run our lives, would suddenly lose all sense of time and logic the moment the clock struck midnight was both fascinating and hilarious to me.

The county took the whole thing seriously, though. As part of our emergency preparedness efforts, essential staff—including myself—were issued beepers, just in case civilization as we knew it crumbled at the stroke of midnight. I accepted mine with a smirk, clipped it to my belt, and carried on as usual. While some people stockpiled canned goods and bottled water like an impending apocalypse was upon us, I had my own priorities—I was heading to a New Year's Eve party.

There I was, surrounded by laughter, music, and champagne, with my trusty beeper securely fastened to my waist—ready to leap into action should the world go dark. But deep down, I didn't buy into the alarmist frenzy. As the countdown began, I braced for either complete societal collapse or just another round of drinks.

And then—midnight struck. We all held our breath for a moment. The lights stayed on. The music kept playing. The world kept spinning. And most importantly—my beeper remained silent. No emergencies, no frantic calls to action, just another New Year's Eve filled with celebration.

Looking back, the Y2K scare was one of the most overhyped non-events in modern history, but at least it gave us something to laugh about. I had a fantastic night, partied worry-free, and rang in the new millennium with friends—beeper and all.

## A Day That Changed Everything: September 11, 2001

It was the morning of September 11, 2001—a day that began like any other but would soon be seared into our memories forever. Our stormwater business agencies team had gathered for one of our routine meetings in a large conference room, discussing plans, policies, and the usual administrative matters. The atmosphere was calm, focused—just another day at work, or so we thought.

Suddenly, the door burst open.

Our administrative assistant, normally composed and professional, was frantic. Her voice trembled as she uttered words that sent chills through the room:

*"Turn on the TV now—the world is coming to an end."*

A stunned silence fell over us. Those words, spoken with such urgency and fear, felt surreal. We quickly scrambled to switch on the television, and there it was—a scene straight out of a nightmare. One of the Twin Towers of the World Trade Center was engulfed in flames, black smoke billowing into the clear blue sky. The initial reports were chaotic, uncertain. My first thought was that this had to be a tragic accident—perhaps a small plane had veered off course and crashed into the tower.

But then, before we could even fully process what was unfolding, a second plane appeared on the screen. It was heading straight for the South Tower.

Time seemed to freeze!

We watched in horror as the aircraft slammed into the second tower, erupting into a massive fireball. A collective gasp filled the room. This was no accident. This was deliberate. An attack! The realization hit like a punch to the gut.

No one spoke. No one could. We were glued to the screen, absorbing every word of the frantic news reports, the speculations, the desperate calls for help. Panic filled the airwaves, reporters struggling to keep their composure as they relayed the events in real-time. Then, to our utter disbelief, the first tower began to collapse. It folded in on itself, crumbling to the ground in what looked like a controlled demolition—except this wasn't a movie. This was real. And there were thousands of lives inside.

Shock turned to grief. Grief turned to terror!

And then—the second tower fell.

Just when we thought we had seen the worst, another explosion rocked the news feed. Reports came in that a plane had crashed into the Pentagon, just miles from where we stood in Fairfax County. This was no longer just a national crisis; it was now dangerously close to home. As we processed the news, we could hear a deep, distant rumble—the eerie, thunderous sound of the impact. The Pentagon, a symbol of our nation's military strength, was now a target.

Chaos erupted around us. Emergency alerts blared, and we were told to take cover, uncertain of what might come next. Were there more planes? More attacks? Where would they strike next? Sirens wailed in the distance, and the fear in the room was palpable. We looked at each other, wide-eyed, searching for some reassurance that none of us could provide.

As emergency response personnel, we had no time to process our emotions—we had to act. The rest of the day became a blur of urgent calls, emergency plans, and crisis management discussions. We had to prepare Fairfax County for whatever might come next. The usual business of stormwater management and infrastructure planning was suddenly overshadowed by the grim reality that we were now part of a national emergency.

That day changed everything!

The world as we knew it was different now—shattered by an unimaginable act of terror. Airports shut down. Fighter jets patrolled the skies. Streets emptied as people rushed home to be with their families. The entire nation was gripped by fear, uncertainty, and an overwhelming sense of loss.

Over the days that followed, the shock slowly gave way to grief. The death toll climbed. Stories of unimaginable loss and incredible heroism began to emerge. Firefighters, police officers, and everyday citizens had given their lives to save others. Strangers comforted one another, united in sorrow and resilience.

As I look back on that day, I remember the fear, the disbelief, and the deep sadness that settled over the country. But I also remember the way people came together—the way communities rallied to support one another, the way first responders worked tirelessly without hesitation, the way an entire nation stood in solidarity.

The memory of September 11, 2001, will forever be etched in the minds of those who lived through it. It was a day of infamy, a day of sorrow, a day that reminded us all how fragile life can be. But it was also a day that revealed the strength of the human spirit—a strength that carried us through the darkness and helped us rebuild, not just our cities, but our sense of unity and purpose.

Even now, more than two decades later, the weight of that day remains. The world changed forever, and so did we. But in remembering, we honor those we lost, and we remind ourselves to cherish each day, to stand together in the face of adversity, and to never take for granted the peace and security that we so often assume will always be there.

## The Anthrax Crisis

The 2001 Anthrax attacks, also known as the Anthrax Crisis, took place in the weeks following the September 11 terrorist attacks, adding to national anxiety. Beginning on September 18, anthrax-laced letters were mailed to media offices, including ABC News, NBC News, CBS News, and the *New York Post*, as well as the offices of U.S. Senators Tom Daschle and Patrick Leahy. The letters contained a fine powder with *Bacillus anthracis* spores, which cause inhalational and cutaneous anthrax, a severe and often fatal bacterial infection.

The attacks resulted in five deaths and 17 infections, prompting widespread fear. Government buildings, postal facilities, and media offices were decontaminated, and public confidence in mail safety was severely shaken. I remembered the fear I experienced during the Anthrax Crisis—every piece of mail felt like a potential threat, and the sense of vulnerability was overwhelming. The crisis led to a surge in bioterrorism-related security measures, including improved detection technology and emergency preparedness.

The FBI launched "Amerithrax," an extensive and costly investigation that initially focused on foreign terrorism before shifting to domestic suspects. Years later, investigators honed in on Dr. Bruce Ivins, a microbiologist at the U.S. Army Medical Research Institute of Infectious Diseases (USAMRIID), who had worked with anthrax. Despite circumstantial evidence, Ivins died by suicide in 2008 before he could be formally charged, leaving some questions about the case unanswered.

The Anthrax Crisis underscored vulnerabilities in national security and public health preparedness. It led to significant improvements in biosecurity, increased research on anthrax vaccines, and changes in how government agencies respond to bioterrorism threats. The incident remains one of the most infamous examples of bioterrorism in modern U.S. history.

## The D.C. Sniper Attacks

The D.C. Sniper Attacks were a harrowing chapter in the Washington D.C. region's recent history, a period when the fabric of everyday life was torn apart by senseless violence and fear. It was October 2002 when the Metropolitan D.C. area found itself besieged by a series of random shootings that left communities on edge. The attackers, John Allen Muhammad and Lee Boyd Malvo—a young man originally from Jamaica—targeted ordinary citizens, turning the most mundane routines into life-threatening risks. Gas stations, parking lots, sidewalks, and even quiet residential streets were transformed into potential danger zones. Every trip outside, no matter how short or routine, became a gamble with one's safety.

During those tense weeks, the pervasive atmosphere of paranoia infiltrated every aspect of life. People began to question the safety of their neighborhoods, and the very act of commuting became an ordeal. Schools were placed on lockdown, public events were canceled, and residents found themselves trapped in a climate of constant vigilance. The sense of security that many had taken for granted was shattered overnight, replaced by an ever-present anxiety about when, or where, the next shot might ring out.

I distinctly recall one personal experience that encapsulated the terror of that time. I had a critical meeting with state officials in Richmond, and the drive down I-95 was fraught with tension. Each mile felt longer than the last, as I watched the scenery pass by with a nagging sense of impending danger. When I pulled off the highway for a much-needed lunch break, the anxiety hit me hard. The simple act of leaving my vehicle became a monumental challenge. I sat in the car for what seemed like an eternity, scanning my surroundings, and watching with apprehension as other travelers hurried between their cars and the restaurant. Eventually, after gathering every ounce of courage I could muster, I stepped out—but even then, my movements were deliberate and quick, always alert, always scanning for any sign of danger.

This personal ordeal was mirrored by the collective experience of the entire region. The sniper attacks brought an abrupt halt to the normal rhythms of life. Families stopped planning outings, and businesses were forced to adjust their operations in response to the pervasive fear. Every siren and every distant sound sent ripples of alarm through communities that had never before experienced such a direct assault on their daily routines.

In the midst of this terror, law enforcement agencies mobilized on an unprecedented scale. The manhunt for Muhammad and Malvo was one of the largest in the area's history. Officers from multiple jurisdictions collaborated in an intense investigation that spanned across state lines, using every resource available to track down the elusive perpetrators. Their eventual capture brought a measure of relief to a community that had endured weeks of uncertainty and dread.

Yet, even as the shooters were apprehended and the immediate threat subsided, the scars of those dark days remained. The events of that October left an indelible mark on the D.C. area, serving as a stark reminder of how fragile our sense of normalcy can be. The collective trauma experienced by the community continued to influence behavior and policy long after the crisis had passed. Increased security measures, a greater emphasis on emergency preparedness, and an ongoing dialogue about public safety emerged as part of the legacy of the sniper attacks.

For many, including myself, the D.C. Sniper Attacks were more than just a series of violent incidents—they were a profound lesson in the resilience of the human spirit. Amid the pervasive fear, there was also an outpouring of solidarity. Neighbors looked out for one another, local organizations mobilized to offer support, and many individuals found strength in the face of adversity. It was a time when ordinary citizens became heroes in their own right, whether by comforting those in distress or by simply standing firm in the face of overwhelming fear.

Reflecting on that period, I realize how significantly it reshaped my understanding of vulnerability and courage. The terror of not knowing when the next attack might occur forced all of us to reconsider what it means to feel safe and secure. In a way, the sniper attacks exposed the raw nerves of our society, prompting a collective reevaluation of priorities and security. It taught us that even in moments of profound darkness, there can be unexpected light—an enduring sense of community and mutual support that helps us heal and move forward.

The D.C. Sniper Attacks will forever remain etched in the memory of those who lived through them. They serve as a powerful reminder of the unpredictable nature of life and the importance of preparedness, and vigilance. While the scars of those terrifying days may never fully fade, they also underscore our capacity to come together and to overcome.

## The Evolution of My Career at Fairfax County

Between the late 1990s and 2001, Fairfax County underwent a major government reorganization that significantly reshaped its public works and environmental management structure. This restructuring led to the merger of the Department of Public Works (DPW) and the Department of Environmental Management (DEM), forming the Department of Public Works and Environmental Services (DPWES). As part of this transformation, my role evolved as well. A newly established agency, the Stormwater Planning Division (SWPD), was created by consolidating several units, and I was appointed as the Branch Chief of the Watershed Planning and Assessment Branch within SWPD.

In this leadership role, I managed an internal team of up to 15 professionals, along with multiple consultant contractors, overseeing the planning and execution of stormwater management programs. A key responsibility was directing the county-wide watershed management program, a critical initiative aimed at mitigating the increasing degradation of local streams caused by rapid urban development.

Fairfax County's stormwater infrastructure and policies had remained unchanged for decades, and the effects of expanding impervious surfaces were becoming evident through erosion, flooding, and declining water quality. Recognizing the urgency of the situation, the county adopted an innovative approach—utilizing physical and biological stream assessments to evaluate stream conditions and identify key water quality indicators.

The first step in this process was developing the Stream Protection Strategy (SPS), a baseline biological assessment, which was published in 2001. This report classified the county's watersheds based on stream water quality into five categories: Excellent, Good, Fair, Poor, and Very Poor. The findings revealed that just 25% of county streams exhibited good to excellent biological health, while 75% were negatively impacted by development.

The next step involved conducting a county-wide Stream Physical Assessment, which used observable physical metrics to further evaluate watershed health. These studies laid the foundation for developing detailed watershed plans aimed at addressing the decline in stream health and implementing sustainable management strategies.

The implementation of this program was unprecedented in Fairfax County and a first in the Commonwealth of Virginia. Over the course of a decade, we developed comprehensive watershed management plans for 30 distinct watersheds, with a total investment exceeding $20 million. These plans provided a science-based framework for stream protection and restoration, ensuring that the county could implement effective long-term solutions. A key component of this initiative was public involvement. We launched a robust community engagement effort, incorporating public meetings, stakeholder workshops, and outreach campaigns to educate residents on watershed health and secure their support for restoration projects. Given the scale and complexity of the effort, this was the first time Fairfax County had undertaken such an extensive watershed planning initiative in over 20 years.

A key question is: How do we measure progress toward healthier streams? To answer this, we developed a program to conduct representative sampling of county streams each year. Fairfax County continues to collect biological data from 40 randomly selected stream locations annually. The Stream Quality Index (SQI), an innovative method we created, assesses water quality based on benthic macroinvertebrates—small, bottom-dwelling organisms that serve as indicators of stream health. Each location is rated (excellent, good, fair, poor, or very poor) based on the organisms found, with higher SQI scores indicating better water quality. Since the program began, over 75% of the county's streams have been rated fair, poor, or very poor, highlighting widespread impairment and low biological diversity. These findings reinforce that reversing environmental degradation is a long-term process that may take decades to achieve meaningful improvement.

Leading this program was a pivotal experience for me. Not only did I gain valuable expertise in managing large-scale consultant contracts, but I also honed my skills in public outreach and engagement. I learned how to communicate technical information effectively to diverse audiences, fostering collaboration between government agencies, community groups, and environmental organizations. Under my leadership, the program achieved significant milestones, setting a new standard for watershed management in the county. This initiative reinforced my belief in the importance of proactive environmental planning and community-driven solutions to address the challenges posed by urban development.

I also led the county's efforts to comply with the Municipal Separate Stormwater System (MS4) Permit, a key component of the National Pollutant Discharge Elimination System (NPDES) program. NPDES regulations mandate the management of pollutants in stormwater runoff, specifically from impervious surfaces, as they enter storm drainage systems. These regulations have far-reaching implications for urban infrastructure and environmental quality, addressing every aspect of the built environment typically found in urban landscapes. Under my leadership, the county took a proactive approach, exceeding the minimum regulatory requirements at times, to ensure improved ecological health and a cleaner environment for the community.

I led the initiative to secure consultant expertise for a comprehensive Stormwater Needs Assessment Study, a critical effort aimed at identifying sustainable funding mechanisms to support the county's growing stormwater management needs. As development expanded and stormwater infrastructure aged, it became increasingly clear that existing funding sources were inadequate to address pressing issues such as flooding, erosion, and declining water quality. The study provided a detailed evaluation of future program requirements and explored viable funding alternatives to ensure the county could meet its stormwater management obligations effectively.

A key outcome of this study was the successful recommendation and adoption of a dedicated "Penny" on the local real estate tax assessment by the Board of Supervisors in 2006. This dedicated funding source provided over $20 million in new revenue during its first year, significantly enhancing the county's ability to plan, implement, and maintain critical stormwater infrastructure projects. With these additional funds, the county was also able to adequately fund the development of complete watershed management plans.

Over time, the dedicated "Penny" tax has increased, generating additional revenue that has allowed the county to expand its stormwater management programs, further improving water quality and flood resilience. This forward-thinking approach positioned the county as a leader among urban jurisdictions, demonstrating a strong commitment to environmental stewardship and long-term sustainability. By proactively addressing stormwater challenges, the county not just met but sometimes exceeded regulatory requirements, putting it on the path of a healthier and more resilient environment for future generations.

My responsibilities extended to supporting the development and implementation of local Total Maximum Daily Loads (TMDLs), which are regulatory plans designed to reduce and ultimately reverse the impact of specific pollutants in streams and rivers. These plans were critical in addressing water quality impairments and required extensive coordination with state and federal environmental agencies to ensure compliance with the Clean Water Act (CWA). A key component of these efforts involved robust public outreach and education initiatives aimed at engaging community stakeholders, advocacy groups, and local businesses. Public participation was essential to fostering a shared responsibility for watershed stewardship and achieving measurable improvements in water quality.

Beyond regulatory compliance, my role included working closely with various governmental departments to establish and promote innovative stormwater best management practices (BMPs). This involved advancing policies for Low Impact Development (LID), Environmental Site Design (ESD), and Green Infrastructure (GI), all of which emphasize sustainable stormwater management approaches that mitigate stormwater runoff impacts, enhance groundwater recharge, and improve overall ecosystem resilience. These strategies were integrated into both new development and redevelopment projects to create a more environmentally sustainable urban landscape.

Additionally, I was an integral member of the county's emergency management operations team, especially during severe weather events such as hurricanes, extreme rainfall, and flooding. My responsibilities included coordinating with emergency response agencies to ensure community readiness and resilience in the face of climate-related disasters. I also played a key role in reviewing major floodplain studies, ensuring their compliance with the Federal Emergency Management Agency's (FEMA) National Flood Insurance Program (NFIP) regulations. This work was crucial in protecting residents and businesses from flood hazards, minimizing economic losses, and maintaining the county's eligibility for federal disaster assistance programs.

These multifaceted efforts underscored the county's commitment to environmental leadership, regulatory compliance, and community resilience, positioning it at the forefront of sustainable stormwater and floodplain management practices.

Some of my proudest moments came from developing and delivering numerous presentations for webinars, public meetings, conferences, for the County Board of Supervisors, stakeholder groups, and professional training sessions. These opportunities allowed me to communicate complex stormwater management concepts to diverse audiences, bridging the gap between technical expertise and public understanding.

As a member of Fairfax County's Stormwater Leadership Core Team, I played a key role in shaping critical policies and initiatives. I contributed to the development of the Stormwater Business Area Strategic Plan in the early 2000s, the establishment of Performance Standards, and other leadership-driven efforts aimed at enhancing the county's stormwater management programs. These initiatives not merely strengthened regulatory compliance but also set a proactive vision for sustainable water resource management in the county.

I was fortunate to be a part of this organization for much of my professional career, where I had the privilege of working alongside a highly talented and dedicated team of engineers, planners, and scientists. The collaborative environment fostered innovative solutions to complex environmental challenges, making every project a rewarding experience. The sense of satisfaction I derived from my work extended far beyond personal achievements—it was deeply rooted in the meaningful service provided to the broader community. Knowing that our efforts directly contributed to improving water quality, mitigating flood risks, and enhancing environmental sustainability was profoundly fulfilling for me.

## Hiring and Development of Highly Skilled Employees

I played a key role in the hiring and development of dozens of highly skilled employees, carefully selecting individuals who not just possessed the necessary technical expertise but also demonstrated strong character and a commitment to excellence. Many of these employees worked under my leadership for decades, becoming invaluable members of my team and contributing significantly to our collective success.

Beyond those who remained under my supervision, several individuals I hired were later recognized for their talents and promoted to higher positions throughout the organization. They went on to serve in various capacities, taking on greater responsibilities and continuing to make meaningful contributions.

Seeing their growth and professional advancement has been incredibly rewarding, as it reaffirms my ability to recognize potential and cultivate talent.

This experience stands as a testament to my keen eye for identifying individuals with not just the right skills, but also the right attitude, work ethic, and integrity—qualities that are essential for long-term success in any organization.

Throughout my tenure, I was honored to receive recognition and accolades for my contributions. However, I firmly believe that these achievements were not mine alone but were a reflection of the collective dedication, professionalism, and expertise of the incredible staff with whom I had the good fortune to work with. Their unwavering commitment to public service and environmental stewardship made every success possible.

## Notable Awards and Recognitions

Throughout my career at Fairfax County, I was fortunate to receive several prestigious awards and recognitions that highlighted my contributions to engineering, leadership, and public service. These honors not just acknowledged my professional achievements but also reinforced my commitment to excellence in civil and environmental engineering, watershed management, and community engagement.

In 2016, I was honored with the Robert S. Hopson Leadership Service Award from the Mid-Atlantic Chapter of the American Public Works Association (APWA). This award recognized my dedication to leadership in public works and my efforts in advancing best practices within the field. Receiving this award was a significant moment, as it underscored my role in guiding teams, implementing innovative solutions, and fostering professional growth within the public works community.

Earlier in my career, in October 2011, I was the recipient of a North American Lake Management Society (NALMS) Achievement Award. This award was granted for a successful Public Education and Outreach Program related to watershed management planning. The initiative focused on engaging the community in understanding the importance of watershed health and implementing strategies to protect water quality. It was rewarding to see the impact of this program in raising awareness and promoting responsible environmental stewardship.

My long-standing affiliation with the American Society of Civil Engineers (ASCE), which began in 1980, culminated in a special milestone when I was designated a "Life Member" in January 2021. This recognition reflected over four decades of professional dedication and contributions to the field of civil engineering.

Within Fairfax County, I received several awards that acknowledged my performance and contributions. In July 1993, I was honored with an Outstanding Performance Award (OPA) for my work in public infrastructure and environmental initiatives. Additionally, I was a recipient of the Department of Public Works and Environmental Services (DPWES) Champion Awards in May 1996, December 2011, and July 2015. These awards were especially meaningful as they recognized my efforts in implementing key projects and leading initiatives that improved the county's water resources, environmental sustainability, and public engagement strategies.

Each of these recognitions represents a milestone in my professional journey—one marked by a commitment to engineering excellence, leadership, and public service. These awards serve as a testament to the dedication and teamwork of the many individuals I had the privilege of working alongside throughout my career.

## Mentorship of Young Students

Beyond my work in public service, I have always been passionate about mentoring and inspiring future engineers. Throughout my career, I have sought opportunities to share my knowledge, experiences, and insights with young minds, fostering an appreciation for engineering and its role in shaping the world around us.

One of the most rewarding experiences in this regard came in 2014, when I had the opportunity to serve as a judge for the Mid-Atlantic Regional Future City Competition, an event sponsored by the National Society of Professional Engineers (NSPE). This competition is a prestigious national initiative that challenges middle and high school students to design and present futuristic cities that address real-world issues related to urban planning, sustainability, and infrastructure. Students work in teams, guided by educators and engineering mentors, to develop innovative solutions for creating livable, resilient, and technologically advanced cities.

As a judge, I had the privilege of reviewing detailed models, written reports, and presentations from highly motivated and creative students. Their enthusiasm for engineering was evident in the way they approached complex issues such as transportation, energy efficiency, environmental conservation, and water management. Many of their ideas were remarkably forward-thinking, incorporating elements of green building design, smart technology, and climate adaptation strategies.

What stood out to me most was the depth of research and problem-solving skills these students demonstrated. The competition not just tested their technical abilities but also required them to think critically about how engineering solutions impact society. They had to consider questions such as: How can cities be designed to be both environmentally sustainable and economically viable? How do we balance technological advancement with cultural and social needs? How can engineers create infrastructure that is resilient to climate change and natural disasters?

Beyond the technical aspects, I was extremely impressed by the students' teamwork, communication, and ability to articulate their ideas effectively. Seeing their passion and dedication reinforced my belief in the importance of early exposure to STEM (Science, Technology, Engineering, and Mathematics) education. By participating in this competition, these young minds were not just gaining valuable technical skills but also learning how to collaborate, innovate, and think like future leaders in the engineering field.

For me, this experience was more than just an opportunity to evaluate projects—it was an affirmation of the critical role that mentoring and education play in shaping the engineers of tomorrow. The experience also reminded me of my own journey into engineering, recalling the mentors and educators who encouraged my growth and helped me realize my potential.

This event was just one of many instances where I have engaged in mentoring and outreach efforts, and it continues to inspire me to support initiatives that promote engineering education. Whether through judging competitions, speaking at events, or simply offering guidance to aspiring engineers, I remain committed to encouraging the next generation to pursue careers that make a lasting impact on communities and the world at large.

Another rewarding experience came sometime during the late 90s, when on behalf of the National Society of Professional Engineers, I had the privilege to mentor some very talented and smart high school students to design a solution for the "Sleight of Hand" for participation in a state regional competition. It was a challenge that required ingenuity, teamwork, and a structured approach to problem-solving.

From the outset, we established a team with each member assigned a different task. I guided them through the brainstorming process, encouraging them to think creatively and critically about the problem at hand. We explored various concepts and strategies, ensuring that every voice was heard and every idea considered. The students showed an impressive level of enthusiasm, and their ability to collaborate effectively became one of our greatest strengths.

As the project progressed, we delved deeper into robotics and automation, integrating mechanical and electronic components to refine our solution. The students displayed remarkable adaptability, fast grasping complex engineering principles and applying them in practical ways. Through trial and error, they learned the importance of perseverance and continuous improvement, refining their design to enhance efficiency and effectiveness.

Throughout the journey, I made it a priority to instill a sense of discipline, responsibility, and problem-solving skills. By fostering an environment of open communication and mutual respect, I helped them appreciate the power of teamwork. We held regular meetings, tested different configurations, and encouraged one another to push beyond perceived limitations. Each student brought their unique strengths to the table, whether in programming, mechanical design, or project management, and together, they built a cohesive and well-functioning system.

The final product was a testament to their dedication and ingenuity. When competition day arrived, the team executed their solution with precision and confidence. Their hard work and commitment paid off when they secured 2nd place at the state championship—a remarkable achievement that reflected not solely their technical skills but also their ability to work as a unified team.

I was incredibly proud to have played a role in their success. Seeing their faces light up with excitement and pride reinforced the value of mentorship and leadership. The experience not just strengthened my passion for engineering education but also reaffirmed my belief in the next generation's ability to innovate and solve complex problems. It was a moment that underscored the impact of guidance, encouragement, and a shared vision of success.

To this day, I cherish the memories of that competition and the lessons we all learned. The students' achievements were a testament to the power of hard work, perseverance, and collaboration. I have no doubt that many of them went on to pursue careers in STEM fields, and I remain grateful for the opportunity to have contributed to their journey in a meaningful way.

As I reflect on the early years of my engineering career, beginning in Fairfax and extending throughout the Washington, D.C. metropolitan area, I am filled with gratitude for the friendships forged, the lessons learned, and the opportunities seized. This region provided an ideal setting for professional and personal growth, becoming a place, I am proud to call home. Beyond my career, I remain actively engaged in the community, mentoring the next generation of engineers and advocating for continued investment in sustainable infrastructure.

My journey stands as a testament to the transformative power of education, perseverance, and a supportive community. It has shaped not just my career but also my broader life experience, reinforcing the belief that meaningful work—especially when done in collaboration with dedicated professionals—can leave a lasting impact on both the built environment and the people it serves.

My journey from Jamaica to the United States, through education and early career challenges, has been defined by resilience, determination, and a passion for engineering excellence. Each step, from my days at Dinthill Technical High School to studying at Howard University and establishing myself in the D.C. area, has shaped my professional identity and reinforced my dedication to making meaningful contributions to a wide array of impactful projects and public service.

## Evolution of the Work Environment at Fairfax

As I reflect on my decision to accept a job with Fairfax County in 1990, I recall the organization's strong reputation as one of the most desirable places to work. It was a large, well-managed entity that prioritized employee benefits, safety, career advancement, and workforce diversity. These qualities made it an attractive workplace, and I was eager to join an organization that valued its employees and fostered professional growth.

This commitment to employee development was especially evident in the leadership of the Department of Public Works (DPW) during my early years there. The management team at the time demonstrated a genuine interest in supporting their employees, actively promoting diversity in hiring and promotional opportunities while fostering a productive and motivating work environment. Their efforts reflected significant changes implemented in response to a lawsuit filed by the U.S. Department of Justice in the 1980s against the County for discriminatory practices in hiring, retention, and promotion of minorities.

A Letter to the Editor published in *The Connection Newspaper* on January 19, 2009, described the lawsuit's impact, and I quote:

"The lawsuit was settled with Fairfax County being placed on probation for a number of years. As part of the settlement, the county was required to initiate programs to recruit and retain minority employees. In 1982, the county started to implement programs to increase diversity in the workplace. Efforts were focused on hiring minorities in professional, non-professional, and administrative roles, recruiting interns from colleges and graduate schools, and promoting qualified minorities into mid-management and leadership positions. Considerable progress was made until the mid-to-late 1990s. Sadly, the gains that were made have systematically been reverted by subtle but effective discriminatory practices, including but not limited to:

1. Shortlisting highly qualified minority applicants for positions but using the job interview process to disqualify them. *Lack of communication and leadership skills"* is often used as an excuse to deny minorities into supervisory or management positions.

2. Using post-9/11 security measures as an excuse to impose tougher screening processes on candidates hired or promoted within agencies.

3. Limiting the promotion of minorities into supervisory, middle management, and leadership positions.

4. Strategically promoting and placing Caucasian men and women into middle management and leadership roles, even when they were not the most qualified candidates.

5. Implementing workplace reorganizations that, rather than improving efficiency, systematically removed minorities from supervisory and management positions, restricting their advancement into senior roles."

While my experience with DPW during the early years reflected a positive shift towards inclusivity and professional development, it is evident that these progressive policies did not fully withstand the test of time. The structural changes made in the 1980s laid a foundation for workplace diversity, but as the letter suggests, systemic barriers gradually re-emerged, reinforcing historical challenges faced by minority professionals in the County.

At the turn of the century, significant organizational changes reshaped the structure of Fairfax County's Department of Public Works and Environmental Services (DPWES). A new management framework was introduced, emphasizing stormwater management and regulatory compliance. By 2001, a newly appointed director introduced a vision statement:

*"Stormwater is the Gateway to the Environment."*

His objective was to consolidate and elevate key agencies to form the Stormwater Planning Division. At the time, I was leading the Stormwater Management Branch, which was responsible for over 70% of the key functions of the new division and I had previous experience in another 25% of the functions. This placed me in a strong position to qualify for the director's role.

I applied for the position and successfully advanced through two rounds of interviews. I later learned that I was the top-ranked candidate and was invited for a one-on-one meeting with the DPWES director. The interview was scheduled for a Saturday morning in his office.

What transpired during and after this meeting was a disheartening display of power abuse, racial discrimination, and professional disrespect. Instead of a fair evaluation, the director used the opportunity to belittle, demean, undermine my qualifications and showed a lack of serious interest in my candidacy as the interview merely lasted about 15 minutes. Shortly thereafter, he re-advertised the position and ultimately hired a retired federal government employee with no prior experience in urban stormwater management or Fairfax County regulations.

Despite my repeated requests for feedback—supported by the Human Resources (HR) Department policies—the director flat-out refused to provide an explanation regarding the selection process. His actions were never challenged by upper leadership or HR, even after I formally filed complaints.

Unfortunately, this incident was just the beginning of a painful pattern in my career at Fairfax County. Over the next eight years, I was denied promotional opportunities on three additional occasions, including twice for the same Stormwater Planning Division director position. The systemic racial biases I experienced in each case were undeniable. Upper management repeatedly offered feeble, unconvincing excuses—insulting both my intelligence and my professional contributions. It was evident that these discriminatory practices were deeply embedded, supported by multiple layers of leadership, and carried out with impunity.

## Seeking Justice: The EEOC Complaint

By 2011, after much deliberation, I decided to file a complaint with the Equal Employment Opportunity Commission (EEOC). However, I swiftly realized that the burden of proof rested entirely on me, requiring substantial evidence to meet a legal standard akin to "beyond a reasonable doubt." This, in turn, necessitated expensive legal representation without any guarantee of success. Regrettably, I also faced challenges in obtaining full cooperation from HR to access crucial data that would have been vital in substantiating my case. I was then forced to abandoned my pursuit for justice through the EEOC.

Ironically, during this same period, the County introduced a new initiative promoting "High-Performance Organizations" (HPO). This approach emphasized employee empowerment, diversity, and career advancement, aiming to create a workplace where employees were encouraged to take initiative, contribute ideas, and feel ownership of their roles.

I initially saw this as a positive and necessary step toward fostering high morale, increasing employee engagement, and opening up pathways for advancement. When properly executed, these principles could lead to a more inclusive and high-functioning workforce.

## The Reality: A Systemic Disconnect

Unfortunately, while the County's rhetoric emphasized employee empowerment, engagement and inclusivity, upper management failed to genuinely embrace these principles. In practice, leadership remained resistant to diversity, and systemic biases continued unchecked. The promised workplace empowerment was largely performative, leading to growing frustration among employees who had once been hopeful about these changes.

One of the most glaring issues was the lack of diversity in leadership roles. Decision-making positions were disproportionately occupied by a homogeneous group, and despite public commitments to diversity, qualified minority professionals were systematically overlooked. This failure to implement true empowerment strategies led to diminished morale, leaving many employees feeling ignored and undervalued.

The true tragedy lies in the missed opportunity to deliver optimal service to the residents and taxpayers of Fairfax County. By denying myself and others the chance to fulfill our potential and implement innovative visions and practices, the community ultimately paid the price.

## A Shift in Leadership and Hope for the Future

Over time, I have remained engaged in monitoring organizational changes within DPWES. I became aware that, following the COVID-19 pandemic of 2020, the County's leadership underwent a significant transformation.

I had an enlightening discussion with the new DPWES leadership, who assured me that they were actively working to correct the systemic failures of the past decades. They emphasized a renewed commitment to diversity, equity, and inclusion (DEI) and were implementing training programs to reshape the organizational culture.

I have been made aware of a countywide initiative call "*One Fairfax: Equity Impact Plans*". The document outlines the efforts aiming to achieve a community where all residents can thrive by addressing inequities. Key points include:

1. Investigating the roots and trends of inequity actively.

2. Collaborating across departments and with the community to dismantle structural barriers.

3. Implementing Equity Impact Plans (EIPs) across agencies to operationalize commitments to racial and social equity.

4. Enhancing capacity within departments for equitable planning and decision-making.

These efforts are intended to drive institutional and structural change towards a more equitable Fairfax County.

I believe these recent efforts signal a path toward rehabilitation. If fully realized, these reforms could help restore Fairfax County's workplace culture and reputation, ensuring that future employees experience a fairer, more equitable, and more inclusive work environment.

## Acknowledgement of Special Friendships Forged

Beyond the immediate support of family and friends, I must express my sincere gratitude to a group of extraordinary individuals who became much more than just colleagues during my time at Fairfax County. Over the years, our professional interactions blossomed into enduring friendships, enriching my life in countless ways. To Demetrius, Johnson, Koenig, Murray, Abernathy, Gordon, Shirey, Burdick, Meyers, Kent, Cannon, and Curtis, thank you for your unwavering camaraderie, your shared laughter, and the countless moments of support that made even the most challenging days brighter. I would also like to take a moment to remember the late Colonel Ray Willis. Ray was a consistent source of inspiration to work out in the gym. His wisdom, guidance, and the unique spirit he brought to our circle left an indelible mark on us all. I am extremely fortunate to have these special people in my life.

Chapter 10

# Highlights of Notable Events

### Celebrating a Family Member's Outstanding Achievement

In May 2014, under the brilliant skies of Yale University in Connecticut, I experienced a moment of profound joy and pride. Surrounded by loved ones, I gathered to celebrate the remarkable achievement of my younger sister, Leonie Rose Bovino. It was a day etched with significance as she was honored with the conferral of her Doctorate Degree (PhD) in nursing during Yale's prestigious commencement ceremony.

Before the commencement, Leonie was also recognized with the Anthony DiGuida Delta Mu Research Prize for her groundbreaking dissertation titled *"Continuous ST-Segment Ischemia Monitoring in the Emergency Department"*. Her dedication to advancing medical research and her scholarly accomplishments marked this day as a testament to her tireless commitment and academic excellence.

This moment was the culmination of years of relentless hard work, perseverance, and an unshakable determination to succeed. From the time she first arrived in America, in the early 2000s, Leonie faced countless challenges, yet she never wavered in her pursuit of excellence. She embraced every obstacle as an opportunity to grow, proving time and again that resilience and dedication could turn dreams into reality.

I have always admired my sister for her incredible strength and tenacity. She tackled difficulties head-on, never allowing setbacks to define her journey. Her unwavering commitment to her goals, coupled with her deep sense of purpose, made her an inspiration to all who knows her. Watching her walk across that stage, receiving the highest academic honor, was not just a proud moment for her—it was a testament to the power of perseverance and an inspiration to our entire family.

Beyond her academic and professional achievements, Leonie has been more than just a sister to me—she has been a constant source of encouragement, wisdom, and understanding. Our sibling bond is one of the greatest treasures of my life. Through every phase, she has been a pillar of support, always there to uplift and inspire.

That day at Yale was not just a celebration of her academic success, but also of the incredible woman she had become. It was a defining moment, not just for her but for all of us who stood by her side, witnessing the fulfillment of a dream that she had worked so hard to achieve.

## The Grief of Losing Key Family Members

### Mama G

The 2000s brought unbearable loss and sorrow to my life, beginning with the untimely passing of my beloved mother in July 2003. She was taken from us far too soon, at just 70 years old, in Virginia. Her death was swift and unexpected, a cruel reminder of how fragile life can be, shaking the very foundation of our family. The pain of losing her was unlike anything I had ever experienced—it was as if the steady anchor of my life had suddenly been removed, leaving me adrift in a sea of grief.

My mother was my rock, my source of unwavering love and protection. Just her presence alone covered me with warmth and reassurance, making me feel that no matter what challenges came my way, I would always have a safe place to turn. She had an incredible ability to comfort, nurture, and guide with both wisdom and kindness. Even now, I can still hear the gentle cadence of her voice, offering encouragement and love in ways only a mother can.

One of my most treasured memories is of the last Christmas we spent together. That year, she gave me a complete set of fine chinaware and glasses for the china cabinet—a thoughtful and symbolic gift, one that represented not just her care and generosity but also the traditions and values she held dear. To this day, I have preserved and cherished that set in her honor, a tangible reminder of her love and presence in my life. Also, she had created several highly admired pieces of fine art, which are displayed in my home and the homes of several relatives.

We affectionately called her "Mama G," and she was more than just a mother to her children—she was a nurturer to all who crossed her path. Her kindness and selflessness knew no bounds; she cared deeply for others, always willing to lend a helping hand or a listening ear. Whether it was family, friends, or even strangers in need, she embodied the spirit of generosity and compassion, leaving a lasting impact on everyone who had the privilege of knowing her.

Losing her to cancer was devastating, altering my perception of life forever. The ruthless nature of the disease left me with a profound awareness of life's unpredictability and the harsh reality of loss. It was as if the world had shifted in an instant, and nothing would ever feel the same again. Her absence created a void that no one else could fill, but her love, wisdom, and the values she instilled in me remain an enduring part of who I am. Though she is gone, her spirit lives on in the countless lives she touched, in the lessons she taught, and in the love that will forever bind us together.

## Joyce Toomer

In June 2012, my uncle Les' beloved wife, Joyce Toomer, passed away in Queens, New York, after a courageous battle with cancer. Her passing was a deeply saddening moment for me, marking the loss of a remarkable woman whose kindness and generosity had left an enduring impact on my life.

My connection to Joyce stretched back to my early years in Kingston, long before I moved to the United States. I will always cherish the memories of her warmth and care, especially during a pivotal time in my life. In 1977, as I prepared to embark on my journey to the U.S., Joyce and Les graciously welcomed me into their home, providing a safe and supportive place for me to stay until my plans were finalized. Their generosity and hospitality made an immeasurable difference, easing my transition into a new chapter of my life.

For decades, their home in Queens remained a sanctuary of comfort and love, a place where I always felt welcomed. It became one of my favorite places to stay whenever I visited New York, largely because of Joyce's warm and giving spirit. She had a way of making everyone feel at home, her hospitality woven effortlessly into everything she did. Whether it was through a home-cooked meal, a heartfelt conversation, or her quiet acts of kindness, Joyce embodied the essence of unselfishness.

Beyond her role as a gracious host, she was deeply spiritual, a woman of faith who never hesitated to extend a helping hand to those in need. Her passion for serving others was evident in her everyday life, and those who knew her could always count on her unwavering support and compassion.

Since her passing, Uncle Les has admirably maintained the family home, doing his best to preserve the sense of warmth and tradition that she had cultivated over the years. However, it is clear that he feels the weight of her absence every single day. Joyce was not just his wife—she was his confidante, his partner, and the heart of their home. Though time has passed, her memory continues to live on in the lives she touched, the love she gave, and the indelible mark she left on our hearts.

## Daddy Rose

As if that wasn't enough to bear, in July 2013, I was struck by the heart-wrenching loss of my father, who was taken by a sudden illness at his home in Carron Hall, Jamaica. Though he had lived a long and fulfilling life, reaching the remarkable age of 91, the pain of losing him was no less profound.

Just a year earlier, my father had joyfully celebrated his 90th birthday, an occasion that turned into a cherished community event. The celebration was proudly sponsored and hosted by GraceKennedy, one of the Caribbean's largest food processing and distribution companies based in Jamaica, as part of their initiative to honor elders reaching significant milestone birthdays.

The celebration was attended by many, a testament to the deep love and respect the community held for him. To them, he was more than a neighbor—he was a leader, a mentor, and a man of unwavering faith and service.

My father had dedicated himself to uplifting those around him. He founded a church in the community and worked closely with a missionary group from the U.S. to improve living conditions for families in need. He volunteered his time and resources to address the severe lack of adequate housing, ensuring that those most vulnerable had a safe place to call home. On one of my visits shortly before his passing, he proudly took me on a tour of the community, pointing out the newly built homes that stood as a testament to his efforts. As the main liaison for the project, he had personally assessed the families in dire need and compiled lists to ensure the right people received assistance.

I distinctly remember telling him how proud I was of his selfless dedication, especially considering his declining health. Despite the physical challenges he faced, his spirit remained strong, his heart committed to serving others. At his funeral, I reflected on his life of service and the lasting impact he left behind. In that moment, I realized that my father was more than just a parent—he was one of my greatest inspirations. He had lived by example, showing me the true meaning of compassion, generosity, and leadership. Without a doubt, he had emerged as *My Hero*. His famous words still resonate clearly: *"God helps those who help themselves"*.

## Sister Althea

On April 1st, 2014, my world was shaken by the heartbreaking loss of my beloved younger sister, Althea, who succumbed to cancer at the age of 54. For eight long years, she waged a brave and unyielding battle against the disease, facing each challenge with remarkable courage and resilience. Despite her strength, the illness eventually took its toll, leaving an immense void in our hearts and another profound loss for our family to endure.

Althea was more than just my sister—she was a radiant soul, a source of joy and warmth to everyone who knew her. A naturally gifted educator, she dedicated much of her life to teaching home economics and craft in Jamaica, imparting both knowledge and creativity to her students. Teaching wasn't just her profession; it was her passion, one that she carried with her even after migrating to the U.S. in 2004.

Losing her, especially so soon after the passing of our father, was an indescribable burden—one that tested the very fabric of our family's strength. However, in those difficult moments, one person stood unwaveringly by Althea's side: her only son, Demal. With steadfast devotion, he remained her rock, providing care, comfort, and unconditional love during her most vulnerable times. His presence in her final days was a testament to the deep bond they shared—a mother and son connection built on love, sacrifice, and mutual support.

The pain of losing a mother at such a young age was an unimaginable weight for Demal to bear. I witnessed firsthand the depth of his sorrow, the way grief left its mark on him. But through it all, our family has come together to surround him with the love, encouragement, and guidance he needs. Over the years, he has grown into a mature and determined young man, carrying forward his mother's strength and resilience.

Though Althea is no longer with us in body, her spirit remains ever present. She lives on in the values she instilled in her son, in the lives she touched as a teacher, and in the cherished memories we hold close to our hearts. Her unwavering love for family, her passion for education, and her quiet strength will never be forgotten.

## Son Wynton

And to my deepest sorrow, in March 2022, I suffered an unimaginable loss—the passing of my son, Wynton, in a tragic accident, just months before his 30th birthday. The grief has been overwhelming, and his absence has left a void in my heart that no amount of time can ever really heal.

Wynton was an extraordinary soul; a young man whose brilliance and talents left a lasting impression on everyone he met. His intellect was sharp, his skills versatile, and his competitive spirit in sports was matched only by his creative genius in music and art. Among his many creative musical works, two stand out to me— "90s Baby" and "Angels," a heartfelt tribute to his beloved late grandmother and grandfather, which stirs deep emotions within me every time I listen to it.

Beyond his remarkable abilities, he possessed a deep spiritual awareness that guided his path and touched the lives of those around him. More than anything, Wynton had a warmth and gentleness that made everyone in his presence feel comfortable, valued, and at ease. He had a way of connecting with people that was effortless and sincere, leaving behind cherished memories and an enduring impact on those who knew him.

The weight of this loss, compounded by others I have endured, has been almost unbearable. Yet, through the pain, I have been forced to find strength, resilience, and a deeper understanding of life's fleeting nature. Each day is a reminder of how precious our time is, and though Wynton is no longer physically with me, his spirit lives on in the countless ways he touched my life and the lives of so many others.

## Stepfather Sam Forbes

Then, in November 2022, grief struck once more with the passing of my stepfather, Sam Forbes, at the age of 87. After a lengthy and courageous battle with illness, he finally succumbed, leaving an irreplaceable void in my heart and in the lives of those who knew and loved him.

Sam was more than just a stepfather—he was a pillar of strength, a man of unwavering dedication, and, without question, the other rock of our family. His presence was one of reassurance, always there to support and uplift us during life's challenges. No matter the situation, we could count on him for his wisdom, his kindness, and his quiet yet steadfast leadership.

I observed firsthand how deeply he was affected when his beloved wife, Mama G, passed away. The loss was profound, and though he carried on for nearly two more decades, it was evident that life at the family home was never quite the same without her. Still, Sam did his best to preserve the traditions they had built together. Determined to maintain a sense of family unity, he made it a priority to keep our cherished holiday gatherings alive for as long as he was physically able.

One of his greatest sources of pride came during the Christmas season when he would meticulously bake the traditional Jamaican Black Cake. With a level of care and precision that reflected his love for family, he decorated it beautifully with vibrant, colorful icing—a sight that always brought joy to our celebrations. This ritual was more than just a culinary tradition; it was a heartfelt expression of his devotion to family and the values he held dear.

Even as time moves forward, his memory and the traditions he upheld will forever be woven into the fabric of our family's story. His unwavering love, generosity, and resilience will continue to inspire us, reminding us of the strength he embodied and the legacy he leaves behind.

I am deeply grateful to the many friends and relatives who have taken the time to support and uplift me with their prayers. The grieving process is neither easy nor brief, but I find strength in the support I've received and will continue moving forward.

## Major Global Events between 1990 and 2020

Between 1990 and 2017, the world witnessed profound political, economic, and social transformations. The decade of the 1990s marked the end of the Cold War with the collapse of the Soviet Union in 1991, reshaping global geopolitics. The

Gulf War (1990-1991) saw the U.S.-led coalition force Iraq out of Kuwait, while globalization accelerated with the establishment of NAFTA in 1994. However, the decade also saw acts of terror, including the 1993 World Trade Center bombing and the 1995 Oklahoma City bombing, foreshadowing a growing threat. The 1994 Rwandan Genocide was a tragic humanitarian crisis, while the Asian Financial Crisis of 1997 highlighted the vulnerabilities of emerging economies. Meanwhile, the 1999 introduction of the Euro currency signified economic integration in Europe.

The Rodney King incident occurred on March 3, 1991, when Rodney King, a Black man, was violently beaten by the Los Angeles Police Department officers after a high-speed chase. A bystander recorded the beating, and the video sparked national outrage.

Despite the footage, the officers were acquitted in April 1992, leading to the Los Angeles riots, which lasted six days, caused over 60 deaths, and widespread destruction. The incident became a powerful symbol of police brutality and racial injustice in the U.S.

In 1994, former football star O.J. Simpson was charged with the murders of his ex-wife Nicole Brown Simpson and her friend Ron Goldman in Los Angeles. After a highly publicized trial filled with dramatic moments—including the famous glove demonstration, *"if it don't fit, you must acquit"*. Simpson was acquitted in 1995.

The case divided public opinion and raised major issues around race, celebrity, and the criminal justice system. It remains one of the most famous and controversial trials in American history.

The 2000s ushered in an era of heightened security concerns and economic instability. The controversial 2000 U.S. presidential election ended with a Supreme Court decision, bringing George W. Bush to office. The September 11, 2001, terrorist attacks changed the course of global history, leading to the War on Terror and U.S. military interventions in Afghanistan and Iraq. Natural disasters also left their mark, including the devastating 2004 Indian Ocean tsunami and

Hurricane Katrina in 2005. The 2007-2008 Global Financial Crisis triggered the Great Recession, impacting economies worldwide.

## An Historical Presidency

In 2008, Barack Obama made history by being elected the first African American president of the United States, a moment that represented a transformative milestone in the nation's long struggle with race and civil rights. His election inspired millions across the country and around the world, symbolizing progress toward a more inclusive democracy. It marked a profound shift in American politics and culture, breaking a centuries-old racial barrier and offering hope to those who had long been marginalized in the political system.

The 2010s saw political upheavals, technological advancements, and pressing global challenges. The Arab Spring uprisings (2010-2011) led to major regime changes in the Middle East, while the killing of Osama bin Laden in 2011 was a defining moment in the fight against terrorism. The 2012 Sandy Hook school shooting reignited debates over gun control in the U.S., while Russia's annexation of Crimea in 2014 strained international relations. The 2015 Paris Climate Agreement marked a global commitment to addressing climate change, though the U.S. later withdrew from it under President Donald Trump, who won the 2016 election in a major political shift. Natural disasters, including Hurricanes Harvey, Irma, and Maria in 2017, tested the resilience of affected communities.

## Major Technological Achievements, 1990 to 2020

During the decades of the 90s and 20s, the world experienced groundbreaking technological advancements that reshaped communication, transportation, healthcare, and everyday life. The internet revolution transformed how people accessed and shared information, with the World Wide Web becoming publicly available in 1991 and search engines like Google emerging in 1998. The expansion of broadband internet replaced slow dial-up connections, enabling streaming, cloud computing, and e-commerce platforms such as Amazon and eBay to flourish. The rise of social media, with Facebook (2004), YouTube (2005),

Twitter (2006), and Instagram (2010), changed global communication, making the world more interconnected than ever.

The evolution of flat-screen and high-definition (HD) televisions began in the late 1990s and gained mainstream popularity in the early 2000s. The transition from bulky cathode-ray tube (CRT) TVs to sleek, lightweight plasma, LCD, and later LED screens was driven by advancements in display technology and consumer demand for better picture quality. By the mid-2000s, HD resolutions (720p and 1080p) became standard, revolutionizing home entertainment. The 2010s saw the rise of 4K Ultra HD and OLED technology, offering even greater clarity and vibrant colors. Today, with 8K resolutions and smart TV features, flat-screen TVs continue to dominate the market, providing immersive viewing experiences and seamless integration with streaming services.

The evolution of mobile technology saw basic cellular devices give way to smartphones, spearheaded by Apple's iPhone (2007) and Android devices. Wireless connectivity improved with Wi-Fi and Bluetooth, while the introduction of 4G LTE networks in the early 2010s brought high-speed internet to mobile users, enabling streaming, mobile banking, and cloud-based applications. Meanwhile, artificial intelligence (AI) and automation advanced significantly, leading to the development of virtual assistants like Siri (2011), Alexa (2014), and Google Assistant (2016). AI-driven machine learning and big data analytics revolutionized industries, while companies like Tesla and Google's Waymo pushed forward with self-driving car technology.

In the field of biotechnology and healthcare, the completion of the Human Genome Project in 2003 paved the way for personalized medicine, while breakthroughs in stem cell research led to advancements in regenerative treatments. The development of CRISPR gene-editing technology in the 2010s enabled precise genetic modifications, offering hope for treating inherited diseases. Wearable health devices, such as the Fitbit (2009) and Apple Watch (2015), allowed individuals to monitor their health in real time, making wellness tracking more accessible.

Space exploration also saw remarkable progress during this period. The International Space Station (ISS) became fully operational in 2000, serving as a global research hub for space sciences. NASA successfully landed the Curiosity rover on Mars in 2012, furthering planetary exploration. Private space travel gained momentum, with SpaceX launching reusable rockets in 2015, revolutionizing the space industry and making commercial space missions a reality.

In response to climate change and energy demands, the development of renewable energy technologies has expanded rapidly. Hybrid and electric vehicles, such as Toyota's Prius (1997) and Tesla's electric cars (2008 onward), gained popularity, reducing dependence on fossil fuels. Advances in solar and wind energy helped drive global sustainability efforts, while improvements in battery storage technology made energy management more efficient for homes and businesses.

The period between 1990 and 2020 was one of rapid technological progress, laying the foundation for even more transformative advancements in the years to come. From the internet and AI to space exploration and renewable energy, these innovations not just reshaped industries but also changed how people lived, worked, and connected with the world.

## The Evolution of Popular Culture in US, 1990-2020

Between 1990 and 2020, American popular culture evolved dramatically, shaped by technological advancements, shifting social norms, and major historical events. This period saw the rise of new music genres, blockbuster films, social media, reality television, and a growing emphasis on diversity and representation in entertainment.

## 1990s: The Rise of Digital Media and Counterculture

The 1990s saw the transition from analog to digital culture, with the internet beginning to influence entertainment and communication. The grunge movement, led by bands like Nirvana, Pearl Jam, and Soundgarden, dominated rock music, reflecting the disillusionment of Generation X. Meanwhile, hip-hop and rap grew into mainstream culture, with artists like Tupac Shakur, The Notorious B.I.G., and Dr. Dre influencing both music and fashion. Pop music also flourished, with boy bands like *NSYNC and the Backstreet Boys* and pop stars like Britney Spears and Christina Aguilera defining teen culture.

Television in the '90s was heavily influenced by sitcoms, with shows like *Friends, Seinfeld,* and *The Fresh Prince of Bel-Air* shaping humor and storytelling. The decade also saw the rise of cable networks like MTV, which played a crucial role in music and youth culture. Meanwhile, blockbuster films became bigger and more technologically advanced, with movies like *Jurassic Park (1993)* and *Titanic (1997)* pushing cinematic boundaries. The influence of video games expanded with the launch of the Sony PlayStation (1994) and Nintendo 64 (1996), turning gaming into a dominant form of entertainment.

## 2000s: The Digital Revolution and Reality TV Takeover

The early 2000s ushered in the digital age, dramatically changing the way people consumed entertainment. The rise of iTunes (2001) and the iPod (2001) revolutionized music, while illegal file-sharing services like Napster disrupted the traditional music industry. By the mid-2000s, YouTube (2005), Facebook (2004), and Twitter (2006) introduced new ways for celebrities and everyday people to connect with the world.

Reality television exploded in popularity, with shows like *Survivor (2000), American Idol (2002), The Bachelor (2002), and Keeping Up with the Kardashians (2007)* changing the entertainment landscape. Meanwhile, hip-hop fully dominated mainstream music, with artists like Jay-Z, Eminem, Kanye West, and Lil Wayne redefining the genre. Pop music also evolved, with Beyoncé, Rihanna, and Lady Gaga rising as global superstars.

Hollywood embraced big-budget franchises, with superhero films beginning to take over box offices, thanks to the success of *Spider-Man (2002)* and *The Dark Knight (2008)*. The launch of the Marvel Cinematic Universe (MCU) in

2008 with *Iron Man* set the stage for a new era of interconnected blockbuster storytelling. In television, the golden age of prestige drama took off with *The Sopranos (1999), The Wire (2002), and Breaking Bad (2008),* demonstrating a shift toward complex storytelling and antihero characters.

## 2010s: Social Media, Streaming, and Diversity in Entertainment

By the 2010s, the dominance of social media had fully transformed pop culture, making celebrities more accessible and influencing everything from fashion to political movements. Platforms like Instagram (2010), Snapchat (2011), and TikTok (2016) changed how entertainment was created and consumed. Streaming services such as Netflix, Hulu, and Spotify disrupted traditional television, film, and music industries, allowing for more independent content creation and binge-watching culture.

Music in the 2010s was shaped by a mix of hip-hop, EDM, and pop, with artists like Drake, Kendrick Lamar, Taylor Swift, and The Weeknd defining the era. The rise of K-pop with groups like BTS signaled the globalization of pop music. Meanwhile, representation and diversity became major cultural themes, with Hollywood facing pressure to include more diverse stories and actors. Films like *Black Panther (2018)* and *Wonder Woman (2017)* highlighted the push for inclusivity.

The 2010s also saw the explosion of meme culture and viral content, with internet challenges, GIFs, and Vine/TikTok videos influencing everyday communication. Superhero films became the most dominant genre, with the MCU culminating in *The Avengers* series, while TV saw the rise of high-budget fantasy epics like *Game of Thrones (2011-2019).*

## The COVID-19 Pandemic

The COVID-19 pandemic, caused by the SARS-CoV-2 virus, began in late 2019 and quickly became a global health crisis, officially declared a pandemic by the WHO on March 11, 2020. Originating in Wuhan, China, the virus spread rapidly, causing a wide range of symptoms from mild to life-threatening and resulting in millions of deaths worldwide.

Governments responded with lockdowns, travel bans, and mask mandates, which disrupted daily life, economies, and education systems. Healthcare systems were overwhelmed, and frontline workers faced extreme conditions amid shortages of personal protective equipment (PPE).

Vaccines were developed at record speed, with mass vaccination efforts beginning in late 2020, significantly reducing severe illness and death. However, vaccine hesitancy and unequal access, especially in poorer countries, presented challenges. Variants like Delta and Omicron caused new waves of infection, prolonging the crisis.

The pandemic also brought a mental health toll, accelerated remote work and digital learning, and triggered a global economic downturn. Governments, including the U.S., introduced stimulus packages to cushion the blow.

By mid-2022, thanks to vaccines and natural immunity, many countries began returning to normalcy. Still, COVID-19 remains a concern, emphasizing the need for stronger global health systems, early response mechanisms, and international cooperation in future emergencies.

## The George Floyd Killing

In May 2020, George Floyd, a Black man, died in Minneapolis, Minnesota, after a police officer, Derek Chauvin, kneeled on his neck for over nine minutes during an arrest. Floyd repeatedly said, *"I can't breathe,"* but the officers did not intervene. The incident was captured on video and quickly spread worldwide.

His death sparked global protests and renewed focus on systemic racism and police brutality. The movement galvanized support for *Black Lives Matter*, which became a powerful voice advocating for justice, police reform, and racial equality. The officer was later convicted of murder in 2021.

## The January 6th Incident

On January 6, 2021, a violent mob of supporters of then-President Donald Trump stormed the U.S. Capitol in Washington, D.C., in an attempt to overturn the results of the 2020 presidential election, which had been won by Joe Biden. The attack occurred as Congress was in session to certify the Electoral College vote.

The rioters breached security, vandalized offices, and clashed with police, leading to the deaths of several individuals, injuries to more than 140 law enforcement officers, and significant damage to the Capitol building. Lawmakers were evacuated, and proceedings were halted for several hours.

This unprecedented assault on the seat of American democracy was widely condemned across the political spectrum and around the world. It led to a historic second impeachment of Donald Trump for incitement of insurrection, though he was later acquitted in the Senate. The event has had lasting political and legal consequences, including extensive investigation that resulted in hundreds of arrests and convictions.

The January 6th Capitol riot is considered one of the darkest days in modern U.S. history, marking the first time the peaceful transfer of presidential power was violently challenged within the Capitol itself.

# Chapter 11

# Legacy and Journey Ahead

## Entering Retirement

In 2017, after four decades of a fulfilling career in engineering, I made the decision to retire from my regular job at Fairfax County. It was a moment filled with mixed emotions—pride in what I had accomplished, excitement for what lay ahead, and a hint of uncertainty about stepping away from a profession that had shaped so much of my life. However, my passion for engineering and my desire to stay engaged in meaningful work led me to take on a part-time role as a Senior Engineer with a global engineering consulting firm with a local office in Alexandria, Virginia. This position provided me with the perfect balance—continuing to apply my expertise to impactful projects while enjoying the flexibility to explore new interests and embrace a different pace of life.

One of the most rewarding aspects of my post-retirement career has been the opportunity to mentor young engineers. Sharing my experiences, guiding them through technical challenges, and offering insights on leadership and problem-solving has been immensely fulfilling. It is a way to give back to a profession that has given me so much while ensuring that future generations are prepared to tackle the challenges ahead. Engineering is an evolving field, with new technologies, methodologies, and sustainability initiatives reshaping the way we build and manage infrastructure. By mentoring, I can pass on both foundational knowledge and real-world wisdom, helping young professionals navigate an industry that demands both technical excellence and adaptability.

Beyond engineering, I found a new passion in real estate, becoming a licensed real estate agent. The transition was natural in many ways—both fields require analytical thinking, meticulous attention to detail, and a deep understanding of regulations and processes. More importantly, real estate gave me a different kind of satisfaction: the ability to help individuals and families navigate one of the most significant decisions of their lives. Whether assisting first-time homebuyers, helping investors find the right property, or guiding retirees toward their dream home, I take immense pride in making the process smooth and rewarding for my clients. Real estate has allowed me to combine my love for problem-solving with my commitment to helping others achieve their goals.

In the early days of retirement, I seized the opportunity to sharpen my tennis skills. I had the perfect partner in my son, Wynton, whom I convinced to join me on the court. Though he hadn't played in years, he quickly reminded me of both his talent and my age—I struggled to keep up and had to beg for mercy more than once! These days, I'm mostly content as a fan of the sport, enjoying matches on TV from the comfort of my couch. Still, I fondly recall the thrill of watching live action at the Billie Jean King National Tennis Center during the US Open in New York on a number of occasions.

## Reflections on a Career

As I reflect on my journey—from the vibrant streets of Jamaica to the academic halls of Howard University, from working on impactful infrastructure projects in the Washington, D.C. metropolitan area to stepping into new ventures in consulting and real estate—I feel immense gratitude. Every experience, every challenge, and every success has been a building block, shaping a life of purpose and fulfillment. My career has never been about titles or accolades but about making a difference, whether in the lives of individuals, communities, or the environment.

One of the pressing issues that has captured my attention in recent years is climate change. The evidence is undeniable: rising global temperatures, increasingly intense natural disasters, and the widespread impact of environmental degradation. I have always believed that meaningful change begins with individual action. My role as a consultant engineer has given me the opportunity to delve deeper into solutions, examining how sustainable engineering practices and innovative infrastructure designs can help mitigate climate risks.

On a personal level, I have taken steps to align my lifestyle with my environmental values. I installed solar panels on my home, reducing my reliance on electricity from fossil fuel-generated sources. I transitioned to an electric vehicle, cutting down on carbon emissions from daily travel. I actively practice recycling, repurposing materials, and upgraded to energy-efficient appliances whenever possible. These may seem like small actions, but I firmly believe that collective individual efforts can drive broader systemic change. We still have a long way to go, but every step in the right direction matters.

Retirement, for me, has not meant slowing down—it has meant shifting gears, exploring new passions, and embracing opportunities that align with my values. I remain committed to making a positive impact, whether through mentoring, real estate, engineering, or environmental advocacy. The lessons instilled in me during my early years in Jamaica continue to guide me: resilience, curiosity, and an unwavering commitment to excellence.

One of the most valuable lessons I've learned in my professional career is to never let others diminish your joy or dampen your sense of accomplishment. While some may be dismissive, the majority will recognize and appreciate your dedication, efforts, and the genuine heart you put into improving the community.

Retirement is not the end of the road; it is the beginning of new possibilities. It is about finding ways to stay engaged, to keep learning, and to continue making a difference. This chapter of my life is proving to be one of the most exciting yet, and I am eager to see where the path leads next.

## A Retirement Gift to Myself

Immediately after retiring in January 2017, I wasted no time fulfilling a long-held dream—I finally got myself a fast sports car! It wasn't just any car; it was a sleek, head-turning machine in a stunning shade somewhere between red and orange, aptly named *"sunset orange"*. The moment I got behind the wheel, I knew this car was built for speed and excitement. The engine's roar, the smooth grip of the steering wheel, and the way it hugged the road sent a thrill through me like nothing else.

Not long after picking up the car in February, I decided to take it on a real adventure. I booked a trip on the Amtrak Auto Train to Florida, eager to test my new ride on the open roads of the Sunshine State. The overnight journey was exhilarating—though I barely got any sleep. The anticipation of the long drive from Orlando to Fort Lauderdale kept my adrenaline pumping. I lay awake, imagining the rush of acceleration, the wind against the car, and the endless highway ahead—mostly at the regulated speed limits.

Once I arrived, I wasted no time hitting the road, reveling in the car's power and speed. Every press of the gas pedal was a reminder that I had finally made this dream a reality. Over the next couple of weeks, I explored Florida, taking in the beautiful coastal highways, zipping past palm-lined streets, and feeling the sheer joy of driving without a care. I clocked well over 1,000 miles, including a memorable drive from Fort Lauderdale to Jacksonville to visit friends. Each stretch of road added to the excitement, solidifying this trip as one of the most thrilling experiences of my life.

As I look back, one thing stands out—this was my first time owning and driving a true sports car, and it was absolutely sensational. The speed, the freedom, the adventure—it was everything I had imagined and more. I couldn't have been happier knowing I had finally turned this dream into reality.

Then in 2020, I had the unfortunate experience of being involved in an automobile accident that left a lasting impact on me both physically and emotionally. My prized car was hit from behind with great force, suffering significant damage, and I sustained injuries that required immediate and ongoing medical attention. The aftermath of the accident was overwhelming, as I faced months of physical pain, medical consultations, and rehabilitation.

This period was made even more challenging by the circumstances of the COVID-19 pandemic. At the time, many medical facilities were either closed or operating under severe restrictions, making it difficult to access necessary treatment. The uncertainty surrounding healthcare availability added to the stress of recovery, forcing me to seek alternative methods to heal. Determined to regain my strength, I took charge of my rehabilitation, dedicating myself to recovery exercises and self-care at home.

Through this ordeal, I gained a deeper appreciation for the unpredictability of life. It was an awakening moment for me, a stark reminder that "in the midst of joy, there can be sorrow." The experience reinforced my resilience and gratitude, teaching me to value health, patience, and perseverance even in the face of adversity.

## My Passion for Real Estate

My passion for real estate began in the early stages of my professional engineering career, long before I formally entered the field as a licensed real estate agent. The seeds were planted when I moved to Fairfax County, Virginia, and purchased my second home in 1989. This experience introduced me to the intricacies of home ownership, property valuation, and the long-term financial benefits of real estate investment. At the time, I viewed home ownership primarily as a means of securing stability for my family. However, as I navigated the process of buying and maintaining my home, I developed a keen interest in the broader aspects of real estate—particularly the potential for investment, wealth-building, and community development.

As I became more established in my engineering career, I started to explore real estate as an avenue for financial growth. The idea of property investment intrigued me, especially after recognizing the opportunities that existed in acquiring, improving, and reselling homes for profit. Over the years, I gradually built a portfolio of properties, each presenting unique challenges and learning experiences. Some of these properties were kept as long-term rentals, generating steady passive income, while others were *"flipped"* for a profit.

Flipping properties is both an art and a science. It involves purchasing homes significantly below market value—often distressed properties in need of major repairs—renovating or upgrading them and then reselling them at market value or higher. This process requires a deep understanding of the real estate market, construction and renovation costs, and buyer preferences. During my initial ventures into flipping, I fast realized that the success of each project depended on careful planning, cost control, and having the right team of contractors and professionals to execute the vision efficiently.

One of the biggest lessons I learned early on was the importance of accurate market analysis. Understanding neighborhood trends, home values, and buyer demands was critical in ensuring that a property would sell quickly and at a desirable price. Additionally, I had to familiarize myself with the complexities of financing and deal structuring. While some properties were purchased outright, others required creative financing strategies, such as leveraging home equity or working with private investors. These experiences not merely sharpened my business acumen but also deepened my appreciation for the real estate industry as a whole.

As I continued my journey in real estate investment, I identified a key area where I could optimize my operations—real estate commissions. Every time I bought or sold a property, I had to pay agent commissions, which, over time, added up to a significant amount. It became clear that obtaining my own real estate license would be a strategic move, allowing me to handle transactions independently and save on these costs.

However, like many things in life, the decision to become a licensed real estate professional took time to materialize. My engineering career was demanding, and real estate remained more of a secondary pursuit. Then, in 2020, the world changed. The COVID-19 pandemic forced much of daily life into a standstill, with lockdowns keeping people at home and shifting perspectives on work and career choices. It was during this period of uncertainty and reflection that I made the bold decision to pursue my real estate license. With the additional time at home, I immersed myself in real estate coursework, studying market laws, financing strategies, contracting principles, property management principles, and client representation techniques.

In June 2021, I obtained my state license as a real estate professional in Virginia. This milestone marked the beginning of a new chapter—one that expanded my role from investor to agent, allowing me to help others navigate their real estate journeys.

What intrigued me most about being a real estate agent was the opportunity to assist clients in finding their dream homes. Home ownership is one of the most significant financial and emotional investments a person can make, and I wanted to be part of helping them in that journey. My background in engineering had equipped me with a unique perspective—an ability to assess a property's structural integrity, identify potential risks, and guide clients through the decision-making process with confidence. I also understood the importance of teamwork and effective communication, skills I had honed through years of leading engineering projects. These experiences translated seamlessly into real estate, where collaboration with buyers, sellers, lenders, inspectors and contractors are essential for success.

Beyond technical expertise, I genuinely enjoy meeting new people and building meaningful relationships. Real estate is not just about transactions; it is about understanding people's aspirations, guiding them through complex processes, and ensuring they make informed decisions. I relished the opportunity to use my vast public engagement experience to connect with clients, anticipate their needs, and provide solutions tailored to their specific goals.

Having lived in Northern Virginia since 1990, I developed extensive knowledge of the region's economic drivers, cultural diversity, and evolving market trends. This insight has been invaluable in helping clients choose neighborhoods that align with their lifestyles and long-term investment objectives. Northern Virginia is a dynamic area, home to a mix of urban, suburban, and rural communities, each with its own unique charm and market conditions. Understanding these nuances has enabled me to advise clients effectively, whether they are first-time homebuyers, seasoned investors, or individuals relocating to the area.

Since obtaining my license in 2021, my real estate journey has taken me to numerous properties, helping clients buy and sell homes across a wide radius. Each transaction has reinforced my belief in the power of real estate as a tool for financial growth and stability. I have had the privilege of assisting families in securing their first homes, guiding investors toward profitable opportunities, and working with sellers to maximize their property's value. Every success story adds to my passion for the industry and motivates me to continue delivering the highest level of service.

I take immense pride in the quality of service I provide. Real estate is a highly competitive field, but my commitment to professionalism, integrity, and client satisfaction sets me apart. I am fully dedicated to devising and executing the best strategies for achieving the most satisfactory outcomes for my clients. Whether it is negotiating the best price, identifying off-market opportunities, or providing expert guidance on property improvements, I go above and beyond to ensure a seamless and rewarding experience.

Looking ahead, I am excited about the future of my real estate career. The industry continues to evolve, with new technologies, market trends, and investment opportunities emerging. My goal is to remain at the forefront of these changes, continuously learning and adapting to provide the best possible service. More importantly, I want to continue helping individuals and families achieve their real estate dreams—whether that means finding the perfect home, building a robust investment portfolio, or navigating the challenges of buying and selling in an ever-changing market.

One of my most memorable real estate transactions involved representing a seller who was navigating a difficult chapter in her life. Her husband had recently passed away, leaving her with the overwhelming responsibility of maintaining a large house on her own. Understandably, she was in distress, not just grieving her loss but also facing the daunting task of selling the home and finding a more manageable living arrangement. Recognizing her challenges, I stepped in to provide guidance and support, helping her through each step of the process with care and professionalism.

Before listing the property for sale, several issues needed to be addressed. The most pressing challenge was ensuring that the home's water well and septic system were properly assessed and obtaining past maintenance records to provide to potential buyers. Additionally, we identified necessary repairs and improvements to enhance the home's appeal and market value. Once all the preparation work was completed, the house was professionally staged and listed on the Multiple Listing Service (MLS). Within a week, we received an offer at the full asking price, a testament to our thorough preparation and strategic marketing.

The transaction proceeded smoothly to settlement, thanks to my meticulous attention to detail. I made sure that every inspection requirement was met and that no stone was left unturned in preparing the property for a seamless sale. My client was relieved and grateful for the positive outcome, as the successful sale provided her with financial security and peace of mind.

The next challenge was finding her a new home that fit her needs. Timing was crucial, as she wanted to transition into her new residence as soon as possible after vacating her previous home. The search required persistence and problem-solving, especially when it came to negotiating necessary repairs with the seller of the new property. While working with the listing agent presented some challenges, we built a professional rapport throughout the process, ultimately ensuring a smooth transaction. In the end, both our clients benefited, making it a true "win-win" situation.

This experience reinforced my belief that real estate is about more than just transactions—it's about helping people navigate life's transitions with confidence and ease. Being able to provide solutions, alleviate stress, and guide my client to a successful outcome made this one of the most rewarding transactions of my career.

Real estate is more than a profession for me—it is a passion that has shaped my journey, provided financial empowerment, and allowed me to make a tangible impact in people's lives. As I move forward, I remain committed to excellence, innovation, and the unwavering belief that real estate is one of the most powerful tools for building wealth and creating a legacy.

## My World Travels

After transitioning into a more flexible professional life, I finally found the time to indulge in one of my greatest passions: world travel. Exploring diverse cultures, landscapes, and histories has always fascinated me, and I've been fortunate to experience the wonders of many incredible destinations beyond the United States and Jamaica. My travels beyond Jamaica have started since the commencement of my professional career in the early 90s and continued since. Each country has left a unique imprint on me, offering unforgettable sights, sounds, and flavors that have enriched my understanding of the world.

## Negril, Jamaica

Negril Beach, often regarded as one of Jamaica's most beautiful and iconic destinations, has undoubtedly earned its place as my favorite vacation spot in Jamaica. The beach stretches for about 7 miles along the island's western coast, offering breathtaking views of turquoise waters and soft, powdery white sand. The calm, shallow waters make it a perfect spot for swimming, snorkeling, and relaxing, with a gentle breeze swaying the palm trees along the shore.

The beach's laid-back atmosphere is one of its defining features, allowing visitors to unwind without the hustle and bustle of more crowded resort areas. The famous Seven Mile Beach is lined with resorts, charming beach bars, and restaurants where you can savor authentic Jamaican cuisine, especially fresh seafood, and jerk dishes. As you stroll along the beach, you'll often see locals offering handmade crafts or inviting you to enjoy a traditional jerk chicken or fresh fruit.

Negril is also known for its stunning sunsets, which paint the sky in vibrant shades of orange, pink, and purple as the sun sets into the horizon over the Caribbean Sea. The sunset views are truly stunning when seen from the iconic vantage point of Rick's Café. The evening views, accompanied by the sound of the waves gently lapping against the shore, create a serene and magical atmosphere. Whether you're lounging on the beach with a drink in hand or exploring the surrounding areas, Negril Beach offers a perfect blend of natural beauty, tranquility, and cultural charm. I will never get tired of going back to Negril Beach.

## Kingston, Jamaica

Carnival in Kingston during the '90s was nothing short of electrifying—a whirlwind of color, music, and unrestrained revelry! Having lived in Kingston during my early college days at CAST and visiting frequently after migrating to the U.S., some of my most unforgettable experiences came from actively participating in this grand celebration, not just as a spectator, but as a reveler fully immersed in the exhilarating chaos.

The weekend kicked off with high-energy parties leading up to the ultimate spectacle—Sunday's grand street parade. The pulsating rhythm of Soca music filled the air as bands of revelers, women and men, clad in dazzling, feathered costumes, danced their way through the streets. Starting on Hope Road, we moved like a wave of vibrant energy through the packed streets of Half Way Tree, onto Constant Spring Road, and finally down to New Kingston. The journey culminated at National Heroes Park, where a massive stage awaited, ready to host the final showdown of music, dance, and sheer celebration.

The parade itself was an explosion of sights and sounds. Dozens of bands, each boasting at least 50 members, competed for the most stunning costumes and the most electrifying dance performances. Towering music trucks rolled between the groups, blasting the hottest Soca anthems, driving the crowd into a euphoric frenzy. The energy was contagious—hips swayed, flags waved, and the intoxicating mix of rhythm, movement, and free-flowing liquor kept spirits soaring.

Jamaica's Carnival, the brainchild of the late Byron Lee, was a masterful fusion of local flair and the legendary Trinidadian Carnival experience. Taking place right after Easter, it embodied the same spirit of uninhibited joy, vibrant creativity, and cultural pride that made its Caribbean counterpart world-famous. Each visit, I would find myself completely swept up in the magic—losing track of time, surrendering to the rhythm, and making memories that would last a lifetime.

## Mexico

Mexico was one of my first international adventures outside of Jamaica and the U.S., and it did not disappoint. From the stunning beaches of Cancun to the historical marvels of Chichén Itzá, Mexico is a country that seamlessly blends ancient history with modern vibrancy. The food alone—authentic tacos, tamales, and chiles rellenos—was worth the trip. I have also visited Cozumel on another occasion as a stop on a cruise. It was a fantastic way to experience more of Mexico's coastal beauty and culture.

## Canada

Just to the north, Canada impressed me with its vast landscapes and cultural diversity. Toronto, with its towering skyline and multicultural food scene, felt like a bustling metropolis, while Niagara Falls was a breathtaking natural wonder. During the 90s, I first visited Toronto and stayed with in-laws while we attended the annual Caribbean Carnival. The sights in Toronto were captivating, and the highlight of the city tour was enjoying the view from the top of the CN Tower, the tallest building at the time. It was a perfect blend of urban excitement and natural beauty.

In 2016, I had the chance to visit my Aunt Pat in Montreal to celebrate her retirement. It was a special occasion, and I thoroughly enjoyed the visit—meeting new friends and exploring the city. Montreal's European charm, paired with the French-speaking locals, made it feel like I was stepping into a different world within North America.

## Dominican Republic

My visits to the Dominican Republic have always been nothing short of unforgettable. Having traveled there at least three times, I've had the chance to explore both the rich historical charm of Santo Domingo and the breathtaking beauty of Punta Cana—each offering a unique and vibrant experience.

Walking through Santo Domingo's Zona Colonial felt like stepping back in time. The cobblestone streets, lined with centuries-old buildings, led me to remarkable landmarks like the Alcázar de Colón, the former home of Christopher Columbus' son, and the Catedral Primada de América, the first cathedral of the New World. Yet, despite its deep historical roots, the city pulses with modern energy.

What struck me most was the music and social life—merengue and bachata rhythms seemed to float from every street corner, drawing people into spontaneous dance. I embraced the local flavors, savoring dishes like mangú, mofongo, and the rich, hearty sancocho. And of course, no trip was complete without sipping on a glass of mamajuana, the Dominican spiced rum that locals swear by!

Punta Cana, on the other hand, was all about relaxation and adventure in paradise. The white sandy beaches and turquoise waters were straight out of a postcard. I spent my days lounging by the shore, taking in the sun, playing games staged by our resort hosts and occasionally venturing out for some snorkeling and catamaran cruises.

The nightlife here was electric—beachfront bars and lively dance clubs created an atmosphere that was both thrilling and laid-back. Each visit left me with new memories, from the friendly locals to the incredible food and music that made every moment feel alive. What draws me back to the Dominican Republic is not just the stunning landscapes, but the warmth and passion of its people. It's a place that truly captures the heart—and keeps calling me back.

## The Caribbean Islands

The Caribbean has always felt like home, with each island offering its own unique charm. I've had the pleasure of visiting several islands, either on individual trips or as part of a cruise itinerary.

Puerto Rico welcomed me with its blend of Spanish, African, and Taíno influences, seen in the colorful streets of Old San Juan and felt in the rhythms of salsa music. The Eastern Caribbean islands, including Barbados, Trinidad and Tobago, St. Lucia, St. Kitts, St. Marten, St. Thomas US Virgin Island, Grenada and Antigua, each had their own distinct beauty—whether it was the Pitons of St. Lucia, the white sandy beaches of Antigua, or the rich cultural heritage of Barbados. The Bahamas was a sun-drenched paradise with turquoise waters and endless opportunities for relaxation, but it also had a rich history, from the bustling markets of Nassau to the quieter, picturesque Out Islands.

Traveling to Trinidad and Tobago in the early '80s for the annual Carnival was an electrifying experience filled with vibrant music, dazzling costumes, and non-stop festivities. From the rhythmic beats of Soca and calypso to the pulsating energy of J'ouvert, where revelers danced through the streets covered in paint and mud, the celebration was pure exhilaration. Port of Spain came alive with elaborate masquerade bands, steelpan competitions, and the grand Parade of the Bands, showcasing breathtaking artistry and cultural pride. The warmth of the people, the rich flavors of doubles and roti, and the infectious spirit of Carnival made it an unforgettable adventure.

St. Thomas is a vibrant island in the Caribbean, known for its stunning beaches, crystal-clear waters, and lively tourism industry. The island's capital, Charlotte Amalie, is a historic port city with colonial architecture, duty-free shopping, and beautiful views. St. Thomas is a popular destination for cruises, water sports, and exploring natural attractions like Magens Bay and Coral World Ocean Park.

Grenada, often referred to as the "Spice Isle," is located in the southern Caribbean. It's renowned for its aromatic nutmeg and spice production, lush landscapes, and picturesque beaches. The island boasts a rich history and vibrant culture, with landmarks like Fort George, the historic town of St. George's, and Grand Anse Beach. Grenada is also known for hiking, particularly to the crater lakes of Grand Etang National Park. An amazing opportunity awaited to snorkel in the stunning and mesmerizing coral reefs just off the coast.

Visiting the Dutch Caribbean islands of Aruba and Curaçao was a treat. Aruba's desert landscapes and striking rock formations were unlike anything I had seen in the Caribbean before, while Curaçao's pastel-colored buildings in Willemstad made me feel like I was walking through a European postcard set in the tropics. The relaxed island culture, combined with Dutch colonial history, made these destinations a fascinating contrast to the other Caribbean islands I had explored.

One of my more adventurous travels took me to Belize, a country where history and nature intertwine beautifully. I marveled at the ancient Mayan ruins of Xunantunich, snorkeled in the crystal-clear waters of the Belize Barrier Reef, and even explored the famous Great Blue Hole from above. Belize's laid-back atmosphere and commitment to eco-tourism made it a haven for nature lovers like me.

## Suriname, South America

Suriname, the childhood home of my former wife, Judith, is one of South America's lesser-known gems, and it surprised me with its incredible cultural diversity. This small yet vibrant country, nestled between Guyana to the west, French Guiana to the east, and Brazil to the south, is a captivating fusion of Indigenous, Dutch, Javanese, African, Indian, and Chinese influences, all blending seamlessly into a rich and harmonious cultural society. Everywhere I went, I could see how these cultural threads were woven together—whether in the architecture, cuisine, or daily life of the people.

Our journey centered around Paramaribo, the capital, which felt like a piece of the Netherlands transported to the tropics. The city's beautifully preserved Dutch colonial buildings, many made of wood and painted white with green shutters, gave it a distinctive charm that set it apart from any other country's capital I had visited. Walking through the historic center, I marveled at landmarks like the Presidential Palace, Fort Zealandia, and the Saint Peter and Paul Cathedral, one of the largest wooden churches in the world. But beyond its colonial past, Paramaribo was alive with energy—from bustling markets filled with the aroma of exotic spices to the lively waterfront where locals gathered to socialize and enjoy Suriname's unique street food.

One of the highlights of my visit was venturing into the country's lush rainforest interior, a place of untouched natural beauty that felt worlds away from the city. The dense jungle, teeming with diverse wildlife and towering trees, showcased Suriname's rich biodiversity. We visited a public bathing spot in a blackwater river, its dark, tannin-rich waters a stark contrast to the vibrant greenery surrounding it. The experience of immersing myself in these natural waters, so deeply connected to the land and the local way of life, was both refreshing and humbling.

Our explorations also took us along the Suriname River, a major waterway stretching from the central interior to the Atlantic Ocean. The river is a lifeline for many communities, supporting transportation, agriculture, and fishing. Its banks were lined with dense rainforests, where we caught glimpses of exotic birds, monkeys, and other wildlife. Beneath its surface lurked piranhas—small yet notorious fish known for their sharp teeth and carnivorous feeding habits. While their fearsome reputation precedes them, locals reassured me that they rarely pose a threat to humans unless provoked. The Suriname River was more than just a body of water; it was a vital artery of the country, sustaining both people and nature in an intricate balance.

One of the most personal and enriching aspects of the trip was visiting several of Judith's relatives and friends. Each stop was a memorable experience, punctuated by warm hospitality and the joy of sharing meals together. Surinamese cuisine is a delightful fusion of its multicultural heritage, and I eagerly indulged in dishes that combined flavors from Javanese, Creole, and Indian traditions. Among the many delicious foods I tried, one stood out as my absolute favorite—a pastry called "fiadoe." This delightful Surinamese layered cake, which originated within the Jewish community, was unlike anything I had tasted before. Its rich, spiced flavors and slightly chewy texture made it a truly special treat, and I found myself savoring every bite.

Beyond its stunning landscapes and delicious food, what fascinated me most about Suriname was its people. The multi-ethnic population lived harmoniously with each other, embodying a spirit of unity and resilience that was really inspiring. Whether through their charm, kindness, or sheer determination, the people of Suriname left a lasting impression on me.

Suriname may not be a typical travel destination, but for me, it was deeply rewarding to explore. It felt off the beaten path, yet every moment spent there was rich with discovery. The memories of my visit—of the vibrant city, the tranquil rainforest, the flowing river, and the warmth of the people—will always hold a special place in my heart.

## England

Europe was another region that captured my imagination, with its deep history and architectural wonders. England, in particular, was a classic destination that offered a mix of both grandeur and charm. I walked through the historic streets of London, stood in awe of Buckingham Palace, and took in the magnificence of Big Ben and the Tower of London. I also enjoyed the experience of riding on the iconic double-decker buses and navigating the subway, where the famous warning "Mind the Gap" was a constant reminder to stay alert as passengers moved between trains and platforms. A cruise down the River Thames was another unforgettable highlight, offering a unique perspective of London's landmarks from the water.

Outside the city, the rolling green countryside and picturesque villages were a peaceful contrast to the urban bustle. Historical sites like Stonehenge added another layer of fascination, offering a glimpse into England's timeless beauty. England also holds personal significance for me, as it is home to my extended family on my mother's side. Some relatives have settled in Birmingham, while others are in the southern part of London, adding a special connection to my visits.

## Netherlands and Belgium

I had two family visits to the Netherlands, where I was instantly captivated by the charming canals of Amsterdam, the world-class museums filled with Rembrandt and Van Gogh masterpieces, and the unique Dutch cycling culture. This country held special significance as it was the birthplace of my former wife, Judith. Beyond Amsterdam, we explored several cities including The Hague, Zoetermeer, Volendam, Breda, Groningen, and Amstelveen. However, it was in Zoetermeer, where Judith's uncle (Oom) Guido and his family resided, that we spent most of our time. Zoetermeer was a laid-back and charming city, perfect for cycling along its extensive bike paths, complete with their own traffic signals, making them main thoroughfares for non-vehicular traffic—a standard feature in the Netherlands. Experiencing an entire country seamlessly functioning on two wheels was really special!

Another amazing treat I indulged in was the incredible variety of Dutch beers. From light and crisp pilsners to rich and complex Belgian-style brews, the different types and flavors available were remarkable. Whether enjoying a cold Heineken in its home country or sampling craft beers at a local brewery, the Netherlands offered an impressive selection that enhanced the experience of the trip.

One of the most notable things I observed was that a significant number of the people were tall, and most had a warm disposition. One of Judith's cousins had a son, Francisco, who towered at an impressive 6 feet 10 inches and earned a basketball scholarship to George Washington University in the U.S. He fast became an idol for my son Wynton, and we made it a point to attend as many of his local basketball games as possible.

Whether in the cities or smaller towns, I found the Dutch to be generally friendly, welcoming, and helpful, making my time there even more enjoyable.

Nearby Belgium provided an equally enchanting experience with its medieval towns, the breathtaking Grand Place in Brussels, and, of course, its renowned chocolates, waffles, beer, and relatively affordable jewelry.

## France

I have visited France on three separate occasions, each offering a unique and unforgettable experience. My first visit was in 1997 when I traveled to Paris via train from the Netherlands. This journey itself was breathtaking, as it provided a scenic view of the picturesque countryside, charming villages, and small towns along the way through Belgium and into France. The anticipation built as the train sped toward the iconic city, and once I arrived, Paris turned out to be everything I had imagined and more. The city's grandeur, from the soaring Eiffel Tower to the world-renowned Louvre, the stunning Notre-Dame Cathedral, and the atmospheric cafés lining the Seine, embodied a perfect blend of romance, history, and culture. One of the most enjoyable aspects of the trip was indulging in the vast variety of exquisite French wines and shopping along the famous Avenue des Champs-Élysées, where luxury and elegance were on full display. Taking a tour bus was a fantastic way to navigate the city, allowing us to see most of its famous landmarks with ease while soaking in the vibrant Parisian atmosphere. Beyond the sights, the food alone was enough to make me want to return—starting the day with a perfectly flaky croissant, savoring a rich coq au vin for dinner, or simply enjoying a baguette with fine cheese and wine in a cozy bistro.

My second visit to France was a more personal one, as I traveled back to Paris to visit my son Wynton while he was living in the country for a couple of years. This time, I spent a longer time and had the opportunity to experience Paris more through the lens of a resident rather than just a tourist, giving me a deeper appreciation for the city's day-to-day charm, local markets, and hidden gems that one might overlook on a first visit.

The third time I visited France was during a Mediterranean cruise in 2019, when we made a day stop in the port city of Marseille. Though my time there was brief, I was captivated by the city's stunning coastal views, vibrant markets, and historic architecture. Marseille had a distinct character compared to Paris—its blend of French and Mediterranean influences was evident in the food, the people, and the overall atmosphere. Strolling through the Old Port, taking in the sea breeze, and sampling fresh seafood made the stop an especially enjoyable experience.

Each visit to France left me with incredible memories, and it remains one of those places I would always be happy to return to, whether for its world-class art and architecture, its exquisite cuisine, or simply the charm of French culture.

## Italy

Then came Italy, a country that felt like an open-air museum, where history, culture, and breathtaking landscapes blended seamlessly. My first visit was in 2002 on a family trip to attend a soccer tournament for Wynton. It was an unforgettable experience, filled with awe-inspiring sights, delicious food, and the warm embrace of Italian hospitality.

Our journey began in Rome, a city where history seems to come alive at every turn. Walking through the ancient ruins of the Colosseum, the Pantheon, and the Roman Forum, I felt transported back in time, imagining the grandeur of the Roman Empire. The Vatican City was equally mesmerizing, with the magnificent St. Peter's Basilica and Michelangelo's masterpiece on the ceiling of the Sistine Chapel leaving a lasting impression. The bustling piazzas, charming cafés, and the unmistakable aroma of Italian espresso added to the city's allure.

From Rome, we traveled to the coastal town of San Benedetto del Tronto, a journey that showcased the diversity of Italy's landscapes. Leaving behind the energetic streets of the capital, we passed through the picturesque rolling hills of the Italian countryside, dotted with vineyards, olive groves, and medieval villages. As we neared the Adriatic coast, the scenery transformed into a serene coastal paradise.

San Benedetto del Tronto, nestled in the Marche region, sits on the breathtaking Adriatic Sea, known for its long sandy beaches, swaying palm trees, and clear blue waters. The town had a relaxed and welcoming atmosphere, making it the perfect place to unwind. This was where the soccer tournament took place, but beyond the matches, I found immense joy in strolling along the palm-lined promenade, feeling the fresh sea breeze, and indulging in some of the freshest seafood I had ever tasted. The historic center of the town, with its charming streets, bustling markets, and friendly locals, offered an authentic taste of Italian coastal life. And the food—every meal was a celebration of Italy's culinary excellence. From rich, homemade pasta and crispy, wood-fired pizza to creamy gelato that melted in my mouth, every bite was unforgettable. However, one particular indulgence stood out—limoncello. The bright, citrusy liqueur quickly became my favorite, and I made sure to bring bottles of it back home to enjoy long after the trip ended.

My second visit to Italy was in 2019, this time as part of a Mediterranean cruise. We had daily stops in three different ports near Florence, Rome, and Naples. Having already explored Rome on my previous trip, I was eager to discover the other cities and their surrounding areas.

The most memorable discovery of this trip was the enchanting coastal town of Sorrento, located near Naples. Sorrento was simply magical, with its dramatic cliffs, panoramic sea views, and charming streets lined with artisan shops and cafés. We spent the day sightseeing, shopping, and immersing ourselves in the vibrant atmosphere of this bustling yet picturesque town. Of course, my fondness for limoncello was reignited here, as Sorrento is known for producing some of the best varieties of the drink. I couldn't resist tasting different flavors and once again found myself bringing back several bottles of my favorites.

Italy left an indelible mark on me, with its incredible history, stunning landscapes, delectable cuisine, and, of course, its signature limoncello. It remains one of the most captivating places I've ever visited, and I would return in a heartbeat to relive its magic once more.

## Ghana, Africa

One of the most profound and soul-stirring journeys of my life was traveling to Ghana, Africa—not just once, but twice. My first visit in 2019 was an experience unlike any other, one that awakened something deep within me. The moment I stepped off the airplane, an overwhelming sense of something sacred and spiritual washed over me. It was as if the very land itself was calling out to me, whispering the stories of my ancestors. In that instant, I fully grasped the magnitude of where I was—I had set foot on the ancestral soil of my fore parents, Africa, the "Motherland." It was more than just a trip; it was a homecoming, a reconnection with a past that had always been a part of me, waiting to be embraced.

Walking through the historic slave castles of Cape Coast and Elmina was an emotional and sobering experience. As I stood in those dimly lit chambers where countless enslaved Africans were once held, I couldn't help but reflect on the immense suffering and resilience of those who endured the horrors of the transatlantic slave trade. The weight of history was palpable, yet it was a necessary journey—one that deepened my understanding of the past and its enduring impact on the present. Ghana is known to be the ancestral homeland of many Jamaicans, whose fore parents were taken from these very shores centuries ago. This connection made my visit even more meaningful, as I contemplated the shared heritage between Ghana and the Caribbean.

At the same time, Ghana's vibrant culture, warm hospitality, and rich traditions made for an unforgettable experience. Exploring the bustling markets of Accra was a sensory delight, with the sights, sounds, and aromas of street food, artisan crafts, and lively conversations filling the air. I was especially thrilled to find an abundance of natural skin care products, including my favorite shea butter, renowned for its healing and moisturizing properties. I was also excited to acquire a few traditional art canvases. While the poverty in some areas was striking by Western standards, what stood out even more was the incredible resilience, strength, and joy of the Ghanaian people. Their sense of community and determination to thrive despite hardships was extremely inspiring.

Beyond Accra, I had the pleasure of visiting the town of Mpraeso, nestled in the mountains of Ghana's Eastern Region. This town is steeped in history and known for its vibrant Easter celebrations, where families from across the country return to their mountain cabins to reunite and partake in festive traditions. I was welcomed with open arms by the Mireku family, who showed me unparalleled hospitality, making me feel as though I was truly at home. Their kindness, generosity, and eagerness to share their culture left a lasting impression on me.

I also had the pleasure of visiting the seaside village of Prampram, a beautiful coastal area located well outside of Accra. This quiet and picturesque village offered a refreshing escape from the city's hustle and bustle. The serene beaches, rolling waves, and unspoiled natural beauty provided a sense of peace and tranquility. It was a reminder of Ghana's diverse landscapes, from its bustling cities to its serene seaside retreats.

During my second visit to Ghana in 2022, I became even more immersed in the social and cultural environment. One of the highlights was attending a traditional Ghanaian wedding—a grand celebration that spanned four days. The entire experience felt like a beautifully orchestrated movie or TV production, with dazzling outfits, vibrant local music, and an endless array of traditional dishes at every event. It was an unforgettable experience, and I am deeply grateful to the Mireku family for inviting me to be part of their private celebrations. Among the many culinary delights, two of my favorites stood out: the perfectly roasted tilapia and the flavorful, spicy goat meat—both of which left a lasting impression on my taste buds and memories.

Ghana was more than just a travel destination—it was a journey of connection, history, and cultural immersion. It touched me on both a personal and historical level, leaving me with a deep sense of appreciation for its people and heritage. The bond between Ghana and Jamaica remains strong, and my visit reinforced the significance of these shared roots. I will forever cherish the memories and the lessons I gained from my time in this remarkable country.

## Alaska

The most fascinating place I have visited in the United States was Alaska. I had the opportunity to travel to Anchorage on a few occasions, and each visit left a lasting impression. The breathtaking scenery, with its vast wilderness, snow-capped mountains, and pristine rivers, made for an unforgettable experience. One of the highlights was a scenic tour through the countryside, where I marveled at the untouched beauty of nature. The summer solstice never fails to amaze with its nearly 24-hour daylight, while the winter solstice brings about its opposite effect.

A specially memorable part of the trip was a boat ride along a river in Seward, where I had the chance to observe swarms of puffin birds in their natural habitat and spot wild animals roaming the hillsides. The incredible variety of wildlife and pristine landscapes transported me to another realm. It evoked thoughts of encountering the famed bears wandering freely. However, the only bears I encountered were preserved ones displayed in glass cases at the airport, standing tall with their formidable gaze.

Another highlight was getting fresh salmon fillets to take back home. Alaska is known for its world-class seafood and being able to enjoy freshly caught salmon straight from its source was a special treat. The entire experience—from the warm and hospitable people, stunning landscapes to the wildlife encounters and the delicious local food—made my visits to Alaska really remarkable and unforgettable.

Each of these places I had traveled, has added a new dimension to my worldview, offering lessons in history, culture, nature, and humanity. Travel has been more than just an escape—it has been an education, an adventure, and a way to connect with people from all walks of life. As I continue my journey, I look forward to discovering even more corners of the world, embracing the diversity that makes our planet such a fascinating place to explore.

# Chapter 12

# Parting Thoughts

## Reflections and Outlook

Reflecting on my journey, the lessons of resilience, curiosity, and the pursuit of excellence have been paramount. As the title of the book, **My Hill and Gully Ride**, implies, the journey is rarely smooth. There are mountains to climb, ravines to cross, and steep valleys to navigate or avoid. I will say, *"Stay mindful of where you come from and where you're headed, but remember, it's crucial to focus on the path ahead—because without careful attention, you might never reach your destination."*

As I continue this journey, I am excited for what the future holds. There are always new challenges to tackle, new knowledge to gain, and new ways to contribute. This new chapter is not just about career transitions; it is about purpose, lifelong learning, and making a lasting difference in the world around me.

I believe and trust that future generations will continue to expand the use of technology, including artificial intelligence (AI), as integral tools to tackle the challenges of the future. Innovations in AI, data analytics, and automation have already transformed industries, and I am confident that the next wave of leaders, engineers, and visionaries will harness these advancements to address pressing global issues—from climate change to infrastructure resilience and beyond.

The role of AI and technology in shaping our world cannot be overstated. We are living in an era of rapid technological advancements, where machine learning, automation, and data-driven decision-making are revolutionizing every industry.

The engineering field is no exception. AI-powered design tools, predictive analytics, and automation are transforming how infrastructure is planned, built, and maintained. Smart cities are no longer a concept of the distant future but a reality being implemented today, with AI helping optimize traffic flow, energy consumption, and resource management.

Beyond engineering, AI and machine learning are reshaping real estate as well. Data-driven insights are allowing buyers and sellers to make more informed decisions. Predictive modeling is enabling investors to anticipate market trends. Automation is streamlining administrative processes, making transactions more efficient and seamless. The real estate industry, much like engineering, is evolving to incorporate these technological innovations, enhancing both efficiency and customer experience.

The challenge moving forward is ensuring that these technological advancements are used ethically and sustainably. The integration of AI must not replace human ingenuity and problem-solving but rather complement and enhance it. The younger generation, with their digital fluency and innovative mindset, will be at the forefront of leveraging these tools responsibly. I trust in their ability to navigate this technological shift, applying it to address some of the world's most urgent challenges.

I look forward to embracing these advancements while remaining committed to my core values. Whether in engineering, real estate, environmental advocacy, or technology, my goal remains the same: to contribute to meaningful change, to mentor and inspire the next generation, and to ensure that the legacy I leave behind is one of positive impact and purpose.

As I look towards the future, I remain committed to the cause, continuously seeking ways to contribute positively to the world around me. Let us all be stewards of change, working hand in hand to create a legacy of hope and progress for the next generation.

Our actions today will shape the future of our planet. By taking conscious steps to reduce waste, conserve energy, and protect natural habitats, we can make a significant difference. Planting trees, supporting renewable energy projects, and advocating policies that address climate change are just a few ways we can contribute to a healthier environment.

Education and awareness play a crucial role in this endeavor. By educating ourselves and others about the importance of sustainability, we empower communities to make informed decisions. Schools, workplaces, and local organizations can all be platforms for spreading knowledge and encouraging sustainable practices.

Moreover, addressing social issues such as inequality and injustice is integral to creating a sustainable world. Ensuring that marginalized communities have access to resources and opportunities is essential for building a just society. We must stand against discrimination and support initiatives that promote inclusivity and equality.

One of the most powerful tools we have is our ability to connect with others. Building strong, supportive networks can amplify our efforts and create a ripple effect of positive change. By working together, sharing ideas, and supporting one another, we can achieve greater impact and foster a sense of global solidarity.

As individuals, we should also strive to lead by example. Our actions can inspire those around us to adopt more sustainable and compassionate practices. Whether it's through everyday choices like using reusable products or larger commitments like participating in environmental advocacy, every action matters.

In conclusion, the path to a better world requires collective effort, empathy, and unwavering commitment. Let us embrace the values of resilience, curiosity, and the pursuit of excellence as we navigate the challenges ahead. Together, we can create a world where the environment is protected, diversity is celebrated, and every individual has the opportunity to thrive.

As I continue my own journey, I am filled with hope for the future. The experiences and lessons from my travels, professional endeavors, and personal reflections have reinforced my belief in the power of positive change. I am committed to contributing to a sustainable and just world, and I invite you to join me in this mission. Let us all be catalysts for change, working towards a brighter, more equitable future for all.

Thank you for accompanying me on this journey. Your support, encouragement, and shared commitment to making a difference have been invaluable. Together, we can create a lasting impact and leave a legacy of hope, compassion, and sustainability for generations to come.

As I expand on these reflections, I am reminded that life itself is an ongoing process of growth and transformation. Each experience, each challenge, and each moment of triumph serves to shape our character and refine our purpose.

My own journey, much like the winding roads of the Jamaican countryside, has been filled with unexpected turns, steep inclines, and moments of breathtaking beauty. The resilience I have cultivated along the way has enabled me to weather storms, overcome obstacles, and remain steadfast in my pursuit of excellence.

Looking back, I see how every setback was a lesson, every failure an opportunity to learn, and every success a milestone that prepared me for the next stage of my journey. I encourage those who walk similar paths to embrace these experiences, for they are the true architects of growth and transformation.

The road ahead remains uncertain, but I face it with optimism, knowing that the values of resilience, curiosity, and purpose will continue to guide me. As I write this chapter, I extend an invitation to you, dear reader, to embark on your own journey with courage, conviction, and a steadfast commitment to making a difference.

The world needs bold thinkers, compassionate leaders, and tireless advocates for progress. Let us rise to the occasion, armed with knowledge, fueled by passion, and inspired by the boundless potential that lies within each of us.

This is not just my journey; it is our collective journey. And together, we can build a future that is not just brighter but filled with hope, opportunity, and lasting impact.

As I embrace the next stage of my life, I do so with a deep sense of gratitude. Gratitude for the people who have shaped me, the lessons that have strengthened me, and the opportunities that have propelled me forward. Though the journey may continue to be filled with hills and gullies, I will face it with unwavering resolve, hoping that every step forward is a step towards a better world.

As I reflect on my journey—the trials, triumphs, and the many hands that have guided me along the way—I am reminded of Maya Angelou's powerful words: *"I've learned that people will forget what you said, people will forget what you did, but people will never forget how you made them feel."* My greatest hope is that through my work, my teaching, and my friendships, I have left a positive mark on those whose paths have crossed mine. With gratitude for the past and excitement for the future, I embrace the next chapter, knowing that life's greatest rewards come from the connections we make and the lives we touch.

My message to the younger generation is simple yet powerful: education is undeniably a pathway to a better life. It is the key that unlocks doors to opportunities, empowerment, and personal growth. No matter what challenges or hardships you may face today, never allow them to define your future. Instead, use them as stepping stones to propel yourself forward. Strive to rise above adversity, reaching as high as possible, and view every setback not as a failure but as the next rung on the ladder toward eventual success.

Success is not always immediate, nor is the journey smooth, but perseverance, discipline, and a thirst for knowledge will carry you through. As Nelson Mandela so wisely stated, *"Education is the most powerful weapon which you can use to change the world."* Arm yourself with knowledge, embrace every learning opportunity, and keep climbing. Your dreams are within reach—keep pushing forward and never stop believing in your potential.

*"Let this be your ray of sunshine and a beacon of hope for the future."* – *Fred Rose*

# About the Author

F red's early life was steeped in the rhythms of rural Jamaica, where lessons came as much from the land and community as from school. At Carron Hall Primary and later Dinthill Technical High School, he stood out as a gifted student with a growing passion for Building Construction and applied sciences. In 1972, fresh out of Dinthill, Fred returned as a teacher, stepping into his mentor's shoes. With strong support from the principal Mr. CV Philips, he guided students to Dinthill's first-ever GCE pass in Building Construction—a landmark achievement.

Fred's worldview was shaped not only by personal experiences, but also by the seismic events of his era—the civil rights movement, the Cold War, Jamaican independence, and the rise of Black consciousness across the Caribbean and diaspora. These moments sparked his sense of purpose and pride in both his heritage and his aspirations.

He pursued engineering at CAST, then moved to Washington, D.C., in 1977 to attend Howard University. There, he earned both bachelor's and master's degrees in Civil Engineering, overcoming culture shock and personal adversities with faith and determination. Fred became a licensed Professional Engineer in 1984 and built a distinguished career in both the private and public sectors. Fred has made substantial contributions to water resources and environmental engineering.

A traveler, educator, real estate professional, and now writer, he shares a message of resilience, hope, and transformation in this uplifting memoir. As he would say: *"It's not where you start—it's how you ride."*

# Index

**The complete Index follows this page!**

# *C*

## T

www.ingramcontent.com/pod-product-compliance
Lightning Source LLC
Chambersburg PA
CBHW071719120626
46550CB00001B/301